Remarkable Russian Women in Pictures, Prose and Poetry

Marcelline Hutton

Zea Books
Lincoln, Nebraska
2013

Copyright © 2013 Marcelline Hutton.
All rights reserved.

ISBN 978-1-60962-044-8 paperback
ISBN 978-1-60962-045-5 ebook

Set in Palatino Linotype types.
Design and composition by Paul Royster.

Zea Books are published by
the University of Nebraska–Lincoln Libraries

Electronic (pdf) ebook edition available online at
http://digitalcommons.unl.edu/zeabook/

Print edition can be ordered from Lulu.com, at
http://www.lulu.com/spotlight/unllib

Preface

I first fell in love with 19th century Russia as a teenager after seeing the film "War and Peace," starring Audrey Hepburn and Mel Ferrer After reading Leo Tolstoy's novel on which the movie was based, I was even more smitten with Russian culture. When I took a Russian history course in college, my lifelong love affair with Russian History began and continued into graduate school and beyond.

Part of the attraction of Russian History was its sense of "Otherness." It was grander than anything I had known living in the Midwest. Moscow and St. Petersburg, as described by Leo Tolstoy and Fedor Dostoevsky, were more exotic than places I had ever known. Russian culture also attracted me because it was more expressive than the subdued Nordic culture in Northern Indiana where I grew up. Only years later did I realize that Russian History embodied not only great mercy, tenderness, and promise, but terrible sadness, suffering, and cruelty as well.

During my studies at the University of Iowa from 1962-1987, I found Russian women, their writings, and history more and more fascinating. I was impressed by their social and political challenges to the status quo. Their personal achievements and troubles also attracted me. I wrote my Master's Thesis on the "Woman Question" in the 1860s, following it with a dissertation entitled "Russian and Soviet Women, 1860-1939: Dreams, Struggles, and Nightmares." My first book was entitled *Russian and West European Women, 1860-1939: Dreams, Struggles and Nightmares*. This book covered patterns in Russian women's social, educational, political, and economic lives. However, it didn't reveal a lot about their personal lives.

In contrast, this book *Remarkable Russian Women in Pictures, Prose and Poetry* provides glimpses into women's hearts and minds in the late 19th and early 20th centuries. It reveals more about their quests for happy marriages, search for authentic religious life, and desire for education and fulfilling work serving poor peasants and workers as doctors, teachers, and political activists. In many ways, 19th century Russian women's complaints about unhappy marriages resemble modern American women's. Some experienced emptiness, alienation, and even the squandering of their fortunes by unscrupulous husbands. Female poets spoke of their lyrical loves as well as their romantic and marital failures. They criticized their society's tradition of arranged marriage. Several severely judged their country's political oppression in their poems and were punished. The lives of these women writers as well as gentry-class women like Countess Sofia Tolstoy sometimes resembled the arranged marriages depicted in the recent PBS series "Downton Abbey." Where possible, this book showcases the voices and art of women writers, painters, doctors, revolutionaries, peasants, workers, wives, and mothers across several decades, making them visible and their words heard.

Middle and upper-class Russian women left many kinds of written records—novels, poetry, diaries, autobiographies, and interviews. Some of their writings portray a Russian twist to idyllic English gentry-class life depicted in "Downton Abbey." Some of their critiques of marriage highlighted the pilfering of their dowries and the ruining of their personal lives by profligate, philandering husbands. Still, most women in all classes wanted the respectability that marriage offered, and most married. However, some rebelled and wanted different sorts of lives. Some from all classes sought the religious life as nuns or pilgrims. Some found fulfillment in careers such as writing, painting, teaching, medicine, even political activity.

A gifted generation of late 19th and early 20th century women artists known as the Avant-Garde has left an impressive legacy of paintings and illustrations. They portray an array of self-portraits as well as paintings of peasants and working-class women. Much of their work featured abstract paintings, stage designs for innovative theatrical productions, even costume designs for modern ballets.

Wedding laments and folk songs give us a look into illiterate peasant and working-class women's lives, revealing some of their struggles in those epochs. From our perspective, many peasant and working-class women seemed to live lives of quiet desperation and drudgery. Yet, who knows the solace they found in respectable married life and motherhood or the pride they took in their hard work on family farms or in factories. Their survival during the dark days of the 1891 famine, the industrial revolution, WW I, the Revolutions of 1905 and 1917 attest to their remarkable endurance in not merely existing, but even thriving and producing children during hard times. Women's roles as wife, mother, and provider during the harsh circumstances of the late 19th and early 20th centuries were remarkable.

The present book emerges from many influences. One was Sergei Prokudin-Gorsky's impressive color photographs of Russian women prior to World War I. His dramatic pictures show strong peasant women working in the fields, charming peasant girls dressed in holiday frocks, and thoughtful women at rural chapels. Pictures from the Russian Film and Photo Archive in St. Petersburg also show women at home, work, and in society. Wikimedia also supplies some wonderful photographs of Russian icons, Russian religious and political processions, as well as pictures of famous Russian women writers, artists, wives, and revolutionaries. Striking paintings in the Russian State Art Museum in St. Petersburg also influenced me. Teaching at Lithuania Christian College in Klaipeda, Lithuania, from 2000 to 2007 enabled me to visit this museum several times and become familiar with its holdings. Pictures of cultural figures like poet Anna Akhmatova and dancer Anna Pavlova, as well as paintings by Natalia Goncharova and others captivated me. Mikhail Nesterov's painting "The Great Taking of the Vows," fascinated me with its beautiful young nuns. Some of Natalia Goncharova's works depicted powerful women workers and peasants. All of them excited me because I had not been familiar with them when I wrote my dissertation and first book on Russian Women.

Yet another influence is the large body of Russian women's literature and history that Slavic scholars have made available to American readers in the past few decades. It was my privilege to meet and get to know translators and linguists such as Joe Andrew, Toby Clyman, Helena Goscilo, Diana Greene, Birgitta Ingemanson, Mary Zirin and others at the annual Slavic Summer Laboratory held at the University of Illinois in the summers during the 1980s. A host of social historians has also enriched our knowledge of Russian women. Again, I was fortunate to meet Martha Bohachevsky-Chomiak, Ann Kleimola, David Ransell, Bernice Rosenthal, Christine Ruane, Rochelle Ruthchild, Richard Stites, Isabel Tirado, Christine Worobec and others at the Summer Laboratory and at various historical conferences. Their hard work and that of many others cited in the Notes helped make this volume possible. I want to make some of this scholarly material about Russian women available to non-specialists.

Jackie Bartz, a colleague at LCC, read my first book *Russian and West European Women, 1860-1939: Dreams, Struggles, and Nightmares*, and she mentioned how much she liked the quotations of the women writers. Since the book was rather long, I had shortened many of the quotes, but decided the present study can include long ones to give readers better examples of women's voices. Of course, there are "filters" and limitations in using personal, historical sources. Those who wrote diaries, autobiographies, and memoirs were usually educated, unusual women. Sometimes women wrote in their diaries when they were depressed, and we can't assume that their lives were always as miserable as depicted. This is especially true of Countess Sofia Tolstoy, who often complained about her depression and desire to end her life. Yet, if we look at photographs from the same time period, she often looks quite happy and engaged, so perhaps the pictures cloaked her real misery.

In both the Tsarist and Soviet periods, government censors imposed boundaries on writers. Women sometimes also dealt with inner social censors which tempered what and how they wrote. So, let the reader remember that women's publications are their perceptions of reality and their feelings at the time they wrote. Their works are incomplete, but valuable, historical records. All these constraints, as well as the availability and limitations of the holdings at the University of Nebraska in Lincoln, where I lived and did my research from 2009-2013, as well as my own personal choices and understandings of Russian history have shaped the depictions of Russian women presented in this book. I have tried to include not only famous Russian women, but also ordinary ones whose writings have been preserved and are available to English speakers.

My fifty year study of Russian Literature and History has revealed fantastic pluck and perseverance among Russian women. I also resonated with some of the themes and crises in these women's lives and careers, finding them remarkably similar to my own struggles as a married graduate student and mother at the University of Iowa in the 1960s and later decades. Who isn't moved by the idealism of the intelligentsia, the plight of Russian peasant women, or the exploitation of working-class women a century ago? The work most poor women did for their families' survival was phenomenal.

Material for this book sometimes emerged from unexpected sources. Russian ethnographers have provided folksongs of 19th and early 20th century peasant and working-class women, so that we can "hear" their voices. In addition to Russian women's personal writings, there are also English and American women journalists, governesses, and translators who speak of the late Tsarist period.

Acknowledgments

I want to express my gratitude to Lithuania Christian College (LCC) for giving me an office, library, and computer support in the summer of 2008 and the spring of 2009 when I began working on this book. Thanks especially to Roman Shevtsov for computer aid. Thanks to Jean Swetchine for permission to use his grandfather Sergei Prokudin-Gorsky's photos of Russian women, which are available through a web site at the Library of Congress.

Thanks also to archivists Liubov Pyzhova and Elena Liubomirova, for their assistance in obtaining fascinating pictures of Russian women at the St. Petersburg Archive. Thanks to Irina Ivanova, Curator of the Anna Akhmatova Museum, for her gracious provision of pictures of Akhmatova. Thanks also to archivist Janet Weaver at the Iowa Women's Archives at The University of Iowa for the use of pictures from Helena Skrjabina's family archive. Mrs. Skrjabina had been my Russian Language professor at the University in the early 1960s, so it was with great pleasure that I looked at her family photos and re-read her memoir *Coming of Age in the Russian Revolution* for this manuscript.

Thanks to the University of Iowa for assistance in the fall of 2008 when I worked at the Obermann Research Center there. An office, the University library, supportive writing environment, and IT support were very much appreciated. It was a pleasure to work among so many talented and thoughtful people. Thanks to Jay Semel and the late Larry Gelfand, formerly of the University of Iowa, for their support and help when I was doing research at the Center.

Thanks also to the Russian, East European, and Eurasian Center and the Slavic Library at the University of Illinois, in the summers of the 1980s and 1990s, as well as 2009-2010. Their staff and resources are outstanding. Moreover, the Summer Research Laboratory provides opportunities to meet old friends and make new ones when discussing Russian History and Literature. Special appreciation is also due to the University of Nebraska Lincoln Love Library. Its impressive collection of Slavic women's holdings was incredibly useful to me while doing my research. Of course there were also limitations in the holdings which have affected the focus of the book.

ACKNOWLEDGMENTS

Herman Weaver's computer assistance at Pioneer House in Lincoln, Nebraska, has also been incalculable.

Special thanks to my editor Paul Royster for his assistance, kindness, and encouragement in the production of this book. I am also grateful to my former Russian Language Professor Miriam Gelfand for her labor of love in proofreading the manuscript and making thoughtful suggestions. Both have helped me turn the manuscript into a book.

Genuine gratitude is also due to the following for their hospitality, support, and friendship while working on this project: Therese Baker, Tricia Bondurant, Jackie Bartz, Marcelline Breese, Dick and Debra Dorzweiler, Janusz Duzinkiewicz, Chuck and Margaret Felling, Oleg Forbatok, Joyce Gleason, Pat Green, Richard Hansgen, Barbara Hoffman, Kathryn Hutton, Birgitta Ingemanson, Pat Irelan, Michael Johnson, Francis Kezamer, Elaine Kruse, Helmi Mays, Halimah Polk, Tania Simanaitiene, Ninon Shalk, Martin Stack, Tom Tiegs, Jack Wheat, and Janet Yoder. Some read rough drafts of various chapters of this book and made helpful suggestions. Others have provided encouragement, housing, dinners, and computer help. Thanks also to my exercise classes and doctors for keeping me healthy. Thank you one and all.

Technicalities

As usual, Russian names pose some problems. While "aya" is generally used for endings of Russian women's last names such as Bobrovskaya, Kovalevskaya, Krupskaya, and so forth, some famous women are referred to in Western writings without the aya ending such as Countess Tolstoy, Anna Dostoevsky, Catherine Breshkovsky, and Elena Blavatsky. Common usage is preferred. Soft signs are omitted as are people's middle names or patronymics. While patronymics are polite in Russian culture, they are not necessary in American writing and are not used in this book. The Library of Congress system of transliteration is sparingly used.

Confusion also arises when the same name is spelled differently, i.e. Mariia Bochkareva and Maria Botchkareva. She's the same woman, but newspapers, publishers, and scholars transliterate it from the Russian alphabet to the English differently. Mariia, Mariya, and Maria are the same name just presented in different forms. Likewise, the Russian name for one revolutionary is Ekaterina Breshko-Breshkovskaya. Sometimes it is translated by American publishers as Catherine Breshkovsky sometimes Katerina Breshkovskaya. She is the same person. For convenience, I have tried to use the popular American form Catherine Breshkovsky. Likewise, the names Natalia and its diminutive Natasha and Tatyana and Tanya when used in the same section refer to the same person.

Variations in spelling sometimes occur because translators often use British spelling, i.e. honour for honor and so forth. When such spelling occurs in a quotation, it is retained. Likewise, when names like Maria and Wilhelm are anglicized to Marie and William, the names are kept in the quotations, but not the narrative. Likewise, some Russian words like intelligentsia (educated people critical of the government) and gimnaziya (the 19th century Russian elite high school, comparable to the German gymnasium) have become common and are used throughout the book.

For the sake of brevity I have shortened the citation for the St. Petersburg Central Archive of Film and Photo Documents to Photo Archive and likewise abbreviated the citations of some of the photographs of Prokudin-Gorsky and the Photo Archive.

Table of Contents

Introduction 17

Chapter One: Religious Life 19
    A. Piety In Russian Orthodoxy 21
        1. Icons 22
        2. Personal Piety in Women's Writings 24
        3. Religious Visions 30
    B. Russian Religion and Culture 31
        1. Courtship and Church 32
        2. Marriage and the Church 38
        3. Birth and Christenings 40
        4. Pilgrimages and Processions 42
        5. Healing, Magic, and Religion 49
    C. Sorow, Sadness and Death 54
    D. Dissatisfaction with Traditional Religion 56
    E. New Religions 59
        1. Tolstoyans 60
        2. Spiritualists 62
        3. Mme. Blavatsky and Theosophy 63
        4. Zinaida Gippius and New Orthodoxy 65
    F. Conclusion 69

Chapter Two: Marriage 71
    A. The Russian Gentry 71
        1. Unhappy Arranged Marriages 71
            a. Maria Zhukova 72
            b. Evdokiia Rostopchina 73
            c. Karolina Pavlova 76
            d. Elena Gan 79
        2. Other Negative Views of Marriage 81
            a. Nadezhda Durova 81
            b. Grand Duchess Maria 83
            c. Literary Accounts of Marriage 86
        3. Social and Sexual Predators 88
            a. Natalia Sheremetevskaya 90

    4. Happy Marriages 93
        a. Happily Married Writers. 93
        b. Happiness amidst Plenty, the Tolstoy Family . . . 94
        c. Tatiana Tolstoy 107
        d. Happiness in Adversity, Anna Dostoevsky 110
        e. Anna Bek 113
        f. Ordinary Gentry-Class Marriage and Family . . . 115
    5. Fictitious Marriages, 1860s and 1870s 118
    6. Marriage and Women Revolutionaries 121
    7. Liberated Women and Marriage 126
    8. Chaste Marriages 127
    9. Divorced, Remarried Women, and Mistresses 128
    10. Never Married 130
B. Middle Class Women's Marriages 132
    1. Praskovia Tatlina 133
    2. Anna Volkova 134
    3. Nadezhda Khvroshchinskaya 135
    4. Nicholas Dobroliubov: A Woman's Plight 137
    5. Nicholas Ostrovsky: Actresses 138
    6. Middle-Class Painters 140
C. Peasant Marriages 141
    1. Peasant Wedding Laments 145
    2. Peasant Memoirs 147
D. Working Class Marriage 153
    1. Maria Botchkareva 153
    2. A Nameless Working Woman 155
E. Conclusion 156

Chapter Three: Women's Work 159

A. Peasant Work 159
B. Working-Class Women's Work. 164
    1. Maria Botchkareva 167
    2. Clothing and Textile Production 170
    3. Mining 172
C. Commerce 174
D. Education And Employment 178
    1. Governesses 178
    2. Gorstkin Family Governesses. 179
    3. Girl's Education 183

CONTENTS

  4. Higher Education 186
  5. Education for Women in Medicine 194
   a. Anna Bek 195
   b. Vera Figner. 196
   c. Ekaterina Slanskaia 198
   d. Nursing during WW I 200
  6. Writers 202
   a. Poets 203
   b. Prose Writers. 217
   c. Diarists 223
   d. Autobiography 227
  7. Artists 230
   a. Anna O. Lebedeva. 231
   b. Zinaida Serebriakova 233
   c. Natalia Goncharova 236
   d. Olga Rozanova 239
   e. Varvara Stepanova 243
   f. Liubov Popova 244
   g. Aleksandra Ekster. 246
 E. Conclusion 249

Chapter Four: Politics. 251
 A. Gentry and Middle-class Women 254
  1. Social Revolutionaries 255
  2. Social Democrats 264
   a. Konkordia Samoilova 265
   b. Anna Bek 267
   c. Maria Golubeva. 269
   d. Klavdia Kirsanova 270
   e. Ludmila Stahl 271
   f. Tatyana Ludvinskaya 272
   g. Cecilia Bobrovskaya. 274
   h. Vera Broido, Menshevik 278
 B. Feminists 281
 C. Peasant Political Activity 289
 D. Working-Class Political Activity 296
 E. Women Soldiers 300
 F. Conclusion 302

Notes 305

Mikhail Nesterov, "The Great Taking of the Vows," 1898

Introduction

Many fundamental changes began in late 19th century Russia. Women's liberation or the "Woman Question" as it was called in Russia arose in the 1860s, and many women began to look for dignity in work and in "serving the people" as doctors, educators, and political activists. Tangential to the woman's movement was the desire for more authentic marital and family relations. While some women like Countess Tolstoy initially experienced marriages similar to "Downton Abby," others chafed from arranged marriages in which profligate husbands ruined them financially and socially. In the 19th century, more Russian women began complaining about the institution of arranged marriage. By the end of the century, scores earned their living as writers and journalists, several hundred completed medical training, thousands had become teachers, and several hundred revolutionaries.

Radical political movements to overthrow the autocracy and to aid the peasants and the workers also began in the late 19th century. Agrarian socialists called Social Revolutionaries or SRs focused on the peasants and the land question, which the Emancipation of the serfs in 1861 had not really solved. Marxists, or Social Democrats as they were called, focused on relieving the plight of the workers in the cities in the 1890s and later. Women, especially of the gentry-class, took prominent positions in both of these political parties. While most women remained traditional and found holiness in the Russian Orthodox Church, others defined their service to the peasants and workers as their "holy duties."

Looking for meaning, dignity, and authenticity in their lives, some women sought it in the holiness of nuns or pilgrims. Most found it in their ordinary religious lives. In the late 19th century, some intellectuals engaged in unorthodox religious quests. They were different from the Russian Orthodox pilgrims who visited historic sites seeking healing and comfort from traditional religion. Intellectuals like Zinaida Gippius sought to redefine the Godhead, seeking the feminine there. Others sought truth and authenticity in Tolstoy's simpler Christianity. Still others joined religious sects like the Stundists and Molokane (Milk Drinkers) which they found more congenial than the state controlled Orthodox Church. Another unique woman, Madame Elena Blavatsky, developed Eastern esoteric wisdom as a new spiritual path. Chapter One begins with women's religious experiences.

Most Russian women sought meaning and respectability in marriage and motherhood, and Chapter Two analyzes their story. The high regard for Mary as the Mother of God and for fertility in Russian culture meant that most women in all estates married. Indeed, the government forbade women taking final vows as nuns until they had passed childbearing age. While some women in all estates married for love, most marriages included economic considerations, and many were arranged for financial advantage. So, while married life was honored in the Russian Orthodox tradition and Russian society, it had its critics as paintings and writings about marriage show. Some writers were angered at the adultery that arranged marriages entailed. Moreover, the appearance of the "New Woman" in Russian literature and society in the late 19th century showed some embracing marriage and motherhood while others did not.

By mid century, increasing numbers of women were looking for authenticity in their personal and professional lives. Some turned to philanthropy as a way to bind up the wounds of society. Others expressed the values of altruism and self-sacrifice in professional careers as teachers, doctors, pharmacists, and midwives. Others sought to express themselves and their talents in their writing and artistic work. Several w-omen painters became part of the Avant Garde in art from 1900-1930. Like their Western counterparts, many artists wanted to escape from the classical strictures of academic art, and various artistic groups emerged where women played significant parts. Women's careers and work make up Chapter Three.

Some Russian women found philanthropy, medicine, and education mere palliatives and in the 1870s turned to revolutionary struggle to express their altruism and self sacrifice in political struggle hoping thereby to restructure Russian society and improve the lot of the less fortunate. Indeed, some like Catherine Breshkovsky, Vera Figner and Alexandra Kollontai were so outraged by the exploitation of peasants and workers that they left their husbands and children to become fulltime revolutionaries. Women's political activity prior to the 1917 Revolution constitutes Chapter Four.

Chapter One

Religious Life

Russian paintings sometimes show an idealized portrait of women's religious life. Mikhail Nesterov's picture of beautiful young novices surrounded by nuns and priests dramatizes cloistered life. His creation makes us feel the solemnity and sacrifice of religious life.

Still, it was seldom easy for women to shed family obligations and take up the cloistered life. The Russian government forbade women less than 40 years of age from taking final vows. Moreover, providing an initial donation as well as one's support in a women's monastery exceeded the means of most women, especially poor peasant ones. Securing government and church permission to found a new convent was expensive and time consuming. It's a tribute to Russian women that so many persevered in their callings to this sort of holiness. Perhaps it's not so surprising that following their visions empowered them.[1] Despite the difficulties, cloistered religious life attracted over 60,000 women in the late 19th century, while thousands of others lived as religious wanderers and pilgrims. Out of a female population of 62,000,000 this was not such a huge number, but it exceeded the number of women teachers and doctors at the turn of the century.[2] One writer in the late 19th century discussed this matter, saying:

> Frequently girls reject marriage and express the wish to "*spasat'sia*" (to save themselves), "to leave the world." No matter how unpleasant for the parents, in most cases they do not feel they have the right to refuse her. In earlier times such *spasennitsy* went into monasteries; now since state monasteries have seriously diminished and entering a monastery requires a "sacrifice" (*zhertva*), often very large (100 rubles and more, for example, for the Sviatorzerskii women's monastery in Gorokhovetskii district), these *spasennitsy* rarely enter monasteries. More often they set themselves up in their own village

or in the nearest village to be close to the church. Parents are obliged to build her a hut on the outskirts of the village. Sometimes she moves there with 3-5 *spasennitsy*.[3]

Historians Brenda Meehan-Waters and William Wagner argue that Russian convent life changed dramatically in the late 19th century because more peasant women became nuns and more convents were established in the countryside. Wagner noticed over 10,000 new nuns and novices adopting the religious life, and an increase in convents from 202 to 475 prior to WW I. Convent life offered peasant women opportunities for education; a deep religious and liturgical life; and some autonomy in pursuing a religious calling in lieu of traditional family and village life. Rural community living, especially among peasant lay nuns, was not easy. Lay nuns usually took vows of poverty, chastity, and learning. Sometimes lay nuns were pledged by their families, and sometimes they decided on their own to adopt the religious life. They generally shunned monastic living and often read the prayers for the dead and taught village children to read in order to support themselves. Life in a convent was not easy either. Even enclosed nuns might have to help in field work; milk the cows; make clothes and shoes for the community, prepare food; bake bread; care for orphans; educate peasant children; maintain a library; sing in the choir; and pray for the dead (since this was one way the convent earned money). Male emigration from the countryside during industrialization reduced some peasant women's chances of marrying and may have been a factor in some women's choice of the celibate life.[4]

Ivan Turgenev's novella "A Nest of Gentry Folk" (1858) indicates one gentry-class girl's romantic view of monastic life. It portrays a disillusioned young gentry-class woman deciding to enter a convent after a failed romance. Infatuated with a married cousin, she is devastated when his dissolute wife, whom they thought dead, returns, dooming their love. In the short novel, Lisa rejects her mother's marriage plans and rebuffs the handsome yet shallow suitor Panshin in order to remain true to her first love. Lisa believed she could do this by adopting the religious life.

Some women became nuns because of conviction, instead of failed romance, lack of marriage prospects, or economic need. Indeed, elderly widows and unmarried daughters of civil and military servitors, clergy, and merchants constituted a sizeable number of nuns and novices prior to the 1860s. These women often treated the sick, housed the poor, and welcomed pilgrims.[5]

Despite romantic and reverent views of convent life, most Russian women married and participated in the rites and rituals of the Russian Orthodox Church in ordinary family life. Countess Sofia Tolstoy commented in her diary in November, 1890, that it was her habit to pray every evening. Princess Marie, a cousin of Nicholas II, thought that Russians talked familiarly to God and approached him trustfully.[6]

Their behavior as wives and mothers may have been influenced by the Orthodox tradition in which Mary is venerated as the Mother of God, not as Virgin. Moreover, neither the Russian government nor society wanted young girls to become nuns. In one poem, aristocratic writer Evdokiia Rostopchina (1811-1858) reproved a beautiful young woman, telling her that her intention of taking the veil was selfish because God ordered women to be men's consolation and spiritual salvation.[7] Indeed, one gentry-class mother rebuked her daughter telling her she would find "no loving mother, dear family or your own home" there.[8] Since various Tsars raided the treasuries of monasteries and convents, their endowments were smaller than those in Western Europe and economic support of nuns was more limited.

A. Traditional Piety in Russian Orthodoxy

> It has become my habit to pray at much length every evening; it is a good way to finish the day.
>
> Countess Sofia Tolstoya,
> *Diary*, 1890.

Women in all social strata prayed and engaged in pious acts in the 19th century. Peasants usually prayed before the family icon and crossed themselves before eating and before working. According to Page Herrlinger in *Working Souls Russian Orthodoxy and Factory Labor in St. Petersburg, 1881-1917*, workers and factory equipment were blessed by a priest before work began each day and tens of thousands of factory workers regularly participated in religious pilgrimages.[9] Russian life was infused with religion. A chapel on Mount

Blagodat at the Kushvin Works shows the prevalence of holy objects in the work environment.

Peasant culture usually accommodated pious women's desire for a holy life and allowed them to set up huts for themselves in their village near a church. These communities were alternatives to convents since few peasants could afford the donation fee (100 rubles) of joining a monastery. Some women desired a "religious" life, but not necessarily living in a convent. Peasant Nikolai I. Kuznetsov, an observer for the ethnographer Count V. N. Tenishev, tells the story of Anna Sidorova, a literate well-to-do girl with many offers of marriage in a small village near Smolensk in the late 19th century. He remarks:

> Anna stubbornly refuses to marry.... Her family supports her and lets her make pilgrimages even in working periods, giving her money for the road. The old people and the women relate to her in a loving, jocular way. They call her 'our bogomolka.' (holy person.)[10]

The same observer described a village widow who refused to marry again. Although she was a healthy woman, good worker, and courted by good men, she lacked Anna's family protection. When told that she should go to a convent, she answered: What for? Without a dowry I will have nothing but hard work and I will have no time to pray. Now I am a free ...If I need a piece of bread, I will work for it. Good people won't deny me a piece of bread. And there is also plenty of sin in the convent."[11]

1. Icons

> She went into the chapel, right up to the miracle-working icon. She bowed again and again to the ground; it was such a pleasure to watch.
>
> Nadezhda Khvoshchinskaya, *The Boarding-School Girl*

At the turn of the century, Russian women were overwhelmingly Orthodox. Even the poorest peasant hut had an icon corner with candles for personal prayer and probably an icon shelf with ritual towels, holy water from church, blessed Easter bread, incense, and votive lamps. If relatives, neighbors, or family members went on a pilgrimage, they might bring home holy objects for friends and relations. Describing the significance of icons, one Russian theologian suggests:

> A dwelling without icons often affects an Orthodox as empty.... The icon gives the real feeling of the presence of God....The icon is not only a holy picture, it is something greater than a mere picture. According to Orthodox belief, an icon is a place of the Gracious Presence. It is the place of the appearance of Christ, of the Virgin, of the Saints, of all those represented by the icon, and hence it serves as a place for prayer to them.[12]

The liturgy, rites, and rituals of Russian Orthodox Church worship offered comfort to believers. It aspired to "evoke heaven on earth and celebrates the sensual as a manifestation of divine grace and transcendence."[13] People also tried to obtain a similar feeling of holiness by praying at home before the family icons. For believers, the icon opened the door of God's world. Some icons were considered magical and "wondrous." These had special powers for healing, averting calamity, providing blessings and so forth. Many factories provided a chapel, others trained worker choirs. Most work places had icons for blessing the workers, owners, and machinery. Icons also served as reminders of the Divine Presence. Some women workers decorated their looms and barracks with icons and religious artifacts.[14]

In her memoirs, Anna Dostoevsky, the wife of the famous writer Theodore Dostoevsky, remembered being taken to a church in St. Petersburg when she was about three years old and quite ill. There, her mother and she received communion, and her mother prayed before the miraculous icon of the All Compassionate Mother of God. When she saw her mother and nurse praying and weeping, she too crossed herself and sobbed. The next day she began to recover quickly.[15]

Some "wondrous" icons had national significance like the "Vladimir Mother of God," or "Our Lady of Kazan" and some had mainly local recognition such as the "Wonderworking Icon of the Three-Handed Mother of God," in a Voronezh Monastery. Peasants sometimes adopted their own village "wondrous" icon, but they had to seek clerical permission and sanction for this.[16] One reason icons were so important in people's personal religious life was

"Our Lady of Vladimir," icon, 12th century, in Tretiakov Museum.

that the Orthodox Church did not focus on the interpretation of the scriptures themselves, and the Bible was not translated from Church Slavonic into the Russian language of the laity until 1876. Once the Bible became available and more peasants became literate, scripture and the lives of the saints became popular subjects of study among the peasantry and petty bourgeois in the late 19th century.

2. Personal Piety in Women's Writings

> I prayed for only one thing: 'Stay with me, Lord! With Thee I can go anywhere, but without Thee I don't need the ground on which I stand.'
>
> Nadezhda Sokhanskaia, "Autobiography"

Some women writers tell us about their religious life in their diaries, autobiographies, novels, letters and other writings. One passage in provincial writer Nadezhda Sokhanskaya's autobiography tells of her sadness at leaving the Kharkov Girls Institute in the mid 19th century. She remarks:

> I couldn't pray for happiness. If the Lord giveth, then He giveth; and I couldn't even know what form this happiness would take.... But as the day and hour of graduation drew nearer, my vague thoughts of happiness and unhappiness passed, my soul remained strangely free, as though ready for anything.[17]

Likewise, writer Sofia Khvoshchinskaia describes a poignant religious incident at her Moscow boarding school in the 1840s in her "Reminiscences of Institute Life:"

> Collective penitence and forgiveness lifted a heavy burden from our hearts.... by the time we were fifteen, our prayers had become more mystical and more exalted. We no longer expressed heartfelt repentance or forgave our 'enemies' out loud, but shyly and deep within our hearts. Instead of words, tears flowed, but they were tears of feverish emotion without any specific cause. As we waited our turn in church, we shed many tears in front of the icon of our Savior and behind the screen by the opposite window where the priest was quietly hearing confession.[18]

Married, gentry-class writer Lydia Zinovyeva-Annibal gives another view of women's spiritual life in her story "Wolves." She depicts a mother sharing her beliefs with her daughter at their country estate. Having witnessed a wolf hunt, her child returns home traumatized. Comforting her daughter, the invalid mother takes this opportunity to describe the changes in her life that her illness has brought about:

> "You know, Verochka, I've become a completely different person since my illness....It's not important that my illness is taking its course, and that my soul will again grow dark. Whoever has glimpsed just once, will enter his own new world... But why are you crying?..."
> "I'm sorry...that you will die."
> And Mama laughed. "Is dying really so important? Or living? One lives, you see, only to gain understanding. Once one

has understood, that's enough. The little spark has flashed and passed on....How joyous it is to know and to entrust oneself. That's what it means to love God..."

Then her mother cried and had another seizure. Later the author wondered how she recalled this conversation when writing the story years later.[19] This tender mother-daughter exchange provides a touching insight into one woman's inner life.

Many Russian writers and ethnographers recorded women's religious dedication, but Annibal's lyrical description goes beyond the rites and rituals of praying before an icon in one's bedroom. She expresses the "Slavic Soul" in some of its humility. Annibal like Sokhanskaia and Khvoshchinskaia shows that Russian women had meaningful religious lives without living in a convent.

In her novel *A Double Life*, written in poetry and prose, Karolina Pavlova offers the reader many scenes of her heroine Cecily praying before icons. However, as a Protestant, Pavlova depicts God more sternly than many of the mercy inclined Orthodox women writers. At two points, Pavlova describes God as follows:

> He stands, full of stern power,
> He stands motionless and unspeaking,
> He looks straight into her eyes,
> He looks straight into her soul.
> Reproach for what guilt, what mistake
> Clouds his brow?
> On that unsmiling face
> What sad love?[20]

Later, she adds:

> He has given woe to all of us,
> To all a measure of sad days;
> Submit to his laws
> The murmur of your pride.
> Learn to live with outward grief,
> Forgetting youthful dreams of Eden,
> Share no more with anyone
> The secret of inconsolable thought....[21]

In her poem "We Shall Not Overcome Our Sorrows," written almost 20 years later, Pavlova discusses the need for humility and submission. Therein, she more closely resembles her Slavic sisters when she writes:

> We shall not overcome our sorrows
> On earth by struggle proud and grim,
> But only if to God we humble
> Our hearts and lift our souls to Him,
> Shall we, this earthly tribe of mortals,
> Through grief and trouble safely flee,
> As once of old the Jews passed over
> The mounting, salty, evil sea!
> And as the rising wall of waters
> Supported them upon that day,
> So shall our bitter, fateful sorrow
> Be unto us a holy stay.[22]
>
> 1862

Some poets wrote nationalistic as well as religious poetry. Rostopchina wrote some of these in the 1840s and 1850s. During World War One, Anna Akhmatova wrote a poem entitled "Prayer" in which she begged God for Russia's deliverance and offered her health, poetic gift, and family in exchange. It reads as follows:

> Give me comfortless seasons of sickness,
> Visitations of wrath and wrong
> On my house; Lord, take child and companion,
> And destroy the sweet power of song.
>
> Thus I pray at each matins, each vespers,
> After these many wearying days,
> That the storm-cloud which broods over Russia
> May be changed to a nimbus ablaze.[23]
>
> 1915

While most written sources about women's religious lives come from educated gentry-class women, there were some exceptions. An unusual memoir reveals the prayer life of a peasant-born soldier named Maria Botchkareva (1889–1920). She came to the United

States after WW I, and told her story to Isaac Don Levine in New York City. He transcribed her story as she told it to him, and it was published as *Yashka: My Life as Peasant, Officer and Exile* in 1919. Escaping an abusive marriage, Yashka joined the army, with special permission from the Tsar, in November, 1914. Like many Russian Orthodox believers, her mother's and her own prayers were addressed to the Mother of God. When Yashka returned to her parents from exile in Northern Siberia prior to the war, her mother wept and offered prayers to the "Holy Mother." Yashka remembered that in the army, the day began with a prayer for the Tsar and the country before the soldiers breakfasted. Solemn mass for the soldiers was said at the church and conducted by the Bishop before the soldiers went to the front in WW I. The soldiers crossed themselves, prayed, prepared their rifles, and awaited orders before an offensive. In the midst of battle and when wounded, Yashka also prayed to the Mother of God, asking "when will help come?"[24]

As male soldiers began deserting the front after the February Revolution of 1917, Yashka formed the Petrograd Women's Battalion of Death to shame them into continuing the war effort. In June, 1917, the government held a ceremony for the dedication of Yashka's Battalion battle flags. As she describes it in her memoirs hundreds of people came to the blessing of her battalion's standard — President of the Provisional Government Alexander Kerensky, General Kornilov, and other high officials:

> The officiating persons were two archbishops and twelve priests. The church was filled to overflow. A hush fell on the vast gathering as I was asked to step forward and give my name. I was seized with fear, as if in the presence of God Himself. The standard that was to be consecrated was placed in my hand and two old battle flags were crossed over it, hiding me almost completely in their folds. The officiating archbishop then addressed me, telling of the unprecedented honor of dedicating an army standard to a woman. As he spoke and said the prayers, in the course of which he sprinkled me three times with holy water, I prayed to the Lord with all my heart and might. The ceremony lasted about an hour, after which two soldiers, delegates from the First and Third armies presented to me two icons, given by fellow soldiers, with inscriptions on

the cases, expressing their confidence in me as the woman who would lead Russia to honor and renown.

I was humbled. I did not consider myself worthy of such honors. When asked to receive each of the two icons I fell on my knees before them and prayed for God's guidance. How could I, a dark woman [i.e. peasant], justify the hopes and trust of so many enlightened and brave sons of my country?...

... Women in the throng forced their way to me, kissing my feet and blessing me. It was a patriotic mass of people, and love for Russia was the dominant note of the celebrating crowd....[25]

In Moscow, Archbishop Tikhon held a benediction for the Moscow Women's Battalion of Death on July 2, 1917 on Red Square. St. George's Cavaliers presented the women's battalion an icon of "St. George the Victorious" at the ceremony. During their training most of the women in these battalions participated in both morning and evening prayers. So, religion remained a part of women's lives even when they were preparing to fight in WW I.[26]

When captured by the Bolsheviks and threatened with death in the winter of 1917-1918, Yashka drank a small bottle of holy water, which her sister had given her. Then she prayed on her knees to God, Jesus, and the Holy Mother before a little icon. She begged God for her life for the sake of her elderly parents. As she hugged the little icon and cried, she heard a tender voice say: "Your life will be saved." And she was satisfied that she heard the voice of a divine messenger. It was soothing, elevating. She felt happy and calm and thanked the Almighty for his boundless kindness. She also vowed to have a public prayer offered at the Moscow Cathedral of Christ the Savior at the first opportunity, in commemoration of His miraculous message to her. And she managed to do this after her release from prison.[27]

While Yashka's memoir reveals the traditional faith of a peasant, some villagers participated in local church councils in the late 19th and early 20th centuries. These councils expanded charitable activities, built and repaired local churches and chapels, and tried to discourage others from joining the Old Believers, Baptists, or sectarian movements. After 1905, even village women were allowed to participate in Russian Orthodox Church councils.[28] The picture of Nyrob by Prokudin-Gorsky shows the prominence of the church in the village.

Prokudin-Gorsky, "Village of Nyrob," 1910

3. Religious Visions

> Suddenly she lifted her head and saw above the crucifix a lambent radiance which lit up the whole room and then faded. This phenomenon repeated itself twice more. Mother took it as a sign from heaven...
>
> Anna Dostoevsky, *Reminiscences*

Some Russian women had religious visions, and Anna Dostoevsky tells of one her Swedish Lutheran mother had when praying about her fiancé. She recorded it in her *Reminiscences*:

> On the eve of her final answer to my father, late at night, she was on her knees for a long time in front of the crucifix, praying and asking God to come to her help. Suddenly she lifted her head and saw above the crucifix a lambent radiance which

lit up the whole room and then faded. This phenomenon repeated itself twice more. My mother took it as a sign from heaven that she was to decide her perplexing problem in my father's favor.[29]

Years later, a visiting American recounts a vision that a peasant seamstress told him:

> I dreamed I was back here at home on the river bank with my sister looking up at the sunset clouds, when all at once the heavens broke open like a torn sheet of paper. I felt myself float up in the sky. With me was an old beggar who had loved my father and had sung holy songs by the church. I was terribly hungry. I saw Christ sitting at a table. He was not like the pictures. He looked both wonderfully young and many millions of years old. He said 'You are hungry.' I begged Him for bread. He broke off such a little piece, and I ate it and was hungry still. But He said,
> 'You must be satisfied with the little you received. For the little will be great.'
> I knew what He meant. It was my child. I must work hard for this one small life and do my best to make it great....
> More and more I was sure that my child would be great—for we Russians are a deep people, and there are miracles in our souls, if only we can bring them out.[30]

B. Russian Religion and Culture

> You wouldn't have long to wait for a holy day; and when they came along you should have heard the bells, huge crowds in the churches and you'd stroll out yourself among all these people in your finery...
> Nadezhda Sokhanskaya, "A Conversation After Dinner"

Religion and ritual blended into peoples' lives during courtship, weddings, baptisms, and funerals. While aristocratic women might go to balls or the opera in Moscow or St. Petersburg to see and be seen, the provincial gentry did this at the local church. No matter how weak or strong their faith, church remained an important social and spiritual part of their lives. Allusions to this occur in several women's writings.

1. Courtship and the Church

> I became quite fond of the divine service and always rose for matins even earlier than my aunt. At last my talks with Kiriak attracted my aunt's attention. She began observing us and questioned my cousin...
> Nadezhda Durova, *The Calvary Maiden*

An unlikely account of courtship at church shows up in the journals of Nadezhda Durova (1783-1866), a woman who served in the Tsar's army during the Napoleonic War. One might not expect to find references to religion in such a place, but several occurred. An unusual woman, Durova disguised herself as a male cavalry officer and served in the Hussars from 1806-1815. In the introductory section of *The Cavalry Maiden, Journals of a Russian Officer in the Napoleonic Wars*, she describes her courtship at church around 1800:

> My aunt, like all Ukrainian women, was very devout and observed and followed strictly all the rites prescribed by religion. Every holy day she attended high mass, vespers, and matins, and my cousin and I had to do the same. At first I was very reluctant to get up before dawn to go to church, but in our neighborhood there lived a lady landowner named Kiriakova with her son, and they always came to church too. While we waited for the service to begin, Kiriakova conversed with our aunt, and her son, a young man of twenty-five, would join us, or rather me, because he spoke only to me. He was very good looking, with beautiful black eyes, hair, and brows, and a youthful fresh complexion. I became quite fond of the divine service and always rose for matins even earlier than my aunt. At last my talks with young Kiriak attracted my aunt's attention. She began observing us and questioned my cousin, who at once told her that Kiriak had taken my hand and asked me to give him my ring, saying that he could consider himself sanctioned to speak to my aunt.[31]

This flirtation did not work out, and like many gentry-class women Durova could not marry the man she loved because she lacked a sizeable dowry. So, she was sent back to her grandmother's for the remainder of the summer. When she left her grandmother's, Durova records a typical Orthodox blessing:

> ...On the third day my venerable grandmother hugged me to her breast and kissing me, said: 'Go, my child! The Lord's blessing on your journey and his blessings on your journey through life as well.' She placed her hand on my head and quietly invoked God's protection on me. The prayer of this righteous woman was heard: throughout my turbulent martial life I have often had occasion to experience the clear intercession of the Almighty....[32]

Mid 19th century writer Nadezhda Sokhanskaya's critique of church courtship occurs in "A Conversation After Dinner:"

> 'There were some lovely churches: all made of stone and with five cupolas...You wouldn't have long to wait for a holy day; and when they came along you should have heard the bells, huge crowds in the churches and you'd stroll out yourself among all these people in your finery: a nice colourful frock on and well made: mama's great big earrings and a lovely crimson ribbon round your head with a bow on the side—phew, my darling girl, it was just grand! You felt like there was no one finer than you in the whole wide world! You'd walk along, as if you were floating on air.' ...
>
> 'Well, here's what's really nice, she said. 'After mass, you'd go out into the church-porch, decorously, sedately like; you'd stop in the porch to chat to your friends. You'd stand there chatting, and you wouldn't seem to be looking anywhere at all; but you could still see all the young court officials looking all eyes at you. Then us young ladies, arm in arm, would go off for a bit of a promenade round the church, and they'd follow us on the quiet, like. They'd stop somewhere, so's we'd have to pass them; there they'd be hands in pockets, just waiting for us. As we'd draw level with 'em, they'd say to us: 'What lovelies you are, young ladies: nice and comely! We ought to take the glasses off our judge's big nose so's we could look at you with four eyes.' 'You can look with five if you like,' we'd say back

to them, 'but you won't catch us looking at you even with one eye.' And off we'd trot again, as if we were above all this, but all the same we'd have a sneaky little look at them...That's the way it is, dearie, with a young girl's eye.' Lyubov Arkhipovna concluded: 'it's like she's not looking at all, but she sees what she needs to.'[33]

Likewise, Nadezhda Khvoshchinskaya's novella *The Boarding-School Girl* unsympathetically portrays provincial parents showing off their marriageable young daughters—dressing them up for church so other parents and eligible men could inspect them:

> The next day was a holiday in the parish, and Lolenka's mama to her great surprise, told her that evening that she wouldn't be going to her exams but should get up early and prepare for church. In the morning Mama ironed the ribbons and straightened Lolenka's hat. She added four rosebuds, stored for a long time in the chest of drawers....Lolenka was dressed in all this, along with the white muslin dress prepared for graduation. Anxious and fretful, Mama ordered her to make the sign of the cross and say a prayer over everything she was putting on. They took so long to get ready that the church bells had even stopped ringing. Papa hurried; he was wearing his uniform and was also going to church. Even Pelageya Semyonovna [a matchmaker], who had arrived so they all could go to pray together, hurried and offered her advice about Lolenka's attire....
>
> Her father was conversing with some gentlemen—apparently, Pelageya Semyonovna's sons. It occurred to Lolenka to take a look at them; but she wasn't surprised, although she might have been, that her father was speaking with young men and that three of these young men were accompanying them to the crossroads....
>
> Lolenka didn't even notice how the young men and Pelageya Semyonovna said good-bye and how Papa, Mama, and she herself arrived home.[34]

Church courting did not always go smoothly. The Sunday that the intended groom Farforov intended to impress Lolenka and her mother, he was upstaged by the Treasurer's wife who had arrived in a stunning red velvet cloak, attracting the attention of everyone in the church.

Such elegant attire was a rarity for a remote parish. The lady arrived late and behaved fashionably....She was brought two pieces of communion bread, and at the end of the service the church warden gave her a third piece with a deep bow.

'That's the treasurer's wife,' Mama said to Pelageya Semonovna. 'Why isn't she in the cathedral?'

Mama was so interested in the appearance of such an important person that she barely responded to a bow from the young clerk Farforov. The clerk made an even deeper bow to the honorable treasurer's wife, but this elicited no response at all. He walked up to Lolenka, but she was looking at the treasurer's wife, too.

Later, Lolenka's religious behavior is misinterpreted by various onlookers. Having heard that her beloved Verititsyn was ill, Lolenka prayed at a special icon. Pelageya described the good impression her behavior had on Farforov's mother:

> She marveled at your daughter. 'There, she says, 'is a real zealot. If she bends her head any lower, she'll flip over.' I even said to the old woman, 'Look,' I said, 'what a treasure God is sending your son. As bad-tempered as the old woman is, even she was surprised.'[35]

The eligible bachelor, Farforov the clerk, the same foppish fellow with the watch, a friend of Pelageya Semyonovna's sons, who had come to take a look at Lolenka during church and then was so 'polite' with Papa, had sent Pelageya Semyonovna to ask for permission to marry Lolenka. He would probably get a permanent position this year: therefore it was time to think about a wife. Lolenka would turn sixteen this year: therefore it was time to marry her off. This fop was his mother's only son. The mother was a bad-tempered old woman, but ailing, and had money. Her aunt, her godmother, Alyona Gavrilovna, might bestow a little something....But he was seduced by her beauty. 'I only require music,' he says; 'it's really impossible without it.' When he gets his position, you'll give your blessing.[36]

Lolenka's mother and the matchmaker Pelageya went on a short pilgrimage to a nearby monastery to obtain God's favor for Lolenka's forthcoming marriage that they were secretly plotting:

Mama got ready to make a pilgrimage on foot to a nearby monastery; her companion would be Pelageya Semyonovna; they would return in the evening. Lolenka asked to go with them; the many promises she'd made weighed heavily upon her, but the main thing was that she herself didn't know why she wanted to go away somewhere....Mama refused to take her on very sensible grounds—who would look after the children?[37]

In this case, the parents' machinations came to naught because Lolenka absolutely refused to be married off and ran away from home to live with an aunt in St. Petersburg.

In the 1850s, few girls could escape unwanted, arranged marriages. Nadezhda Sokhanskaya tells the amazing story of one young woman who was beaten by her mother until she consented to a "good match." In her story "A Conversation After Dinner," Sokhanskaya describes the character Liubov, who pines away after an arranged marriage, but who is saved by a pilgrim who miraculously comes to her window to talk with her, pray for her, and feed her. Liubov had refused the food her husband provided and had even turned away from God. She says:

> I couldn't pray to him. I absolutely couldn't, no matter how I tried. I'd stand in front of our icons, and put on my cross, but it would seem so heavy to me, so, so heavy...well, I'd stand there for a while, and then walk away....
>
> 'And so I'd sit and sit by my little window,' she continued. 'For other people there were ordinary days and holy days, for them God's bounty flowered in the fields, but for me there was only my mortal anguish, it utterly destroyed me. I never set foot outside the house, as for going visiting or going for a walk—never! I sat as if on a chain, I'd even completely stopped going to church. One reason was that when I did go people seemed to wonder at me as if I was some alien creature walking among them, and the other was—what was the point of me going to church when I had forgotten how you were supposed to pray to God the heavenly Creator.'[38]

One day a beggar woman, a pilgrim, came by her window, and soon she came everyday to cheer up Liubov. Once she brought wild strawberries and communion bread from church. After some time, the pilgrim left to fulfill a vow to go to Kiev, so Liubov was again

Boris Kustodiev, "Easter Greetings," 1912

alone with her misery. Slightly before Easter, Liubov made an effort to bestir herself and mused:

> God's great festival arrived, bringing heavenly joy down here on earth; I thought, I kept thinking, that even if it wouldn't bring me any happiness or joy, then at least for the sake of Easter, I should try to be like other people. So I set to work on everything, dearie, that was needed for the festival. I baked lovely little paskhas, made an Easter cake for the priest, painted eggs, and at the same time didn't overlook alms-giving and sent money to the prisons—I did everything as I'd learned from mama at home...[39]

After an Easter service, her husband gave her the Easter greeting "Christ is risen," and kissed her three times on the cheeks. For the first time since their marriage, Liubov began to feel reconciled to her husband. They then went on a pilgrimage to thank God for the end of their estrangement.[40] This happy ending in Sokhanskaya's story reminds one of Boris Kustodiev's painting, "Easter Greetings," 1912, in which he depicts a happy couple giving each other the Easter greeting and kiss.

2. *Marriage and the Church*

> Father Philip, who had known me since I was a child, blessed me and wished me happiness.
>
> Anna Dostoevsky, *Reminiscences*

Civil marriage was illegal in Tsarist Russia. If one wanted to marry and have legitimate children, one had to marry in church. Some educated people resented church marriages since they were alienated from the government and the church, but they had to clench their teeth and do it anyway. Dr. Anna Zhukova Bek describes her wedding prior to WW I. Writing in her *Life of a Russian Woman Doctor, A Siberian Memoir, 1869-1954*, she reports:

> ...Evgeny Vladimirovich was strongly opposed to church rituals. During my student years I had also completely renounced church religion. Bearing in mind Evgeny Vladimirovich's firm adherence to principle, I could imagine how difficult it would be for him to subject himself to walking with a crown on his head and to other ceremonies of the ritual, and suggested we manage without a wedding ceremony. He did not want to subject me to ridicule and scorn. In those days women who were not married in the church bore a stigma. Further, Evgeny Vladimirovich wanted to have children, and the sigma of illegitimate birth would fall on them (if we were not married in church). All this made him take control of himself and move to an uncharacteristic compromise. We made no special preparations for the wedding. There was no wedding party except for the necessary two witnesses. On his side Dr. Podtyagin was the witness; on my side was my childhood friend (Tonya) Ryndina. During the whole time of the wedding Evgeny Vladimirovich's dispir-

ited mood was striking. I saw how he pressed his lips together squeamishly when the priest brought him the cup of wine. Not insisting, the priest hurried to pass the cup to me.

On leaving the church his first words to me were: 'Now we are together our entire lives.' Obviously he had lightened his unpleasant state with this thought during the ceremonies.[41]

Of course, most Russian women in the 19th century were not as educated or unchurched as Anna Bek. Marriage was a sacrament in Russian culture and the Orthodox Church, and a wedding icon was often given to the newly weds on their marriage. It was hung in the bedroom, and was sometimes exquisitely decorated with pearls. The richer the family, the more beautiful the icon. A little lamp burnt before it night and day.[42]

Neither Countess Tolstoy nor Anna Dostoevsky note being given a special wedding icon, but both describe being blessed by their mothers before the wedding. Sofia Tolstoy remembered her mother taking down the icon of St. Sophia, and with her brother Michael Islenyev, her mother blessed her with it. Likewise when she arrived at Yasnaya Polyana two days later Lev Tolstoy's Aunt held up the icon of the Holy Virgin, and next to her Tolstoy's brother Sergei stood with the welcoming bread and salt. Countess Tolstoy bowed down to the ground, and making the sign of the cross, kissed the icon and her new aunt. Lev Tolstoy did likewise.[43]

Anna Dostoevsky describes her mother's blessing and her religious behavior the day of her wedding in more detail in her *Reminiscences*:

> All evening we reminisced about the good life we had lived together. Now that we were alone, I asked her to give me her blessing for my new life. Thinking of my girlfriends' example, I said that when the bride is blessed in the presence of witnesses, during all the hubbub before the wedding party leaves for the church, the blessing is sometimes more official than real. She blessed me, and we cried a lot; but to make up for it we gave one another our word not to cry the next day at parting, since I didn't want to arrive at the church with my face all swollen and my eyes red with tears.
>
> On the morning of February 15, I arose at dawn and went to Smolny Monastery to early mass, after which I went to see

my confessor, Father Philip Speransky, to ask his blessing... From there I went to pray at my father's grave in Great Okhta Cemetery.[44]

3. Birth and Christenings

> I have come back from Ilya's, where I christened the baby... With his closed eyes and the happy, contented expression, and his little red face filled with the mystery of his soul and his future life, made me pray for him.
>
> Countess Sofia Tolstoya, Diary, 1891

Birth was a mystical as well as a medical event in 19th century Russia. Midwives used incense, holy water, prayers, and chants to "protect" the mother and baby against the "evil eye" at the time of childbirth. One legend held that a woman named Solomonida assisted the Virgin Mary at the birth of Jesus. And a midwife reportedly told an ethnographer in the 1890s:

> As for helping women in labor, the Lord himself commanded this: the Mother of God gave birth by the Holy Spirit, and the old woman Solomonida was at her side and helped in her labor, and so on the icons she is in second place at the Mother of God's side, and we say a prayer to her: 'Remember, Lord, King David and the old woman Solomonida.' And so it is the Lord God Himself has commanded us midwives to help women in labor....

Women giving birth begged in their prayers:

"Holy Mother of God, ...help me during childbirth."

"Old Solomonida, who delivered Christ, help me."[45]

Midwives had an important place in ritually cleansing the mother and baptizing weak babies. The midwife bathed the mother and child in the bathhouse, and this was as important as the church ritual of "cleansing" which occurred 40 days after childbirth. In the washing ritual, the midwife and mother asked each other's forgiveness, and the midwife often added oats, eggs, and hops to the holy water. Then the midwife might say:

As hops are light yet strong, so too will you be;
As the egg is full, so too will you be;
As oats are fair, so too will you be.

Midwives were honored guests at the christening meal, presiding over the Baptism celebration, and later were always invited to the child's wedding. The church encouraged midwives to name and baptize sickly infants because if a child died unbaptized, it could not be buried in hallowed ground and parents might be forbidden to pray for it.[46]

Christenings did not always go easily, at least in the Tolstoy household. While Sophia Tolstoy does not discuss religion much in her diaries, she did remark on the baptism of her grandson and her religious feelings for him in her diary in 1890:

> I had a wire from Ilya asking me to be godmother. Sophie Andreyevna has refused, so has Tanya, so they are making me, faute de mieux. But I don't mind; I am more interested in my little grandson than in the people around, and I shall be glad to do it.[47]

A few days before she discussed the christening, Sophia mentions some other religious observations. On December 28, 1890, she writes:

> The later part of Rod's book is disappointing. His chapter on 'Religion' is vague, and I don't believe he has actually found that solution, that *sens de la vie* for which I have been searching. But none of us have found it, and *never* will. It is the search for it which *is* life. And afterwards the God-Origin from whom we come will once again take us back. No one can live without that constant sense of the divine within one. I never take a single step without saying in my heart: O Lord, help me; O Lord, forgive me; O Lord have mercy on me....And yet I know that my life is far from holy, though all the time I keep thinking: *now* is the moment to begin to be kind to everybody; *now* the whole world around me will become a world of happiness and kindness. But I cannot do it.[48]

Generally, Sophia was unsympathetic to her husband's writings on religion. She thought him arrogant, and considered his literary writings superior to his Christian and philosophic ones.

4. Pilgrimages and Processions

> The Uspensky processional, which began at night and ended at dawn, made the greatest impression on me. During those splendid processionals with their icons and banners, I often stared at the women in their brocade veils."[49]
>
> Praskovia Tatlina, Autobiography

Memoirs provide glimpses into women's spiritual lives. Both rich and poor took part in pilgrimages and religious processions at Easter and other High Holy Days including Christmas, Epiphany, Palm Sunday, Ascension, Pentecost, The Transfiguration, and the Annunciation. Local and personal feasts included John the Baptist, which coincided with the summer solstice, special feasts for blessing the land and animals, and one's personal name day or Saint's Day, even the anniversary of the founding of a factory. The painting below by Perov shows villagers in a procession celebrating Easter in 1861.

For women of all classes, processions on Holy Days were very important occasions. Gentry-class Irina Tidmarsh remembers an Easter celebration as follows:

> My strongest childhood memories are of the midnight services and feasts we had to celebrate Easter. In the country we would frequently stay with my aunt Zina at her estate called Malashevo. The house was vast, surrounded by an artificial lake where giant carp used to rise to the surface when a bell was rung. She was married to M. M. Kalita, an aristocrat and descendant of one of the founders of the Russian state. When I was older I was taken to the church services; we used to walk to the church in winter. I wore felt boots called *valenki* and fur coats. Flaming braziers were lit in the church. The picture is fixed in my mind. The congregation, after walking in procession round the church, reaches the altar. The golden gates are flung open and the priest sings 'Christ is Risen.' Then the church lights up and the congregation answers 'Yes, indeed. He is Risen.' Everyone kisses each other three times. I always dreaded this because of all the peasants there with prickly beards. At the house a great feast was waiting for us. We broke our seven week fast with *kulich*, special bread blessed in church, *paskhas*, which are sweet cheese cakes made in special

Vasily Perov, "Easter Procession in a Village," 1861 (Wikimedia.)

shapes with engraved letters, coloured eggs, roast piglet, and many kinds of vodka and wine. I always remember the wonderful smell of hyacinths, which were grown in profusion in the greenhouses especially for that procession.[50]

Peasant born Liubov Nikulina-Kositskaia participated in an icon procession, describing it in the following words:

> Everybody knows that every spring the icon of the Vladimir-Oransk Mother of God is brought from Oranki to Nizhny. It is ferried across the river—that is, to the fair and Kunavino for a week or more. Our whole family went to see it off on the ferry. There was a huge crowd of people, all making room for themselves as best they could; we found a spot on rafts, far out from shore....When the icon was put on the boat, everyone who could got into boats, and the boats pulled away from the shore and scattered like light rain across the Oka (River).[51]

Working women and workers' wives also participated in religious marches to monasteries outside the city. Historian Page Her-

Prokudin-Gorsky, "Pilgrims at Church of Tsarevich Dmitry, Uglich," 1910

rlinger estimates that 10,000 to 80,000 went on pilgrimages led by Orthodox priests on summer Sundays. For workers these events occurred after a six day work week. Arising on Sunday at 2 a.m. to dress in their best clothes, they paraded through the city with banners and icons into the countryside to a monastery for a religious service. This showed their special devotion.[52]

Pictures of rural chapels, convents, and shrines by photographer Sergei Prokudin-Gorsky show many as modest yet popular places where people refreshed their souls. Not every village possessed a church, but many had chapels where people could go to hear the scriptures read and partake of communal prayer, which was considered stronger than personal prayer.

Trinity Monastery of St. Sergius

People made pilgrimages, visited chapels and shrines, venerated icons, and went to monasteries for all kinds of reasons. Some sought a blessing or wisdom from a hermit or wise one; some sought healing in body or soul; some sought strength before an undertaking; some wanted a blessing on a forthcoming marriage; some did so because it was fashionable. Countess Tolstoy describes a visit with relatives and friends to the famous Trinity Monastery, near Moscow, in 1860. She was a teenager, about four years before her marriage to the writer Leo Tolstoy. She writes in her diary:

> We reached Troitza at nine in the evening and were given a large, decent room with a fine view of the monastery. The weather is fine, calm, and warm, and inclines one to meditation. The Troitza Monastery made a curious impression on me this time. I never drove into its precincts before with such a feeling of faith and devotion. That's the result of sorrow. I believe that, if I pray, all my cares and sorrows will vanish. It's quite true that 'faith saves.' Although these reflections may seem funny, what can I do when faith and prayer are my only consolation? I have put my trust in God, and shall now tread my path with closed eyes, trusting in

His help and blessing. Life is a hard thing, and I am no good at guiding myself. How often have I made good and firm resolutions, yet each time my powers have failed me and I have had to abandon my intentions. But I'm becoming too pensive. I've got such a queer, silly temperament.[53]

The next morning they went to mass and walked around the historic buildings. The singing at St. Sergius's Church was fine, and one of the monks gave a good sermon on faith and piety. They met a family friend and strolled around with him a bit. Then they bought some icons, toys, and other presents to take home.[54] She never explains why her mother had chosen to go to the monastery at this time, but obviously she was deeply touched by her experience there.

Countess Tolstoy does not write of visiting many shrines or holy places in her diaries for the next 30 years. But after the death of her favorite son Ivan or Vanichka, she recounts a pilgrimage to Pechersk Lavra in Kiev with her sister. It seemed to mitigate her grief a bit. She also mentions praying in many cathedrals and churches after Vanichka's death. However, her grief was so deep and her solace so weak that she didn't write in her diary for two years. It was really the coming of the pianist and composer Sergei I. Taneev and his magical music at Yasnaya Polyana that assuaged her sorrow. Philosophical definitions of God and her husband's religion offered her no consolation. At one point in her diary, she asks: This God is merely an element. But where is the God of love and kindness, God, the spirit, to Whom I pray?[55]

Like Countess Tolstoy, over one million people a year made pilgrimages to Kiev to visit the famous caves of Russian saints. Kiev became more popular and accessible due to the opening of a railway in the 1880s. In her reminiscences, Anna Dostoevsky also tells of visiting Kiev and the holy places there. She took their children there on a pilgrimage in 1877 while her husband was busy one summer publishing his journal *Diary of a Writer*. Approximately 20,000 people a year went to the modest Sepukhov Vladychnyi women's monastery in Moscow in the 1860s.[56]

The aspiring serf actress Kositskaia describes her helpful visit to an Orthodox convent as follows:

> I went to a nunnery where there were nuns we knew. I told them that I didn't want to live in the world anymore and that

I wanted to stay in the nunnery. Of course, they started asking me how and why. I told them that Mama wouldn't let me become an actress. They were horrified at the words and began trying to dissuade me, and I started praying and reading holy books. I wanted to find out whether there was a curse on the theater someplace in them—and what do you think? I opened the first book and read, 'His dominion is in every place.' Not only the nunnery opens the gates of heaven to us, but our good deeds, too! I asked myself who could ban me from doing them when I was in the theater and that made me feel even sadder.'

Emboldened by this discovery, Kositskaia eventually persuaded her mother to bless her career as an actress, and she went on to become a successful one. Apparently Kositskaia sought her mother's permission to become an actress so assiduously because daughters remained under their parent's power until they married, and she was legally as well as morally required to do so.[57]

Religion often shaped the daily lives of peasant women in the forms of certain taboos. On the Fridays before most High Holy Days, spinning and weaving were forbidden. Likewise, these tasks were forbidden between Christmas and the New Year, and sewing and clothes washing were not allowed the week before Pentecost. Menstruating women were not allowed to take communion at church, nor were they allowed to participate in certain agricultural tasks. Pregnant women were also considered "unclean" and could not be a godparent or play a role in a christening. Midwives were usually unmarried or elderly, and only old women were allowed to prepare the communion bread for the Russian Orthodox Church. Women who had given birth were "unclean" for 6 weeks, and were not allowed to enter church, light icon lamps, or touch the icons.[58]

Many working-class women were not free to attend church. While the owners of the Lenzoto Gold Mining Company built several churches and chapels in Siberia, miners and their families often had to work seven days a week and hence had no time for worship. Moreover, some peasants, workers, and other groups were critical of the state run Orthodox Church. One complained to I. S. Aksakov, who was studying the schism between the Orthodox and the Old Believers in Yaroslavl' province: "Your Orthodox faith is a bureaucrat's faith, a townsman's faith, not based on living sincere conviction, but serving as one of the arms of the government to maintain order."[59]

Religious procession, Gatchina 1910

Some peasants and workers were attracted to more charismatic churches like the Brethren which began in St. Petersburg in the 1890s and spread to Moscow after the 1905 Revolution. Shop workers, domestic servants, salesclerks, laborers, and the unemployed flocked to the meetings of the Brethren. At one point the church was led by a skilled metalworker Ivan Koloskov, until he was arrested and imprisoned in 1911. The Brethren urged its members to stop drinking, live moral lives, keep their families together, and stop wife and child abuse. The fervent preaching attracted thousands to this movement.[60] Emphasis on temperance and moral living may have particularly attracted women workers and wives of workers.

Thousands of workers responded to the calls for social justice that the charismatic monk Father Gapon made in January 1905. They joined in a religious/political procession carrying icons and crosses to petition the Tsar to improve their lives, grant an 8 hour day, and generally relieve their sufferings—both spiritual and material. They were horrified when Cossack troops fired on them, wounding and killings hundreds. However, the greatest indignity was that the Tsarist government forbade church officials from burying the dead in consecrated ground. These actions alienated large segments of the working class from the government and church and helped foment the 1905 Revolution.

5. *Healing, Magic, and Religion*

> It happened that I was treated myself and saw how others cure. So I watched closely and began to cure myself: I learned from others.
>
> Marfa, a peasant healer

The lines between miraculous healing, mysticism, and magic were often blurred in Russian society in the 19th century. As the poet Zinaida Gippius phrased it, some "believed in miracles weakly." In Russia, the church sanctioned the invocation of God, saints, angels, and the Mother of God for wholeness. Many peasant healers or znakharki were poor, old women. Most had some training from family members, and many exchanged "recipes" involving herbs for curing the sick. Since illness was often considered a punishment from God, there was also a religious dimension to healing. Sometimes they used charms, chants, and prayers as well as herbs for restoring people to health. An interview with a 19th century peasant healer named Marfa tells about their work. It was presented in an article by Rose Glickman entitled "The Peasant Woman as Healer" and reads as follows:

> 'I remained a widow with six small children, so I had to feed myself somehow.'
> 'Did you learn to cure from someone?'
> 'It's from God.'
> 'Did you begin to cure immediately?'
> 'How can you do it immediately? No, little by little.'
> 'Do you treat with herbs?'
> 'With herbs, with sayings, and I wash with magical water.'
> 'Would you tell anyone these sayings?'
> 'Why not? It's not sinful. I get this from God. So I went among the holy and asked, is it a sin to heal? The old men said, not at all, it's not a sin. You see, I had a dream....I was in

a room and a girl came into the room with a book in one hand and a jug in the other. She looked into the jug and then into the book. Then she says three times, no, it's not a sin. I asked Father Ambrosia about the dream. He said, It's alright, it's given from God. The monks, and the most holy of them, also said it was alright.'[61]

A short story, entitled "The Settlement" by Olga Shapir, also attests to a somewhat magical view of the universe. One of the characters tells her brother who is worried about passing his examinations at the gimnaziya:

"You've lost the way to the Church. Tell you what, you should drop in to vespers tomorrow, and pray as hard as ever you can, and I'll give you five copecks for a candle, then things will take a turn for the better, you'll see. Your fright will disappear as though you'd never felt it, and things (will) turn out all right again."[62]

Similarly in *The Boarding-School Girl*, the writer Khvoshchinskaya portrays a student Lolenka who prays before her classes and before her exams. "She made three deep bows before the icon, recited the prayer 'Before the Beginning of Studies,' and set off for school accompanied by the maid."[63] Normally Lolenka did very well at school, but she had muddled her exams the day before and her classmates were dismayed. Looking at her almost in fear, they asked if someone had bewitched her. "They advised her to pray very hard and promise to light a candle before an icon."[64]

While Russian women often made pilgrimages to pray for their concerns in the late 19th century, some also wrote to revered holy men such as Father John of Kronstadt, a renowned healer and priest. In one letter, a woman asks Fr. John's prayers of intercession for her alcoholic husband:

He never goes past the taverns, *as if he is drawn there by some unseen force*. When he comes home he always goes into his cursing, his foul songs, his dancing...Please pray for us sinners not to perish in this abyss of sin, for the Lord to rescue my husband from this poison, from enemies and destroyers—but above all for the Lord to at least save him from a bad death—at least let the Lord give him death with repentance, as often when he drinks vodka he falls into some kind of delirium, saying *words that recall the unclean spirits...*

According to historian Nadia Kizenko in *A Prodigal Saint, Fr. John of Kronstadt and the Russian People*, Fr. John received bushels of similar letters every day from desperate women, as the following one asking for relief in caring for her young daughter who had been attacked and literally sacred out of her wits:

> Now she spends all day and night on my lap and will not let me step away for an instant, she will not allow others to come near her either. Please pray either for her to die or for her to quiet down and let me go away from her for at least an hour or so. There are idiots in families—I can resign myself to that, and do not murmur at God. I am ready to bear any work, any penance, but just not this.[65]

A well-to-do woman wrote for healing for her husband:

> We have heard so much about your universal help and decided to ask for your holy prayers and healing, and I wrote you for the first time in July. At that time my husband was going to Moscow for business and wanted to seek counsel with doctors again while he was there, but I dissuaded him because I had sent you a letter. And because I was so hoping for your healing, because I believed in it so much, I waited for my husband's return in complete confidence to see him completely well. But what sadness I was in when I learned that he still could not hear! Batiushka! (Little Father) Our only hope is in God! I implore you, pray for him....I will be very, very grateful to you.[66]

Women who were in dire financial straights also asked Fr. John to help them. One confused religious intercession with magic, asking Fr. John to bless her lottery ticket:

> If you are a kind Father and close to God and the Almighty is accessible to you—you have to—your heart has to—feel compassion for me. How many tears, how many torments of the heart have fallen onto my unfortunate lot. O, Lord, enough already!
>
> Otherwise the Lord is vicious, and not merciful. I prayed to Him, prayed to the point of losing consciousness, but He does not hear me. Holy Father! The Lord hears your prayers

and fulfills them. I implore you by the Queen of Heaven, by all the saints, by the Lord Jesus Christ our Savior; I conjure you through the power and might of the Life-giving Cross, the Unfathomable Holiness of the Lords' Body and Blood; I conjure you by the Holy Creed; and beg you to pray for me, may the Lord hear and fulfill my small and modest wish: I have a single lottery ticket: let it win! This will give me the possibility of being further away from people's squabbles and filth. (If I win,) I will put more than a tenth into your disposal, worthy Father.

If the Lord and his inscrutable Mysteries exist, if your prayers are valid, then my wish and my request will be granted, and faith will grow stronger in my soul, and I will glorify the name of the Lord, and yours, too, spiritual father....I conjure you one more time from the depth of my heart, I conjure you by the Holy Gifts of Communion: pray sincerely for my request, which is so possible for the Lord—let Him show his Merciful Mightiness and the Wonder and the Power and the Might of the prayers of the Righteous man who is pleasing to Him.[67]

Apparently Fr. John did not look kindly upon intercessions for winning lottery tickets, but he did direct funds to help impoverished wives and mothers, especially ones like the following from Princess Vera Shakhovskaia for whom he had provided prayer services at her house:

You served *molebens* at our house more than once—but I was rich. And every time you served at our house, God gave us happiness and good fortune. But now all that is changed. My husband has died, leaving me penniless with three sons.... Now I beg you on my knees, as the mother of her children. Do you have any idea of what it is like when children who were brought up in luxury cry, 'Mama, give us some bread!' Now everything is pawned, there is no money to get it back....For you some hundred and fifty rubles is not worth thinking about, for me it is a question of life or death. If this sum should seem too great for any reason, please help us as much as you find possible. ...

You are the first person I am turning to. You will understand me and your responsive heart will say its own word on my behalf kind Batiushka.[68]

A similar request came from Princess Nadezhda Obolenskaia:

> You are our Shrine, your prayers reach the Almighty. I have just buried my brother Boris (Prince Golitsyn), and this has affected my dear son's health so much that he is now sick with a nervous disorder. He is all I have. He has to be taken abroad immediately. I buried my husband not long ago, and who knows when they will start issuing us a pension....
>
> What will a mother not do for her child. So I am asking you for my son's sake, do not refuse me. I am asking you for 225 rubles; if this should be difficult for you, please help as much as you can.
>
> *Not long ago, dear Batiushka, you helped my cousin, Princess Vera Shakhovskaia, and I beg you to respond to my request as favorably as you did to hers*....Your sentence will be the sentence of the Almighty.[69]

Then, as now, "sunshine" Christians—those who loved God when all went well, but shunned the sacraments and church when affliction came—appeared in Varvara's letter below:

> You have been sent by god to all of us who sorrow, now listen to me and my woe, ask god for me for him to help me. I have gone through and am going through so much that my patience is coming to an end....People have taken away all my fortune after a whole series of sufferings. All I have left is one noble's lottery ticket and a three thousand ruble debt of honor. You can ask god for me and He will do it for you; you yourself say: 'Just believe and pray and God will give you whatever you ask for.' Well, I have prayed, to the point of frenzy, to the point of anguish....As I prayed, I believed that there is a God and that He hears me—well, those were just thoughts. There is no happiness for me, but when you look around, you see people, there they go, living and being happy. Is it a sin to want the kind of happiness and life you should have, in the circle you come from?
>
> I haven't gone to confession or communion for—soon it will be three years, and I just can't. If I become fortunate—then and only then will I go to church.[70]

C. Sorrow, Sadness, and Death

> For the sweetest dream is the Kingdom of Heaven after death, and the thought of being united with God, and of meeting again the beloved who have gone.
>
> Countess Sofia Tolstoy, Diary, 1897

Haunted by her beloved son Vanya's death, Countess Tolstoy remarks in her diary that she dreams of heaven where she will be reunited with him.[71] Many Russian lyrical poets wrote about sorrow, sadness, and death. One of the premier poets Mirra Lokhvitskaya was particularly existential in her poem "O, we—the sorrowful,":

O we—the sorrowful,
We—the damned,
Participants in good,
Defeated by evil,
In our dreams—exalted,
In our deeds—deceitful,
In our impulses—wild,
In our tears—pitiful!

Chosen by Fate,
Ignorant of happiness,
We wander—strange ones—
Amidst foul weather,
In love with a star,
By a star protected,
Unsatisfied,
Unsatisfying.

O we—the sorrowful,
We—the damned,
Participants in good,
Born in evil,
Have tasted the fruit
Of knowledge in sin,
Have forgotten our paradise
In the darkness of exile.

1900-1902, IV, 29[72]

In her poem "A Prayer for those who are Perishing," Lokhvitskaya reveals the Orthodox attitude of a merciful God. She implores a forgiving God to pardon the rebellious and those who have fallen away from the faith:

> O, righteous God,
> Hear my prayers
> For the souls of those who are perishing
> Without absolution;
> For all those anguishing,
> For all those suffering,
> For those striving toward You,
> For those ignorant of You!
>
> I do not beg for obedience
> And hope
> For you, the humble,
> Whose life—is silence.
> For you, who are meek in spirit,
> You, who are pure of heart,
> The horny paths
> Are easy and joyful.
>
> But for you, the rebellious,
> Those who have sorely fallen away,
> Who have confused ecstasy
> With madness and evil,
> For the torments of these chosen,
> For the pain of their moment—
> I beg awareness
> And revelation!
>
> 1900-1902, IV, 13[73]

Heavy subjects like visiting a grave are not so morose in the pen of the lyrical poet Poliksena Solovyova (1867-1924). Her poem "In the Crypt," speaks of love and joy:

> A ray of Spring's sun slipped through a low window
> Into the gloomy darkness of the mute crypt;
> Onto the cold floor it threw
> A spot of warmth, like a summons to forgotten merriment.

With a pale smile, the crosses responded,
Their dull silver showing white on the palls;
The wreaths' leaves, withered and decayed,
Sensed through their slumber the breathing of the laurel groves.

The door scarcely opened...with a rush of the breeze
Spring's greeting descended upon the silent graves,
And someone's delicate and slender hand
Laid spring flowers upon the tomb.

All again fell silent, but the bright blooms
Smelled even more delicate in the cold dusk,
Like forgotten yet eternal dreams,
And whispered to the dead of love and joy.[74]

D. Dissatisfaction with Traditional Religion

> I tried to stay away from the Saint-Mary-Appease-My-Grief icon, and other things I felt nothing in common with. Every Sunday in the chapel there was a row of small coffins containing the bodies of newborn infants—six-eight, sometimes even more.
>
> Nina Berberova, The Italics Are Mine

Many students, intellectuals and some workers were disillusioned and refused to go to church in the early 20th century. Some were weak believers, some antagonistic, some reluctant, others alienated. Worker Valentina Petrova's memoir, as presented in Page Herlinger's *Working Souls*, revealed that as a child and youth, her mother and grandmother had coerced her into going to church. A woman in her culture was not considered "good" or "respectable" if she did not learn the Orthodox rites and rituals. She remarked that they "chased us to church and on pilgrimages." Only long after the 1917 Revolution, did she decide that she didn't need to go to church. Many others had lost their faith and religious worldview after the 1905 Revolution when about 100 peaceful worker demonstrators were killed and about 500 wounded by Tsarist troops on Bloody Sunday, and the church authorities did not side with the workers against the government.[75]

Writer Nina Berberova (1901-1993) says in her memoir *The Italics Are Mine* that she didn't go to the Russian Orthodox Church, but was 'taken.' When she grew up and could no longer be forced to go she still remembered all the dead babies laid out in church each Sunday. "Unchristened babies were buried on one side of the cemetery, christened ones on the other."[76] By the age of nine she found poetry, not church, the holier experience.[77]

In *The Book of Happiness*, Berberova's heroine eschews sentimentality and refuses to give a fellow a piece of her braid. He then asks her to make the sign of the cross over him, and she says:

> 'But I...you know...I'm not much of a believer...,' she said clumsily, but she made the sign of the cross at the bridge of his nose. 'May God preserve you and help you. Lord, if You exist, make it so that we see each other again.'[78]

How many unchurched families there were in late 19th century Russia is hard to estimate, but Anna Zhukova Bek described her family's disinterest in religion in her memoirs *The Life of a Russian Woman Doctor*. Her mother did not participate in the rites and rituals of the Russian Orthodox Church, and her father paid homage only on church holidays. She recalled their behavior in Siberia where she grew up as follows:

> I remember Mama's attitude concerning church ceremonies. Once, when Nanny complained to Mama about her own son, Misha, who didn't want to go to church, Mama answered, 'What is he a monk? Why should he waste his time hanging around a church'
> My father, N. M. Zhukov, grew up in an uneducated environment. He was indifferent to questions of religion, but he observed the traditions of the church holidays (attending mass in church, entertaining guests, and drinking). In Gugda, the taiga mine where we lived, there was no village or church nearby. On the mornings of big holidays (Easter and Christmas) my father gathered us children together in a room before the icon, and he himself stood in front of us and prayed silently (he crossed himself and kissed the icon) and we had to pray the same way. This lasted no more than five minutes, and then he took the ladle, previously prepared with incense, and burned it, so that the perfume of incense would be sufficiently dispersed throughout the apartment. After this, we had to ap-

Natalya Goncharova, "Nativity," 1910

proach him in turn and wish him a happy holiday. Mama did not take part in these ceremonies. Father was very hospitable; he always invited guests, and holidays ended with drinking and card games.[79]

Russian artist Natalya Goncharova painted many religious topics, but from a new perspective. Contemporaries thought her paintings of the Evangelists resembled huge peasants more than iconic holy men. Her lithographs for the book *Mystical Images of the War* in 1914 show some of her religious and apocalyptic themes. Her depiction of the Nativity was modern and cubist.

Writing around the First World War, poet Maria Shkapskaya reveals rather negative views towards religion. In one entitled "Magdalene," she reveals her rancor towards God:

> The scroll of my days was not long,
> Its writings were ungodly.
> I went the way of Magdalene
> And repented—as did she.

And, as she, I waited humbly.
But Christ did not come to me,
Nor did He touch kindly
My hair flowing free.

And from that time, day after day,
Performing my daily labor,
I bear a vessel filled to the brim
With never ending rancor.[80]

E. New Religions

> What the upper and educated classes of women seek in the sciences, higher education, and the liberal professions, the poor, ignorant peasant women find in mystical religion.
>
> Marie Zebrikov, "Russia,"

While Russian Orthodoxy remained the predominant religion prior to WW I, it was also a time of new sects like the ecstatic khlysty and Skoptsy, the pacifist Dukhabors, Tolstoyans, and various other scripture based groups in the cities. Some peasants and workers became Baptists some Bible based Stundists. Since more Russians had become literate, many preferred scripture as their authority, not the hierarchical, government dominated Russian Orthodox Church. After the Revolution of 1905 and the October Manifesto of 1906, Russians gained some measure of religious freedom and many took advantage of it to join hitherto forbidden "sects" or groups.

In the late 19th century, some peasant women sought relief from abusive marriages in religious sects where they were treated better. The khlysty often referred to men as "Christs" and women as "Mother of God." The Skoptsy often castrated themselves, and women in this religion often found a community way of life without abusive marriage. According to feminist critic Marie Zebrikov in her article "Russia" (1884), some maidens and some married women fled despotic families to live in a sect, where husband and wife stood on an equal footing, and the marriage lasted as long as both parties were satisfied. Although the sects were sometimes persecuted, women were devoted and heroic, even martyred. Women often preached, and the sects were distinguished by their high moral level, purity and tenderness of domestic life. Some sects were ascetic and women took vows of chastity, consecrating their lives to nursing the sick and studying the Bible.[81]

1. Tolstoyans

> Her whole life is just a fanatical adoration of Lev Nikolaevich. She was once a devout churchgoer; but, after reading Lev Nikolaevich's articles, she took down all the ikons and hung up his portraits all over the place, and collected a whole lot of his prohibited works, and makes a living by copying them out for other people.
>
> Countess Tolstoy, *Diary*, 1897

Around the turn of the 20th century, many artists, writers, intellectuals, even workers were Bogoiskateli or God-seekers, looking for new religious ideas. Some were influenced by Lev Tolstoy and took up simple Christianity and rural living. However, the Russian Orthodox Church excommunicated Tolstoy for his religious writings, and many of his followers had to emigrate to other places. Tolstoy's wife was exasperated by his religion and his followers, describing them as "dark people" and berated them for interrupting life at Yasnaya Polyana. Thinking of the needs of their eight children, spouses, and grandchildren, Countess Tolstoy feared for the extended family's financial survival—especially if the Tsarist government chose to deport them due to Tolstoy's pacifist writings and his condemnation by the Orthodox Church. She was especially concerned for her family's financial welfare because all the revenues of the copyrights of Tolstoy's later writings had been made over to a Tolstoyan foundation in London. In January, 1895, she writes:

> ...That's why I cannot share my husband's *ideas*—which are false and insincere. It is all so strained and artificial, and the basis is all wrong; it is all vanity, this endless thirst for fame, this everlasting desire to become more and more and more popular. No one believes what I say, and everyone's indifference is terribly painful.[82]

Describing a Tolstoyan in 1897, Sofia remarks:

Countess Tolstoya (right) and family circle at Yasnaya Polyana, ca. 1905

> M. A. Schmidt was here...She is terribly thin, and completely wears herself out doing all the work herself and growing wildly enthusiastic about her little garden, her cow, her calf, and the whole world. Women can't live without idols, and Lev Nikolaevich is her idol. Vanichka was my idol...but now life is empty and senseless. As an idol, I have knocked Lev Nikolaevich over. I still feel devoted to him, and it would be terrible to lose his constant care and affection....But *happiness*, real happiness—no, he is unable to give me that.[83]

Describing other followers, she comments:

> To-day's visitors were: Maude, an Englishman, Boulanger; Zinoviev; and Nadya Ferret. Maude is ponderous and dull; Zinoviev bright and clever, but not very pleasant; Boulanger kind and intelligent and deeply devoted to Lev Nikolaevich and to the whole family. He is very busy just now with the *Posrednik* publications. ...
>
> There were crowds of people at home: Dunayev, Dubensky, and his wife (Tsurikova), Rostovtsev, and Sergeyenko. All the rooms are taken up with people and the chatter goes on all day. I found it very trying. All these people are expecting something from Lev Nikolaevich, so he had decided to write an open letter to be printed abroad. The point is that, Nobel, the Swedish

kerosene man, left a will in which he bequeathed all his millions to the man who would do most for the cause of peace—i.e. against war....Then it was said that Lev Nikolaevich deserved to inherit the fortune. Of course, he would not take the money, but he has written a letter saying that the Dukhobor sect—who had refused to do their military service and had severely suffered for it—had done most for the cause of peace. At first I had nothing against the letter, but later I found that Lev Nikolaevich had attacked the Russian Government in it, in the most coarse and aggressive terms, and for no apparent reason—just for the fun of it. This greatly upset me...for it is hard to live under this constant threat; for Lev Nikolaevich might some day write something really spiteful and desperate against the Government, and then we would be deported.[84]

2. *Spiritualists*

> My mother organized a circle of spiritualist devotees, who would often gather at our place. All the spirits summoned forth predicted the destruction of our state by Rasputin.
>
> Elena Skrjabina, *Coming of Age*

At the turn of the 20th century, some intellectuals felt they were living in an apocalyptic time. Many gentry were fascinated by spiritualism and the occult. Gentry-born Elena Scrjabina recalled how popular spiritualism was before WW I. She recalled the meetings at their estate Obrochnoye in the summer:

> During this period in St. Petersburg, there was a great infatuation with spiritualism ... I found these political séances extremely interesting, and I would try to enter the living room where they were taking place. But I would always be turned away.[85]

For a variety of reasons, some Russians flirted with esoteric wisdom and the concepts of the Motherhood of God and the Brotherhood of Man.[86] Some Social Democrats like Anatoly Lunacharsky, Alexander Bogdanov, and the writer Maxim Gorky became Bogostroiteli or God Builders. They wanted to create a humanistic, comforting, and inspiring religion emanating from the ideas of the brotherhood and perfectibility of man in socialist society.

Mme. Blavatsky, Courtesy Wikimedia

3. Mme. Blavatsky and Theosophy

At the turn of the 20th century, some intellectuals responded to the Russian thinker Elena Blavatsky (1831–1891), who developed a new spirituality based on a synthesis of Eastern and Western religion, science, psychology, and spiritualism. She perceived the evolution of the universe and mankind as a spiritual event, not a materialist one. Blavatsky had traveled to Tibet and India, and in conjunction with the American Colonel Olcott founded the Theosophical Society in the U.S. in 1875 and published the *Theosophical Review* in London and the journal *Lotus* in Paris. One of their concerns was transmitting the religious beliefs of Hinduism and Buddhism to the West. Their idea of Divine Wisdom included the Sanskrit literature of the Upanishads and Vedas as well as Christian theology. In some ways, Blavatsky was a precursor of the "New Age" movement in the 20th century. While considered a fraud by some for her spiritualist work, others found solace in her writings like *The Secret Doctrine*, which shows the syncretism of her thought:

> The fundamental identity of all Souls with the Universal Over-Soul, the latter being itself an aspect of the Unknown Root; and

the obligatory pilgrimage for every soul—a spark of the former—through the Cycle of Incarnation, or Necessity, in accordance with Cyclic and Karmic Law, during the whole term. In other words, no purely spiritual Buddha (Divine Soul) can have an independent (conscious) existence before the spark which issued from the pure Essence of the Universal Sixth Principle—or the OVER-SOUL—has (a) passed through every elemental form of the phenomenal world of that Manvantara, and (b) acquired individuality, first by natural impulse, and then by self-induced and self-devised efforts, checked by its Karma, thus ascending through all the degrees of intelligence, from the lowest to the highest Manas, from mineral and plant, up to the holiest Archangel (Dhyani-Buddha). The pivotal doctrine of the Esoteric Philosophy admits no privileges or special gifts in man, save those won by his own Ego through personal effort and merit throughout a long series of metempsychoses and reincarnations. This is why the Hindus say that the Universe is Brahman and Brahma, for Brahman is in every atom of the universe, the six Principles in Nature being all the outcome—the variously differentiated aspects—of the SEVENTH and ONE, the only Reality in the Universe whether cosmic or micro-cosmic, and also why the permutations, psychic, spiritual and physical, on the plane of manifestation and form, of the Sixth (Brahma and vehicle of Brahman) are viewed by metaphysical antiphrasis as illusive and mayavic. For although the root of every atom individually and of every form collectively, is that Seventh Principle or the One Reality, still, in its manifested phenomenal and temporary appearance, it is no better than an evanescent illusion of our senses.[87]

Initially Blavatsky's impact was greater in the U.S., England, and France than in Russia. This was because the Russian Orthodox Church and the Tsarist Government refused to allow Theosophical Societies to register and legally disseminate their ideas in the late 19th century. Still, her book *Isis Unveiled,* while not sold at Russian bookshops, did circulate privately. Despite attacks on her work as plagiarism, artists like Viacheslav Voloshin and writers like Andrei Bely, Olga Forsh, Viacheslav Ivanov, Dmitri Merezhkovsky, and his wife Zinaida Gippius, even Social Democrats like Maxim Gorky and Anatoly Lunacharsky engaged with it. Forsh gave a lecture "On Buddhism and Pythagorus" to a Theosophical Society meeting in

Kiev in 1907. Scores of feminists like philanthropist Anna Filosofova gave their money and prestigious salons for spiritualist discussions, while others like Anna Kamenskaya devoted their lives to spreading Theosophical ideas. Kamenskaya translated the Hindu text of the *Bhagavad-Gita* into Russian and French.

After the 1905 Revolution and the granting of freedom of speech, several Theosophical Societies and their journals opened in the major cities and a few hundred official members registered. Anna Kamenskaya became President of the Russian Theosophical Society, which flourished from 1908 until 1918. In the mid 1920s, the Bolsheviks began confiscating the society's money and imprisoning and exiling their leaders. So Kamenskaya fled to Geneva in 1925, where her French translation of the *Bhagavad-Gita* became her dissertation at the University of Geneva, and where she taught comparative religion, philosophy, and aesthetics until 1950. As Theosophy went underground in Russia, it later reappeared in some of the memoirs of purge victims in the 1930s and in the 1990s after the fall of Communism[88]

4. Zinaida Gippius and New Orthodoxy

The whole world is free to be ruined—or to be saved.

Zinaida Gippius

Unlike Blavatsky who rejected the Russian Orthodox Church, the Russian symbolist writer Zinaida Gippius endorsed the liturgy and Eucharist, but formed a secret religious group called "The Cause." She along with many other artists, intellectuals, and clergy believed that the government controlled Orthodox Church had become stagnant and needed renewal. Like Blavatsky, Gippius thought the Church had participated in the development of humanity but believed that spiritual evolution would produce new concepts and revelations. God-seekers like Gippius and her husband Dmitry Merezhkovsky were building a new Christianity influenced by the mystical ideology of the writer Theodor Dostoevsky and the philosopher Vladimir Soloviev. They believed that old values should not be rejected, but transformed through new ones. Both saw the epoch in which they lived as an apocalyptic one in which Jesus was a Revolutionary. Gippius thought the historical process is revealed, not predestined by fate:

It is indicated, not predestined…Whether this process will lead us into Nothingness, into absolute negation, or to an attainment of the highest level of Being, an absolute affirmation depends entirely on the strength and the intensity of mankind's will and on the unity of this will with the universal, Divine will. It can be said with certainty that each man harbors a tremendous yearning to reach his ultimate destination, since the world ultimately desires to be saved.[89]

Many of her poems show her existentialism, alienation, and struggle. Her poem "Chaos," reveals her spiritual plight in 1907:

> As though wet bluster, you knock the shutters,
> A black-hued bluster, you sing: you're mine!
> I'm ancient chaos, your old companion,
> Your sole companion—so open wide!
>
> I grasp the shutter, I dare not open,
> I hold the shutter, and hide my fear,
> I keep, I coddle, I keep, I treasure
> My last faint light—my caring love.
> But chaos blindly, in laughter, summons:
> You'll die in shackles—break out, break out!
> You know elation, for you are single,
> Your joy's in freedom—and in Unlove.
>
> My blood runs colder. I now am praying,
>   A prayer for loving I scarce can make…
>   My hands grow weaker, I lose the battle,
>   My hands are weaker…I'll open up![90]

Her poem "Monotony," written in 1895, also shows her sadness and anxiety:

> In the evening hour of solitude,
> Despondency and weariness
>   Alone, on unsteady steps,
> I search in vain for consolation,
> Alleviation of my anxiety
>   In the stagnant, freezing waters.
>   …

Zinaida Gippius

> But I know, there is no absolution for this world,
> No oblivion for the sadness of the heart,
> And no resolution of this silence—
> Everything is forever without alteration,
>   Both on earth and in the heavens.⁹¹

Her youthful poetry contained many despondent laments as her poem "A Cry," written in 1896 indicates:

> I grow numb from exhaustion,
>   My soul is wounded and bloody…
> Is there really no pity for us,
>   Really, for us, no love?
>
> We fulfill an implacable will,
>   Like shadows, noiseless, without a trace,

> We walk an unforgiving road
>> And don't even know where we're bound.
>
> And the burden of life, a sacred burden,
>> The further we go, the heavier it grows...
> While an unknown demise awaits us
>> At an eternally locked door.
>
> Without a murmur, without a surprise
>> We do what God desires.
> He created us without inspiration,
>> And after that, could not love us.
>
> We fall down, an impotent lot,
>> Weakly believing in miracles,
> While from above, like a tombstone slab,
>> The blind heavens press down.[92]

Her poem "Psyche" reveals the torment and anguish she wrestled with in her spiritual and intellectual life. Her description of her soul is described as a dark snake, loathsome in the final stanza:

> ...
> With stubborn rings it winds in mute obscurity
> And clings caressingly, its purpose whole.
> And this dead thing, this loathsome block of impurity,
> This horror that I shrink from—is my soul.[93]

As a religious revolutionary, poet, and mystic, she redefined God as Father and Mother, and saw the Mother of God as the revelation of the Holy Spirit. This was a common attitude among 19th century Russian mystics, who spoke of the feminine spiritual essence of the universe in terms such as "the Eternal Feminine," (Vechnaia Zhenstvennost), "the Soul of the World" (Dusha Mira), and "the companion of the Lord" (Podruga Boga). Theologian Nicholas Berdiaev argued: "The fundamental category is motherhood. The Mother of God takes precedence of the Trinity and is almost identified with the Trinity." Critic Mikhail Epstein interpreted Gippius' poetic and personal struggle blending religion with life, making life holy and interpreting the holiness of religion as life.[94]

Critical of the government controlled Russian Orthodox Church, Gippius and Merezhkovsky founded the Religious Philosophical Society where famous artists and high-ranking clergy openly discussed church affairs, art, religion, creative intuition, and the mystery of the spirit. She sought and received Procurator Pobedonotsev's permission for the Society to meet legally in 1901, but he closed it in 1903. What interested Gippius most was the establishment of the Kingdom of God on Earth, not political revolution, and she was very disappointed in the results of the 1905 and 1917 Russian Revolutions.[95]

Many, like Gippius, felt writing was a religious act, a way of praising God. Decades earlier than Gippius, Sokhanskaia noted that writing reveals woman's innermost being and is sacred. Despite social injunctions against women writers in the mid 19th century, she decided to keep writing until God commanded her to stop. She replaced society's laws with a higher authority, defending her writing and accomplishments as gifts bestowed by God. She saw owning her abilities as neither boastful nor egotistical, but a way of praising God.[96]

F. Conclusion

As the above writings and pictures reveal, Russian women had a variety of religious attitudes, practices, and experiences in the late 19th and early 20th centuries. Despite government and social restrictions on women's becoming nuns, tens of thousands did so. Thousands made pilgrimages to special shrines or appealed to holy persons whom they consulted in difficult times. Many expressed a simple, positive belief in God's mercy and comfort. Most peasants remained Orthodox, while some thousands joined new sects to find better lives. Some educated women, followed a variety of paths from the God seekers like the poet Gippius to the followers of Madame Blavatsky's Theosophy, to skeptics like Nina Berberova.

Vasily Pukirev, Unequal Marriage, 1862

Chapter Two

Marriage

A. The Russian Gentry

> Dreams, dreams! Were they never to come true for her? Was she really never to hear: 'I love you!' from lips that were dear to her; would she never know the poetry of love? She had married to please her father...
>
> Maria Zhukova, "Baron Reichman,"

1. Unhappy Arranged Marriages

Vasily Pukirev's painting *Unequal Marriage*, showing an old man marrying a despondent young girl, shocks us today. In 19th century Russia, it depicted a common practice, and Pukirev used his art to criticize society. As was common in many European countries, Russian parents counted themselves successful if they married their daughters to a wealthy man, even if he were decades older than the bride. Few upper-class marriages were based on romantic love, and many women experienced unhappy married lives. In both the 19th and early 20th centuries, many women agreed with the artist Pukirev that marriage was unequal. While many hoped for happy marriages like those illustrated in the recent TV series "Downton Abbey," the most many found was contentment, not happiness or fulfillment. Yet, marriage was the main career open to women, determining their whole existence. Then, as now, weddings produced a mixture of emotions—hopes for a bright future, yet fear that life together might not work out. Unlike the relatively happy arranged marriage depicted in "Downton Abbey" between Lord and Lady Granton, Russian literature provides few such examples.

a. Maria Zhukova

> A woman who wished to seek her happiness outside her designated sphere would discover sooner or later that she was pursuing a will-o'-the-wisp, which will lead the wanderer into a cul-de-sac.
>
> Maria Zhukova, "Baron Reichman"

Marriage might disillusion women, especially if a husband was unable to express romantic feelings to his wife. Several women writers condemned artificial, arranged marriages. While love and marriage were women's whole life, men had life outside the family. Writing about these themes in the early 19th century, Maria Zhukova (1804-1855) depicts a character in her short story "Baron Reichman," complaining as follows:

> ... Serge was good, tolerant, was always thinking of what would please her;...but there was no poetry in him, he did not understand her heart![1]

Influenced by the French romantic novelist George Sand, Maria Zhukova further muses in "Baron Reichman:"

> Love is the main thing in a woman's life; her imagination transforms it into a giant which rules over her whole being. ...
>
> The life of a man is twofold: he is a family man and at the same time the duties of a citizen fall to him. Should he be unhappy at home he may live his life outside the home, he still has purpose, a sphere of activity, which is quite sufficient to occupy his spiritual resources. Woman is created solely for the family; the area of activity beyond it is alien to her; her entering the sphere is quite inappropriate. Her actions are focused on domestic life; she belongs to society like a comforting angel at times of earthly disasters, as pure philanthropy.[2]

Zhukova concedes that men have the law on their side, but contends "marriage is constant warfare, in which mental superiority or strength of character will always win."[3]

In her story "The Idealist," Zhukova laments:

> But what evil genius has so distorted the destiny of women?

Now she is born for the sole purpose of pleasing, flattering, entertaining men's leisure, of putting on her finery, dancing, holding sway in society, although she's only a paper queen to whom the clown bows down while the audience is there, but then chucks into a corner. They set up thrones for us in society; our vanity adorns them, and we don't notice that they're tinsel...Truly, it sometimes seems that God's world has been created for men alone; the universe is open to them, with all its mysteries, for them there are words, the arts and knowledge; for them there is freedom and all the joys of life. From the cradle a woman is fettered by the chains of decency, ensnared by the terrible 'what will people say'—and if her hopes for family happiness do not come true, what does she have left outside herself? Her impoverished, restricted education doesn't even allow her to dedicate herself to important things, and will-nilly she has to throw herself into the maelstrom of society or drag out a colourless existence until she dies![4]

b. Evdokiia Rostopchina

And the secret victims of inconsolable sorrow
Live out, live out their lives—but in their weary hearts
   All is cold, empty, and dark.

Evdokiia Rostopchina, "Winter Evening"

Evdokiia Rostopchina (1811-1858) depicts heartless, arranged marriages in some of her poetry and society tales. This was common in her milieu, and it happened to her in 1833. Like many other gentry-class Russian girls, Rostopchina was not allowed to marry the man she loved, but was married to the wealthy aristocrat Andrei Rostopchin to satisfy her relatives' social schemes. In her story "Rank and Money" (1838), Rostopchina depicts a mother refusing her daughter's beloved because he is poor and without connections. Instead, the mother includes in her list of eligible matches:

> not only all the rich widowers and old men, but even two senators who frequently came to her to play whist who, being decrepit, had prepared graves for themselves in advance in a famous cemetery. Klimova passed not very affectionate verdicts on many; some she left in doubt; she declared two or three

worthy, among whom she included one of the senators, who had close to five thousand unmortgaged souls [peasants].[5]

Describing her daughter's beloved, the mother Klimova says:

> 'Now, there's a fine fellow all around! And attractive too, and has a pleasant manner, but what's the use of him? He's got neither house nor home.'
> Her daughter Vera ventured to ask:
> 'So you like Svirsky, Mama dear?'
> 'Yes, I'm telling you—he'd be a fine follow, only he's no match for you!'
> 'And what would you say, Mama dear, if I were to like him too?'
> 'Ah! The heavens protect us! How would you dare consider somebody without asking me? If such a disaster were to happen, then I'd throw you in the Moscow River as fast as possible; I'd sooner see you underground than give you to a beggar, to trash, to an unsuitable urchin'....[6]

Later, the mother weds her daughter to an elderly General. The daughter dies of a broken heart a few months later since she couldn't marry Svirsky, her soul mate and beloved.[7]

Gentry and aristocratic families often prevented women from marrying the man of their dreams. Living in the early 19th-century when George Sand's romantic notion of a "Great Love" was popular, as well as that of the German Philosopher Emmanuel Kant's idealized view of marriage and the family, many Russian women had high expectations for personal happiness in marriage. Their critiques give us insights into the loveless marriages in that period. Their writings criticized Russian society for marriages based solely on economic considerations. Rostopchina's story "Rank and Money" condemned society for crushing true love and valuing only gold. Her marriage into the aristocracy provided access to high society, but not personal happiness. Her poem "Winter Evening," written in the mid 1830s indicates how sad her married life was:

> More than once suffering has enveloped a young life
> In a burial shroud; quite often a night of sadness
> Usurps a lovely day of happiness....[8]

Evdokiia Rostopchina, by G. Kordik, 1846

Rostopchina's husband usually left her alone, so she spent her time writing poetry and hosting dinners and salons with the literary and artistic elite including Pushkin, Zhukovsky, Gogol, Glinka, and Liszt. Still, she yearned for "true love." As a member of the Russian aristocracy, she was free to indulge in liaisons of her own once she had produced heirs to the family. However, she seemed to only find disappointment, not abiding love in these affairs. Rostopchina's own marriage fell far short of the romantic, idealistic ones touted by popular writers.

Rostopchina attributed women's alienation, isolation, and disillusionment to arranged marriages. Following in Alexander Pushkin's romantic tradition in the 1830s, her poetry initially made her the "darling" of literary circles and critics, but by the 1850s she had lost this distinction. Deploring her situation upon her return to Russia from Western Europe, she asks in her poem "Song of Return:"

> Who greets my arrival with a blessing?
> Who needs me?
> Whose melancholy glance seeks me with desire and longing?....
> Two years have passed without me, and what of it?[9]

c. Karolina Pavlova

> Get used to a difficult path
>   And learn the strength of the weak.
> Learn as a wife, the suffering of a wife.
>
> Karolina Pavlova, A Double Life

Karolina Pavlova (1807-1893) was a contemporary of Rostopchina's, and her family also prevented her from marrying her "true love," Polish poet Adam Mickiewicz. In a poem written just three years into her marriage with Nikolai Pavlov, Karolina wrote about girls' youthful fun that disappeared upon marriage. Her poem "Yes, there were many of us young girl friends," reads as follows:

> Yes, there were many of us young girl friends;
> We would often gather together at a childhood holiday,
> And the hall would thunder for a long time with our pleasure,
> And our circle parted with ringing laughter.
>
> And we did not believe in sorrow or defeat;
> We went to encounter life like a bright-eyed crowd;
> Splendid and wide, the world shone before us,
> And everything that it contained belonged to us.
>
> Yes, there were many of us, yet where's that bright throng?
> Oh, each of us discovered life's burden,
> And we call that time a fable,
> Remembering ourselves as we would a stranger.[10]
>
> 1839

Perhaps like the young girl in Pavel Fedotov's painting *The Major Makes a Proposal*, Pavlova tried to escape the machinations of her family. But it was in vain. Pavlova suffered from a profligate husband who squandered her dowry and lived openly with his mistress. She too condemned the hypocrisy of arranged marriage in her writings. Her novella *A Double Life*, faulted society matrons for marrying off their daughters in "good matches" based solely on economic considerations. She thought even "the best mothers" did this.

Karolina Pavlova, by V. F. Binemann, ca. 1830

The poetic sections of *A Double Life* are rather gloomy, and a "dream spirit" warns her heroine that marriage will stifle her personality, destroying her creativity and talent. The spirit tells her heroine Cecily:

> Understand that the Lord's commandments
> Have doomed you, defenseless ones,
> To unconditional patience
> To a task higher than that on earth.
> Learn as a wife, the suffering of a wife,
> Know that, submissive, she
> Should not seek the path
> To her own dreams, her own desires;
> That her heart protests in vain,
> That her duty is implacable.
> That all her soul is in his power,
> That even her thoughts are fettered.
> Prepare all the strength of youth
> For mute tears, for an obscure struggle,
> And may the heavenly father give you
> An unconquerable love![11]

Pavel Fedotov, The Major Makes a Proposal, 1848

The prose sections of her short novel contain interesting information about marriage traditions common in all estates. Her heroine Cecily doesn't sing the laments that peasant girls did, but she bids farewell to her girl friends at a special "maiden's" party the night before her wedding, as peasant women did. In some ways, Cecily's party resembled modern Bridal Showers where the bride and her friends celebrate her forthcoming marriage.[12]

The night before her wedding, her character Cecily experiences foreboding at leaving home and feels a perplexing sadness. Finally, she goes to the icon corner and falls on her knees before the holy image. She lies prostrate there a long time. When she falls asleep, the dream spirit speaks to her one last time:

> Let us say goodbye today, my poor friend:
> Let life claim its rights!
>
> Go back to the realm of earth,
> Go to your early triumph—
> I give you over to the world,
> With an anxious prayer to the creator.

He has given woe to all of us,
To all a measure of sad days;
Submit to his laws
The murmur of your pride.
Learn to live with outward grief,
Forgetting youthful dreams of Eden,
Share no more with anyone
The secret of inconsolable thought....

You will understand earthly reality
With a maturing soul:
You will buy dear wealth
At a dear price....

So, go as agreed
Strong in faith only,
Not hoping for support,
Defenseless and alone.

Don't disturb the heavens, transgressing,
Silence your own dreams.
And dare to ask of God
Only for your daily bread.[13]

d. Elena Gan

> Everything which I had held dear since I was a child was mocked by his cold reason; everything I respected as a sacred thing was represented to me in a wretched and vulgar light.
>
> Elena Gan, "Society's Judgment," 1840

One of the most tragic stories of the killing of a young woman's spirit through an arranged marriage comes from the pen of Elena Gan (1814-1842). In her tale "Society's Judgment," a beautiful, talented, young girl sacrifices herself to save her brother who has been compromised by his commanding officer. The Major had proposed to Z., but she had refused him until she realizes that only accepting his offer of marriage would save her brother. Still, honor demands she tell the major-general that she doesn't really love him and is offering herself to him to save her brother. At one point she contemplates:

> My brother's senior commander was Major-General N., and he sought my hand; but I knew him so little it seemed to me impossible to give myself to a man I did not love, whom I scarcely knew, so I, without hesitation, declined the honour prepared for me, despite all my aunt's protestations. But circumstances soon changed. My brother committed one of those small misdemeanours which military discipline just cannot forgive. The General had the authority and wished to make him a solemn example of his severity. All the efforts of our family were in vain. And, swallowing my pride, I determined to petition the General![14]

The general refused her pleas, but soon renewed his talk of love, telling her that while he could not pardon her brother who was his subordinate, he could forgive a brother-in-law. Her brother's fate was in her hands! Z. realized that the general thought she would reconsider his proposal, and she did, but not before telling him that she did not wish to deceive a fellow human being because of his blind passion. Z. muses:

> 'He loves me," I reasoned, 'his desire to possess me has made him indiscriminate in the means he is prepared to use to achieve his goal.' But, being so insistent in his desire, he, no doubt, considered me a child with a malleable character, someone who would be influenced by new impressions. ...
>
> He then proceeded to repeat his proposal, and I accepted it. My brother received his pardon, never suspecting what price had been paid to ransom his entire future. N. only required that Vsevolod did not serve under his command and personally arranged for him to be transferred to the guards. Vsevolod left at once for St. Petersburg with letters of recommendation from the General; my father approved of my choice; I was married and I excused the decisiveness of my experienced husband by his passion for me; but soon his concern that my significant dowry be speedily transferred dispelled even this consoling dream. ...
>
> My fate was decided! I had nothing left to desire, nothing to hope for; what could time bring?... Imperceptibly, along with my faith in the beautiful, the refinement and discernment of my ideas also disappeared.[15]

Soon Z. despairs of Russian high society, but begins to cultivate her mind. Eventually even her intellectual brilliance is disparaged as airs of superiority and coquetry by jealous dowagers. After years of unhappy married life with her tormenting husband, Z. meets an injured soldier and falls in love with him. However, when she comprehends that he loves her too, she urges him to leave her father's house where he has been convalescing and where she has been living. Later, this young man confuses Z's brother, thinking him her lover, and in a fit of rage shoots him in a duel. Then the young man retires to the provinces to die of a broken heart, and Z. also dies after writing to him and telling him her life's story and her impossible love for him.

This story suggested that any woman who tried to live an authentic life of the mind and find a soul mate with whom to exchange ideas would be misunderstood and punished by society. So, whether married or not, a woman of ideas could be persecuted and despised in high society. Not only was Z. unhappily married, but her reputation was impugned as well. It seems as though her quest for love resulted in her brother's, her beloved's, and her own untimely death.

2. Other Negative Views of Marriage

a. Nadezhda Durova

A unique rejection of gentry-class marriage came from the pen of soldier-writer Nadezhda Durova, who wrote in the 1830s. An unusual woman who disguised herself to serve as a cavalry officer during the Napoleonic War, she never discussed her earlier wedded life and motherhood in her memoirs. Instead, she extolled nature and the free, adventurous life she experienced as a soldier, not that of a wife and mother. In one passage of *The Calvary Maiden*, she advises young women:

> You, who must account for every step, can comprehend the joyous sensations I feel at the sight of most forests, fields, and streams and at the thought that I can roam them with no fear of

prohibition. I jump for joy as I realize that I will never again in my entire life hear the words: *You, girl, sit still! It's not proper for you to go wandering about alone.* Alas, how many fine clear days began and ended, which I could watch only with tear-stained eyes through the window where my mother had ordered me to weave lace. The mournful recollection of the oppression in which my childhood years were passed puts a quick end to my cheerful capers.[16]

In another section of *The Calvary Maiden*, she laments leaving her happy military life to assume family obligations. "As we parted, Papa said to me, 'Isn't it time for you to be quitting the sword? I'm old; I need peace and quiet and someone to take over the household. Think about it.'"

> The suggestion frightened me. I thought that I would never have to quit the sword, and especially not at my age; what will I do at home, condemned so early to the monotony of domestic occupations? But my father wants it that way. His old age! Oh, what else can I do? I will have to bid it all farewell: the gleaming sword and the good steed...my friends...the merry life... drill, parades, mounted formation....all of it will come to an

Nadezhda Durova

end. It will all fade away as if it had never been, and only unforgettable memories will accompany me to the wild banks of the Kama, to the place where I spent my blighted childhood, where I worked out my extraordinary plan (to join the army.) ... To past happiness, glory, danger, uproar, glitter, and a life of ebullient activity—*farewell!*[17]

b. Grand Duchess Maria

> In all time, the marriages of princes have been prearranged; I had been brought up to accept the idea.
>
> Grand Duchess Maria, Memoir

Describing her life at the end of the 19th century, Grand Duchess Maria Pavlovna, a niece of Tsar Nicholas II, disclosed yet another attitude towards marriage—resignation. Since her mother died shortly after she was born, and her father lived in exile in Western Europe, she lived with an aunt and uncle as her guardians in Moscow. Maria records her thoughts about arranged marriage in *The Education of a Princess, A Memoir*:

> I knew that some day I was destined to marry a foreigner; I had always known that only by a stroke of extraordinary luck would I be able to make a choice according to the dictates of my heart[18]

Grand Duchess Maria had not known that her aunt, the Grand Duchess Elizabeth, had sent her niece's photograph to the Swedish Royal family, and that Prince Wilhelm, the second son of the King, was coming to Moscow to meet her. On the fatal day, Elizabeth asked her niece to keep her afternoon free and to don a fresh frock. It was at tea that Maria met her future husband. She describes their getting to know each other later that evening at dinner:

> I dressed for dinner but had not yet, at sixteen, attained the age of true coquetry, and threw only preoccupied and troubled glances at the mirror while Tania fixed my braids. At dinner, the Prince sat beside me. I could feel the attention of the entire table centred on us. Yet I overcame my timidity and we talked with great ease. My aunt sent Dmitri and me to bed about ten o'clock, our usual hour, and kept the Prince by her side, after

Grand Duchess Maria Pavlovna

having dismissed her attendants.

Next morning she summoned me into her drawing-room. I kissed her hand and waited for her to speak; we sat facing each other.

'Listen to me,' she began, looking away from me and crumpling nervously in her hand a handkerchief edged with black, 'I must speak to you of a very serious matter and I want you to think carefully before answering.' ...

Her face was flushed with suppressed emotion and she chose her words with difficulty.

'Prince William came here to make your acquaintance. He likes you, and wants to know whether you would consent to marry him...'

The shock of her words was violent and painful. Although I had been brought up in the idea that I must make a political marriage, I had never expected such abruptness. The rush of my aunt's words, her haste to have me married, and the complete absence of any thought as to the sentimental side of such a compact, revolted me, seemed to me indecent. Noting my stupefaction, she took me by the hand and sought to draw me towards her.[19]

Her aunt tells her to think about marrying the prince. She didn't have to decide at once. Resigned to her fate, Maria decided to accept the Prince since she didn't dislike him. She fantasized that it would be good to organize her own life, to have a home, a family, even children. Her only stipulation was that she not marry until she was 18. She also asked her aunt if she had consulted her father. It turned out her aunt had consulted the Tsar since he was her guardian while her father lived abroad.[20]

Initially, Maria thought only of the fun of having her own household, not of the responsibilities. Like many young girls, she thought that marriage would bring excitement into her boring life. As she mused in 1906: "I was tired of the ordered existence, dull and tranquil, which we then were undergoing in that great house. I longed for movement, noise, excitement, release, for any change."[21]

Grand Duchess Maria had second thoughts about marrying Prince William. She disliked his lack of initiative and realized that others thought and decided for him, just as they did for her. She wondered what would happen when they married? She began to feel remorse because she could only offer him an empty heart and felt she was using him to obtain her freedom. Members of the royal family made it clear that she couldn't back out of the wedding. Having been raised to submit, she did so. She realized that with the exception of her brother, she was leaving little behind—not family, home, nor attachments. In changing her country, she was not changing her milieu. Maria found life in Sweden rather boring, especially since her husband was in the navy and seldom home. She had a son, but finally with the help of her uncle, the Tsar, she had her marriage to William annulled in December, 1913.[22]

During WW I, she threw herself into nursing, and later during the aftermath of the Revolution she met and married a friend Prince Putiatin, whom she loved. Maria described these happy times and her second marriage in her memoir in the following words:

> Feelings that I had never before experienced stirred in the depths of my heart. In spite of the revolution, in spite of all the uncertainty, all the anxiety, our unused youth, our fresh mental forces, leaped to claim their due. Spring was upon us, carrying along living floods of new joy. Above all else, one wanted happiness, one wanted to take from life everything

that was left for life to give. Our very realization of the peril, of the indefiniteness of our situation, our constant personal danger, contributed to the awakening of these feelings and set them aglow. Thus, at the collapse of our old world, we dared upon its wreck to seize at a new chance of happiness, and to live a new life.

I gave myself entirely over to the strange new delight of being really in love. Hesitating to invite him too often to Tsarskoie-Selo, I began going to Petrograd to receive him in my apartment in the palace on the Nevsky.[23]

In 1918 they escaped to the Ukraine, then the Crimea, and eventually left their native land. Like many others they thought Bolshevik rule would be short lived, and that they could return to Russia later. But they were wrong. So, they emigrated first to Romania, then Paris where their marriage unraveled in 1923, and then she came to the United States where she published *The Education of a Princess, A Memoir* in 1930. Despite her high social status, Grand Duchess Maria suffered a lot of loss, her first son in divorcing Prince William; her second son, whom she left with relatives when fleeing Russia with Prince Putiatin in 1918; her father Grand Duke Paul, her aunt the Grand Duchess Elizabeth, her uncle the Tsar and his family, as well as other family members and friends in the course of the Bolshevik Revolution.

c. Literary Accounts of Marriage

In her short novel *The Boarding-School Girl* (1861), Nadezhda Khvoshchinskaya depicts another negative view of marriage in a disillusioned character who is strong willed, runs away from her provincial home to avoid being married off at 16, lives with an aunt in St. Petersburg, and becomes an educated, self-supporting artist. Other decisive women are depicted in short stories such as Maria Zhukov's "Self Sacrifice," in which the heroine Liza becomes a proud, self supporting provincial school teacher when her hopes of marrying her true love are dashed.

Likewise the heroine Feklusha in Avdotya Panaeva's (1819-1893) "The Young Lady of the Steppes" (1855) refuses two offers of marriage to older men. These marriages would have been convenient for her parents, but not for her. She decides not to marry at all until it is to a young man on her own terms. Novelists Ivan Turgenev, Ivan Goncharov, and literary critics like Nikolai Chernyshevsky, Nikolai Dobroliubov, and Dmitry Pisarev all describe strong Russian women in the mid 19th century who are not victims and who do not marry superfluous male heroes. Indeed, Russian censors complained about radical critics' "strange idealization of women" in the late 1850s and early 1860s.

Prior to WW I the famous poet Anna Akhamatova (1889-1966) complains about her husband in a poem entitled "Three Things He Loved:"

> He loved three things alone:
> White peacocks, evensong,
> Old maps of America.
> He hated children crying,
> And raspberry jam with his tea,
> And womanish hysteria.
> ... And I was his wife.
>   Anna Akhmatova (1911)[24]

She wrote this poem one year after they married, and a few years before he deserted her for safari hunting and sexual adventures with other women. Despite their young son and their common commitment to poetry, or perhaps because she was the better poet, they divorced in 1918.

Describing her gentry-class grandparents' marriage in the late 19th century, Russian writer Nina Berberova notes yet another negative view of marriage in her memoir *The Italics are Mine*. She sees her grandfather rarely conversing with his wife and sometimes leaving home to visit his "second family" which lives in Novgorod. His mistress there is much younger than he, and they have three children.[25] As a youth, Berberova noticed that not all was *comme il faut* in her mother's family:

> My grandmother, my mother's mother, had obviously made something of a misalliance in marrying my grandfather, a man who belonged with all his heart to the time of the Great Reforms, and later to the K.-D. Party along with all his friends, all members of the Duma. ... My grandmother came from a fam-

ily of high rank and did not like 'freethinkers'. Some of her relatives were ministers and other high-ranking persons, and all those hospitals and schools that Grandfather helped build were complete anathema to her, I would say. She died when I was twelve, and I think she differed little from her mother or grandmother, who felt serfdom to have been an evil of only average significance.[26]

So, arranged marriages could lead to adultery and even second families in the mid and late 19th century. Of course there were some happy gentry-class marriages, but few writers seem to have written or published works about them. Apparently Lidia Zinoveva-Annibal's second marriage to the symbolist poet Viacheslav Ivanov was a short, but happy one, lasting from 1899 until her early death in 1907. She had been betrayed by her first husband, who despite their 3 children felt entitled to mistresses as well as a wife.[27] Poets like Evdokiia Rostopchina and Mirra Lokhvitskaya imitated their husbands, and after producing family heirs, took lovers to find personal happiness. The struggles of these writers suggest that autonomy and happiness were often incompatible with arranged marriage.

3. Social and Sexual Predators

> Don't dare speak to me of your love! ... Your love gave me tears, poverty, sickness ... children that I didn't want....
>
> Anastasia Verbitskaya, "The Mirage"

While many writers depict gentry-class women as victims of arranged marriages, a few describe them as strong willed, scheming gold diggers. In her short story *Vavochka* (1889), Anastasia Verbitskaya suggests that Russian society is responsible for creating a generation of scheming women whose only aim is to catch a rich husband.[28] Negative views of women as unsavory "gold diggers" also appear in Verbitskaya's play *The Mirage*, (1896). The drama depicts a spoiled gentry-class woman Lyolya, who initially married for love, but eventually becomes disenchanted, saying: "Poverty would kill me... How can one live in three rooms? ... Never travel anywhere?" Scolding her husband, Lyolya complains:

Anastasia Verbitskaya

You're repulsive to me...You thought only of yourself when you dragged me with you into this unhappy marriage...I was a child. I didn't know life. You promised to devote your future to me, you deceived me...Your love gave me tears, poverty, sickness...children that I didn't want....

What right did you have to berate me all these four years for my heartlessness, my shallowness? I didn't promise you anything better...But you?...Remember your vows?...

Oh, you won't be left without work!...Solving learned questions, altering the fate of nations...You'll take Vera for your help mate...Believe me I won't be jealous.[29]

In her early 20th century novel *The Keys of Happiness*, Verbitskaya presents cynical, mercenary, and romantic views of love and marriage. Arranged marriages were still the norm, but she includes a discussion of "The New Woman" who develops her own personality and career and doesn't need marriage to survive economically. She depicts one character taking lovers as men do, loving a partner for a time, but eventually returning to her work. However, her artist heroine cannot carry on this life forever. She grows weary and ultimately returns to an early romantic passion that results in their dual suicide.

Turgenev's play *A Month in the Country*, (1840-50) also depicts two scheming women who marry to avoid poverty. One gentry-class character Natalia marries to make a good match, not for love, and enjoys admirers fluttering around her. Her ward, Vera, initially rejects an arranged marriage to an elderly neighbor, but decides to wed him out of spite after her romance with a young tutor fails. Turgenev doesn't depict happy marriages in this drama. With few exceptions, Russian literature lacks portraits of happily married life.

a. Natalia Sheremetevskaya

> "It would be amusing to win the heart of the brother of the Emperor."
>
> Natalia Sheremetevskaya, *The Grand Duke's Woman*

While there are not many stories about women as sexual predators, there are some. In her account of her grandmother called *The Grand Duke's Woman*, Pauline Gray indicates that her grandmother, Natalia Sheremetevskaya, was beautiful, but arrogant, selfish, and sexually aggressive. Natalia or Natasha as she was called began her love life by taking away a suitor from her sister Olga. At 16, Natasha decided that she liked her sister's suitor Sergei Mamontov, who was sensible and quiet, not like the young peacocks who paraded around showing off. She decided to marry Sergei, and she thought it would be amusing to astonish her family who all believed that Olga would be his bride. She succeeded in her plan, marrying Sergei at age 16 in 1902. Like many other young girls, she saw marriage as an escape from the restrictions and discipline of home. She wanted to become the mistress of a house and have her own servants to order about. Initially, all went well, and Natasha enjoyed married life and having a daughter.

Soon, she became bored with marriage and motherhood and cast her eye beyond her hard working husband. She began stepping out without her husband and fell in love with an officer in the Blue Cuirassiers. Unlike her husband, he had time to accompany Natasha in her shopping, visiting friends, and going to parties. Eventually the officer became infatuated with her and wanted to marry her. After confessing her adultery to her husband, she told him she wanted a divorce to marry Colonel Wulfert. So, Natasha left Mamontov and Moscow in 1906 and took her daughter with her to her new mar-

Natalia Sheremetevskaya

ried life with Wulfert in Gatchina, near St. Petersburg. Gatchina was a garrison town and royal residence of the unattached Grand Duke Michael, who was a fellow officer in Wulfert's regiment.[30]

In Gatchina where the guards were quartered, Natasha enjoyed her new social life full of admiring young officers. She bought new clothes and enjoyed showing them off at parties and receptions. With a nanny to care for her daughter, and servants to run her household, she was free to enjoy life. A month after her marriage to Wulfert, Natasha met Grand Duke Michael Romanov, the brother of Tsar Nicholas II. She decided to make the Duke fall in love with her and so boast of another conquest. As historian Robert Massie observed, "Within a few months Natalia managed to become Michael's mistress. From that moment on, she dominated his life."[31]

The Duke not only fell in love with her, but she with him, and this meant another divorce. The Tsar refused them permission to marry, so no Russian clergy could marry them. After the birth of their son and while vacationing in Europe in 1909, they decided to marry in a Serbian Orthodox Church. Exiled from court, they were allowed to return to Russia at the beginning of WW I. While never accepted by the Imperial family, especially Michael's mother, Natasha had a happy, passionate, romantic and indulgent life with the Grand Duke until the October Revolution forced them out of their Gatchina idyll. Michael was killed along with Nicholas II and his family, in 1918, but Natasha and her daughter, after a brief period of imprisonment, escaped to Kiev, then the Caucasus, and eventually England. In exile, Natasha played the role of the Odalisque as long as her finances permitted.[32]

It appears that many Royals were not blessed with wedded bliss. The Tsar's sister Grand Duchess Olga lived a loveless life in her marriage before falling in love. While her husband Prince Peter of Oldenburg would not consent to divorce her for 7 years, he did allow her to live in a ménage a trois with her lover as his personal aide-de-camp. Apparently they were able to live like this from 1907 until the outbreak of WW I when Olga went to nurse the wounded at the front, and her lover Kulikovsky followed his regiment into battle.

Before WW I, several other sexual scandals and divorces beset the Tsar's family including those of his cousin Grand Duke Michael who had married a commoner despite the Emperor's ban; the Tsar's Uncle Grand Duke Alexis who fell in love with the married Princess Zina. Divorce was not possible in this case, so the scandal was all the greater. In addition, Anastasia, Princess of Montenegro and Duchess of Leuchtenberg divorced her husband and married Grand Duke Nicholas, the Tsar's cousin. A widowed uncle of the Tsar married a divorcee. Then the Tsar's first cousin, Grand Duke Cyril married Victoria-Melita, the divorced wife of the Grand Duke of Hesse, and his own brother Grand Duke Michael married a twice divorced woman. His niece Grand Duchess Maria had her marriage to the Swedish Prince William annulled. So wealth and royal lineage did not necessarily guarantee a happy marriage.

4. Happy Marriages

> I thank you so much my dear love you are always so good to me I kiss your dear hands with great tenderness I still cannot believe that I shall see you in a week these last days are going by so slowly.
>
> Natasha Sheremetevskaya,
Telegram to Grand Duke Michael, 1909

The hundreds of romantic telegrams between Natasha and Grand Duke Michael in 1909 show their love for each other.[33] Writing to Michael, Natasha expresses her devotion as follows:

> I am so unhappy living without you my Misha. I write to you every day. We are leaving the day after tomorrow for Berlin. I kiss you with all my heart. Let me know how your health is at the moment. May God keep you—Natasha.[34]

In one of his telegrams to her, Misha writes:

> My darling, beautiful Natasha, there are not enough words with which I could thank you for all that you are giving me in my life. Our stay here will be always the brightest memory of my whole existence. Don't be sad—with God's help we shall meet again very soon. Please do always believe all my words and my tenderest love to thee, to my darling, dearest star, whom I will never, never leave or abandon. I embrace you and kiss you all over. Please believe me that I am all yours, Misha.

Indeed, it was only the Bolshevik Revolution in October 1917 and his death in 1918 that separated these lovers.

a. Happily Married Writers

> There was a time when he loved me so much that I saw in him my whole world and looked for him in every child we had.
>
> Countess Sofia Tolstoy, *Diary*, 1890

Other examples of happily married couples were the first half of Sofia and Leo Tolstoy's married life, and the 14 year marriage of Anna and Theodore Dostoevsky. (In the sections that follow, Countess Tolstoy and various translators refer to her as Sofia, Sophia, or Sonia and to her husband as Leo, Lev, Levochka, Lev Nikolaevich, etc. In Russia use of the patronymic or second name, in this case Lev Nikolaevich, was the polite way to speak to and about people. Similarly, the diminutives Levochka and Lyova were terms of endearment. In English we do not do this, so I have eliminated the patronymic or diminutive except when it occurs in a quotation. Similarly, Anna Dostoevsky writes of her husband Fyodor Mikhailovich Dostoevsky when we simply say Fyodor or Theodore Dostoevsky in English.)

b. Happiness amidst Plenty, the Tolstoy Family

> With sadness I had to look back and recognize that the nineteen years which we had spent continuously at Yasnaya Polyana were the happiest time of our lives. Besides the family and the copying for Leo Nikolaevich, what a number of good occupations I had in the country!
>
> Countess Sofia Tolstoy

Life on the Tolstoy estate "Yasnaya Polyana" was not as lavish as that portrayed in the modern drama "Downton Abbey," but initially it seemed to have been as happy. While many Russian women writers complained about arranged and unhappy marriages, Countess Sofia Tolstoy (1844-1919) tells in her diaries and autobiography of marrying Leo Tolstoy for love, being loved for 19 years and then enduring 29 years of unhappy wedded life. Indeed, his written marriage proposal to her and his diary entries after falling in love with her show his profound love for her. In his diary for September 12, 1862, he wrote:

> I am in love, as I did not think it was possible to be in love.
> I am a madman; I'll shoot myself, if it goes on like this. They had an evening party; she is charming in everything...
> To-morrow as soon as I get up, I shall go and tell everything or shoot myself.[35]

In their early married life, Sofia loved him equally fervently. In the 1860s and 1870s, they worked together on his manuscripts for *The Cossacks*, *War and Peace*, and *Anna Karenina*. She thoroughly enjoyed copying *War and Peace* and felt she was serving a genius. Her work gave her moral and spiritual strength. She remarked in her *Autobiography*:

> ...When I sit down to copy it, I am carried away into a world of poetry, and sometimes it even seems to me that it is not

Sofia and Lev Tolstoy, 1860s

your novel that is so good, but I that am so clever.' In my diary I also wrote: 'Levochka all the winter has been writing with irritation, often with tears and pain. In my opinion, his novel, *War and Peace*, must be superb. Whatever he has read to me moves me to tears.' In 1865, when my husband was in Moscow looking up historical material, I wrote to him: 'Today I copied and read on a little ahead, what I had not yet seen nor read, namely how the miserable, muffled-up old Mack himself arrives to admit his defeat, and round him sat and the inquisitive aides-de-camp, and he is almost crying, and his meeting with Kutuzov. I liked it immensely, and that is what I am writing to tell you.[36]

Married life was rich and joyous when they only had a few children, but lack of birth control meant that she was continually pregnant, having 13 children between 1863 and 1888. Slowly, her need to simultaneously see to the children's education, the household, and to copy his manuscripts began to take its toll. Her writings explain the everyday life of many married women—teaching her children, nursing them through childhood illnesses, helping her husband, cutting and sewing clothing for the family, doing the accounts, and managing the household.

Tolstoy family, 1887

Her disillusionment with Count Tolstoy occurred during the 1880s and 1890s when she realized that while she had thought she was marrying advantageously since her father had been a mere physician and Tolstoy a Count, she eventually discovered that her husband was not interested in social status and even disdained it. During his time of religious and philosophical searching in the 1870s and 1880s, Count Tolstoy decided that private property was evil. So part of Sofia's dilemma was how to preserve the family social position and income for their household when her husband disliked her doing so.

In her autobiography, written in 1914, Sofia noted that the first two decades of their married life had been full and happy ones. She had born 13 children, and lost four. Since she had prepared to teach French before her marriage, she had tutored their children in French, Russian, German, and even English. She had also taught them history, geography, Church history and liturgy as well as music. She also almost daily copied out manuscripts, letters and diaries that Tolstoy wrote. In addition, she nursed their children through the usual childhood illnesses. But she found herself yearning to be more than a wife, nurse, and mother. She also wanted to be appreciated and respected as a person. Describing the early years of her marriage, Sofia writes in her *Autobiography*:

> Sick peasants used to come to me and, as far as I could, I used to treat them, and I was fond of the work. We planted apple trees and other trees and took pleasure in watching them grow. Once we had a school in the house and the village children were taught with ours as they grew up. But this did not last long, because we had to have our own children educated and we wanted to make their life as varied as possible. In the winter the whole family, including us parents, the tutors, and governesses, skated on the ice or tobogganed on the hills, and we cleared the snow from the pond ourselves. Every summer, for twenty years, the family of my sister, T. A. Kuzminskii, came to Yasnaya Polyana, and our life was so merry that the summer with us was a continuous holiday. There were various games like croquet and tennis, amateur theatricals, and other amusements like bathing, gathering mushrooms, boating, and driving, and besides these, the summer was devoted to music, and concerts arranged by the children and grown-ups, with piano, violin, and singing.[37]

Sofia doesn't dwell on her many household occupations in her autobiography, but she describes them in some detail in her diaries. She discusses making clothes for each of her babies, sewing her husband's shirts and underclothes, darning his socks, knitting, entertaining and making beds for the many guests who came to see her famous husband, managing the estates, keeping the accounts, handling legal problems with peasants who stole wood from their forests, and settling a longstanding dispute with a local priest over land. She did all this besides educating their many children and copying her husband's writings.

She also describes the breach with her husband beginning with his religious crisis in her *Autobiography*:

> But there also came an end to the undisturbed happiness with which we had lived so many years. At the beginning of his spiritual crisis Lev Nikolaevich, as is well known, gave himself ardently to the orthodox faith and church. He saw himself united in it with the people. But gradually he left it, as his later writings show. It is difficult to trace the steps of this crisis in

Lev Nikolaevich, and when it was exactly that I, with my intensely hardworking life and maternity, could no longer live so completely in my husband's intellectual interests and he began to go further and further away from family life. We had already nine children and the older they grew, the more complicated became the problem of their education and our relations to them. But their father was withdrawing himself more and more from them, and at last he refused altogether to have anything to do with the education of his children, on the plea that they were being taught according to principles and a religion which he considered harmful for them.

I was too weak to be able to solve the dilemma, and I was often driven to despair; I became ill, but saw no way out. What could be done? ...

The difference between my husband and myself came about, not because *I* in my heart went away from him. I and my life remained the same as before. It was he who went away, not in his everyday life, but in his writings and his teachings as to how people should live. I felt myself unable to follow his teaching myself. But our personal relations were unaltered: we loved each other just as much, we found it just as difficult to be parted even temporarily...

Only rarely was our happiness clouded and the harmony broken by flashes of mutual jealousy, which had no ground at all. We were both hot-tempered and passionate; we could not bear the thought that anyone should alienate us. It was just this jealousy which woke up in me with terrible force when, towards the end of our life, I realized that my husband's soul, which had been open to me for so many years, had suddenly been closed to me irrevocably and without cause, while it was opened to an outsider, a stranger.[38]

Writing her autobiography at age 70, Sofia Tolstoy did not always remember the past accurately. Reading her diaries for the years 1860-97, it's obvious that she felt estranged from her husband off and on for years. She thought him a sensualist who only sought her out when he lusted after her. She wanted affection and appreciation, not just being his sex object. She suffered from depression, and often wrote in her diary when depressed. At times, she wrote of wanting to kill herself when she felt so alienated from her husband:

In the old days it gave me joy to copy out what he wrote. Now he keeps giving it to his daughters and carefully hides it from me. He makes me frantic with his way of systematically excluding me from his personal life, and it is unbearably painful. This unfriendly existence at times drives me to the depths of despair. I feel like killing myself or running away, or falling in love with someone—anything to escape from a man whom, in spite of everything, for some unknown reason, I have loved all my life, although I now see clearly that I idealized him, without realizing that there was nothing in him except sensuality... But now he has opened my eyes for me, and I see that my life has been wasted. How envious I am now even of such people as the Nagornyis; for, after all, they are together—there is some other link between them besides the mere physical one. Many other people live like that. As for us—good God, it is sufficient to hear his cold, irritable, insincere tone when he is talking to me. To think that he can talk like that to me, when I am so joyful, candid, and so eager for affection! I am going to Moscow to-morrow on business. I find it always very hard and exhausting, but I am glad to be going this time. These hard times are like the ebb and flow of the sea; and when I begin to realize my solitude, I want to weep and to put an end to it—it would be easier then....[39]

Although Sofia read Tolstoy's diaries before marrying him, she loved him and initially closed her eyes to what a sensualist he was. In December, 1890, she wrote in her *Diary*:

There was a time when he loved me so much that I saw in him my whole world, and looked for him in every child we had. I wonder now if it was only a physical matter to him, something which disappeared as time went on, leaving behind only a void.[40]

She yearned for affection from him, but he seemed more lustful than loving. Since his need for sex diminished as he aged, this was another torment of their married life, and she felt more rejected and alienated as they aged. Her endless chores often made her feel overwhelmed, and thirty years after marrying him, she wrote in her *Diary*:

> Yes, I have lost all power to concentrate on any thought, feeling, or action. This chaos of endless worries, stumbling over each other, drives me to a state of complete bewilderment and I lose all my balance. The very thought of all these things, which take up every moment of my life, is overwhelming—children's lessons and illnesses, my husband's physical and, above all, his mental state, the older children, with all their affairs, and debts and posts and children, the sale of the Samara estate, the plans and documents I have to obtain and copy for the purchasers, the new edition, the thirteenth volume, which contains the banned *Kreutzer Sonata*, the proceedings against the Ovsiannikovo priest, the proof of volume thirteen, nightshirts for Misha, sheets and shoes for Andryusha, household expenses, insurance, land taxes, servants' passports, accounts to be kept and copied, etc., etc., etc. Every single one of these things has got to be looked after.[41]

Still, her diaries reveal that she didn't mind all her duties as long as she could see some progress in what she was doing:

> When I do some sewing, I can see the result: I am interested in the process of work and whether it is well or badly done. When I tutor the children, I can see some progress; when I play, I feel I can always discover something new or beautiful in the music. I am not talking of original work—such as the painting of even the most primitive picture: I am just talking of ordinary, everyday work. But when you copy the same article for the tenth time, there is *nothing*. There is no feeling of achievement, and it is hard to see when it will end. For once again it will be taken to bits and the same bits will just be shuffled into some new sequence. And in any case, I am quite unable to be interested in the work as I used to be, copying some work of *literature*. I remember how I would always look forward to copying *War and Peace* after Lev Nikolaevich had finished his day's work. How feverishly would I go on and on, and find some new piece of beauty in every page I wrote! But now I find it boring. I must do some independent work—or else I shall run dry.[42]

Sofia's diaries reveal her life of suffering in silence—the lot of many married women in the 19th century. After copying Tolstoy's work *On Art* for the tenth time, she wrote in her diary entry for July, 1897:

My husband is not a friend to me; he has been at times—and especially in his old age—my passionate lover. But I have been lonely all my life. He will not go out for walks with me, for he likes to ponder over his writings in solitude. He has never been interested in my children—he found them tedious and unpleasant. He would never travel with me anywhere or share any impressions with me—he knew everything and had traveled everywhere before my time. As for me, I have gone silently and obediently through life—a calm, quiet, uneventful and impersonal kind of life. And now I sometimes have a passionate longing for new impressions—new forms of art, new scenery, something new to think about; I want to gain some new knowledge and meet some new people—but again I have to suppress these desires and go on, patiently and silently, as before. And so to the end of life. It is just my fate. My fate has been to serve my husband, the author. Perhaps I ought not to complain; for I have served a man who was worthy of the sacrifice.[43]

Sofia Tolstoy's diaries are heart-breaking when she speaks about her intermittent depression and suicidal thoughts. While she may have suffered from depression before her marriage, it became more intense and she wrote more about it in the 1880s and 1890s. In June, 1897, she writes one especially poignant suicidal piece:

I am feeling unwell; something has been happening within me ever since I arrived. I noticed a strange feeling in my heart—a feeling as though I were waiting for a suitable moment to commit suicide. I have been cultivating this feeling for a long time, and it keeps maturing. But I fear it as much as I would fear insanity—and yet I like it, even though my superstitions and my religious feeling tell me I mustn't. I believe it to be a sin, and I fear that suicide would deprive me of communion with God and the angels—and so with Vanichka [a favorite son, who died]. And as I walked along, to-day, it occurred to me to send a hundred letters to the most varied and unexpected people explaining the motives of my suicide. And as I was composing this confession in my mind, I found it so touching that I nearly wept.... But now I am afraid in case I go mad. Every time I have any trouble or anyone blames me for something, I say joyfully to myself: Now I shall go to Kozlovka and kill myself, and then you can do as you please. I don't want to suffer any longer, and I can't, I can't, I can't, I can't, I can't. I must either live without suffering, or die — and dying is the better course. Oh, Lord, forgive me![44]

While Sofia generally found writing in her diary a solace, she wrote nothing for two years after the death of her youngest and most beloved child, Ivan or Vanichka, in 1895. Later in a manuscript called *My Life*, Sofia describes her reactions to her son's death. At one point she writes:

> Of all my children, Vanichka looked most like his father. He had the same bright, pensive eyes and the same earnest spirit. Once, as I was combing his curly hair, in front of the mirror, Vanichka turned his little face to me and said, with a smile: 'Mummy, I feel I am really like my dad.'[45]

Sofia's *Diary* also describes Vanya's endearing behavior when he was sick before he died:

> A few days before Vanichka died he surprised me by starting to give away his things, attaching little labels to them saying: 'To Masha from Vanya,' or 'To our chef Simeon Nikolaevich, from Vanya,' etc. Then he took all the little framed pictures down from his walls and took them into Misha's room; he was always particularly fond of him. He asked me for a hammer and nails, and hung up all his pictures in Misha's room. He was so fond of Misha that every time they quarreled he would weep bitterly if Misha would not make friends with him again. I don't know whether Misha loved him as much; though later on he called his eldest son after him.
> Not long before his death, Vanichka was looking out of the window, when suddenly he grew pensive and said: 'Mummy, is Alyosha [his little dead brother] an angel now?'
> 'Yes, said I, 'children who die before they are seven are said to become angels.'
> Then he said: 'It might be better for me if I die before I am seven. It'll soon be my birthday, but I may be an angel yet. But if I don't die, dear Mummy, will you let me fast, so that I may have no sins?' I can never forget those words.[46]

Vanya died from scarlet fever a few days after this exchange. The good that came from this evil was that his death temporarily brought the family together. Count Tolstoy tried to comfort Sofia at this time and was attentive and affectionate to her. He also felt profound grief. After the funeral, he burst into tears and told his wife, who wrote in her *Diary*:

> 'And I always thought that, of all my sons, Vanichka alone would carry on my good work on earth. Well, it cannot be helped.'[47]

Sofia wrote to her sister that her husband had grown quite old. He wandered about, stooping with a sad look in his bright eyes, and she felt that the last bright ray of his old age had vanished. After Vanya's funeral, he told his wife that he had lost heart for the first time in his life. Thus, Countess Tolstoy's writings give us insight into some of the sad as well as happy episodes of family life in the late 19th century.

In her later diary, Sofia discusses themes that others generally ignored—mother/daughter difficulties, fear of rejection, disappointment with her children and fear of aging. In one passage in her diary for January, 1891, she discusses her rocky relationship with her second daughter Masha, saying:

> I had a little row with Masha just now, about Birukov. She is trying to get in touch with him again, and I still cannot change my mind on the subject. If she marries him, it will be her death. I was very sharp and unfair, but I simply cannot discuss the matter calmly, and Masha is certainly a curse of God. She has given me nothing but pain ever since the day she was born. She is a stranger to the family, a stranger to God; and her imaginary love for Birukov is a puzzle to me.[48]

Sofia doesn't really come to love Masha until she nurses her through a serious case of typhoid fever.

Sofia wrestled with fears of rejection by her husband in many diary entries. She also worried endlessly about losing her husband's love. In one poignant entry she says she has loved too much, and it would be better not to love so much. Better to dissemble. She writes in September, 1867,

> How can one *attach* anyone to one's self? There is no way. I have always been told that a woman must love her husband

and be honourable and be a good wife and mother. They write such things in ABC books, and it is all nonsense. The thing to do is *not* to love, to be clever and sly, and to hide all one's bad points—as if anyone in the world had no faults! And the main thing is *not* to love. See what I have done by loving him so deeply! And what can I do now with all my love? It is so painful and humiliating; but he thinks that it is merely silly. 'You say one thing and always do another.' But what is the good of arguing in this superior manner, when I have nothing in me but this humiliating love and a bad temper; and these two things have been the cause of all my misfortunes, for my temper has always interfered with my love. I want nothing but his love and sympathy, and he won't give it me; and all my pride is trampled in the mud; I am nothing but a miserable, crushed worm, whom no one wants, whom no one loves, a useless creature with morning sickness, and a big belly, two rotten teeth, and a bad temper, a battered sense of dignity, and a love which nobody wants and which nearly drives me insane.[49]

Sofia tormented herself with re-reading and copying her husband's diaries in which he discussed his affairs with various women before he married her. At one point she confesses in her diary:

Yes, I simply cannot reconcile the ideas of woman's marriage and man's debauchery. It is a constant wonder to me that we have kept it up so long. What saved our marriage was my childlike innocence and my instinct of self-preservation. I instinctively closed my eyes on his past, and deliberately refrained from reading these diaries and from questioning him about his past. Otherwise it would have been the end for us both. He doesn't realize that my purity alone saved us from perdition. But it's perfectly true. His cold-blooded debauchery, and his views on the subject, and all these pictures of a voluptuous life are a poison which could easily have ruined a woman who was even slightly infatuated with somebody else. 'So that's what you were like; you have soiled me with your past—just let me pay you back!' That's what most women would feel after reading these diaries.[50]

While she tormented herself in her mind and in her diary, and some think she only wrote in her diary when she was depressed or sad, her diary writings are none the less true not only for her, but for many women who worried about these issues and had no one to discuss them with. In 1895, Sofia admits her failures as a mother in her diary, saying:

> The struggle with the older boys, and my attempts to make them attend to their duties, has become too much for me, and the worry of this constant struggle makes me dislike them. It is all very painful, just as painful as Ilya's inefficient squandering, Serezha's immoral way of living, (young) Lyova's illness, the unmarried state of my daughters, and this tiny flicker of life in poor little Vanya.[51]

In August, 1897, Countess Tolstoy writes:

> Yes, I have taken care of them; and yet what have I achieved? Nothing! Andryusha has been a complete failure so far, and Misha is weak, and heaven only knows what'll become of him. It is sad, sad, terribly sad....[52]

Later she laments the unwise business dealings of her sons Serezha and Ilya in buying an additional estate. Describing her feelings, Sofia deplores their behavior in her diary in August, 1897:

> All this annoys me and makes me very sad. Ilya is incapable of anything: his studies were a failure, and he is no better at managing his affairs, or at any other work.[53]

Soon after, she complains:

> No luck anywhere. Misha has failed in his exam; and I had another painful scene with Andryusha. The poor boy went off to the Gruzinskys in tears, together with Misha. It seemed to me that he was a bit drunk, for he kept changing in a very queer way from extreme coarseness to extreme tenderness. Misha annoyed me by the way he took his failure. It had no effect on him, for he went into the garden with Andryusha, Mitya Dyakov, and Boris Nagornov, where they sang songs in their loud, uncouth manner.—My children are not at all what I should like them to be: I wanted them to be well educated, and refined in their tastes and with a sense of duty. Lev Nikolaevich [Count Tolstoy] wanted them to lead a simple life, and to do some

hard, rough work, and we both wanted them to have high moral ideals. But it has all failed!⁵⁴

In November, she still has problems with Misha as a day student in Moscow and writes:

> I went to the Lyceum, and was told a lot of unpleasant things about Misha's laziness and bad conduct. It makes me miserable to think that teachers and schoolmasters have always been able to make me blush and feel ashamed of my sons.
> And yet there are some happy mothers who are always told the exact opposite about their children! I had another unpleasant talk with Misha, and I shall try to send him to the boarding-school, as a resident. He is dead against it, but I must try to have it my own way.⁵⁵

She was not fond of her son-in-law Kolya Obolensky, but her daughter Masha's severe case of typhoid fever brought her closer to her daughter. Still, she confided in her diary in September, 1897, that her son-in-law was another disappointment:

> Kolya is a good-hearted boy, though rather lazy and slovenly. He is either unwilling or unable to work—and it's an unpleasant sight.⁵⁶

Countess Tolstoy likewise faulted her daughter Tania's choice in men. Both parents were upset by Tania's morbid love for an unworthy, feeble-minded man—a married man, with a sick wife and several children. Finally, her youngest daughter Alexandra [Sasha] was hopelessly spoiled and behaved badly with all her governesses. While Sofia coached Sasha in essay writing, she still wrote poorly and remained "wild, rough, and obstinate." She hurt her mother's best and most humane feelings.⁵⁷ Eventually, Sofia resolved to take Sasha to Moscow for her education, noting in her *Diary*:

> In six days' time I shall take Sasha to Moscow. I have been trying to put it off, but now it is time she went to school; she hardly does any work, and she is nearly fourteen. I am also worried about Misha, and feel afraid that he will deteriorate morally; the home atmosphere is really the best for a boy. Lev Nikolaevich will stay here with Lyova, and I don't think either

of them fancy the idea. I must try to arrange everything about Sasha as quickly as possible, and come back to Lev Nikolaevich.—It is all so complicated and difficult! May God help me to keep firmly to my duty, to understand wherein this duty lies, and to find the best way to do it in the midst of this hard, intricate existence.[58]

Needless to say it was difficult for Sofia to have several children studying in Moscow while she took care of her husband at Yasnaya Polyana. In October, 1897, she writes in her diary:

> No news from home; and yet I wrote to them all yesterday and sent them money. I am trying not to worry, for it would exhaust me completely if I started worrying about everybody. But no one makes me happy, and I am feeling anxious about them, all the same...[59]

In the same entry, she writes about aging and her need for false teeth at the age of 53:

> Dentist again. I got up late, and am in an unhappy old-age, autumnal mood. I feel as though all the threads around me were broken, as though I were alone and idle, and as though no one needed me any longer....[60]

Often, Countess Tolstoy's musings sound like those of a modern woman, especially when she confesses in her Diary:

> Death is nothing—I welcome it—but helpless old age is horrible[61].

It is strange to us in the 21st century to realize that people in the late 19th century considered people 40 or 50 years old—aged. At one point, Sofia's daughter Tania describes herself as "old" when she is 26 and again when she's in her early 30s. She probably meant she was "old" for getting married since Russians tended to marry early, often before the age of 20.

c. *Tatiana Tolstoy*

> One thing which is indubitable is that it would be very easy for me to marry, and that at the same time I have not the slightest

inclination to do so, and see clearly that I should be unhappy and that it is far more sensible and advantageous for me to remain a spinster.

Tatiana Tolstoy, *Diary*, 1891

Countess Tolstoy's daughter's diary gives us some insight into a young woman's views on love, marriage, and sex. At 27, Tatiana was still rather naïve and Puritanical about sex. In January, 1891, she muses:

> On the way to Kozlovka and back meditated on married life and congratulated myself I am not married. First, I am glad to be a girl still, and not to have gone through that terrible shame which every married woman has to bear, and which I have understood so clearly from what Mamma related, saying that the morning after her marriage she was so ashamed that she did not want to leave the bedroom, but hid her face in the pillows and cried. I am proud not to have been through that and never wish to. I am surprised that it should happen the very first night; if it has to be, one ought first to accustom one's wife to that intimacy, which, moreover, must seem savage and unpleasant; and that the first step in conjugal life should be that which brings the most trying and more painful injury to the spirit. Yesterday it was that Mamma and Masha Kuzminski talked about it, while I sat, without a word, knitting. When some point or other partic-

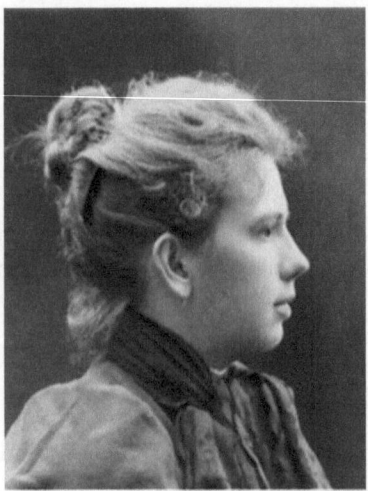

Tatiana Tolstoy

ularly horrified Masha, she would turn to me and ask me what I thought about it; and every time I replied that 'to me it was absolutely all the same.' Yes, I am getting more and more convinced that one ought not to get married. ...

What a powerful, evil lust love is. How can a person live decently and remember his obligations when the whole being is caught up in that egoistic, cruel lust? And, moreover, what absolute indifference to everything and everybody else it does entail! I am sometimes sorry I have never experienced it, because I have never been loved back when I loved, but when I picture myself clearly in that situation, I feel how passionately I should long to get out of it and be free again, to live a full life, and be able to see everything around me, and not be fettered to one single point.[62]

Yet a month later, in a diary entry for February, 1891, Tania admits of how flattered she feels by the attentions of Michael Stakhovich. She realizes that she sometimes craves love and would like to have her own family, especially children:

I am harried by a nightmare thought that I shall almost certainly marry Stakhovich. I believe that were he to try to win my love, it would be easy for him, that he would be capable of fine, powerful love, that it would be impossible not to be moved by it and not to respond to it. I keep imagining this, and when I think about it seems desirable to me, and the feeling gets complete hold of me, my heart throbs and I am both ashamed and terrified by the sensation. But when I cold-bloodedly picture myself as his wife, I am horrified. What would the ceremony alone be like in his family? Benedictions, congratulations, and so forth. Then the upbringing of the children, differing views on life, on religion, on everything—and the principal thing, that I should never be able quite to believe him. Latterly this thought has agonized me almost to madness...with sorrow I feel fated, and the worst of all is that everybody seems to be conspiring to counsel it—even Papa and Mamma....In any case, if he resolved to marry me, that would be a great honour, but I cannot understand why he should choose me....It is difficult to fall into passionate love with me now. I am twenty-six and have become very ugly....I cannot understand what can have made him change so suddenly. I am sure that when he comes to see us next he will try to take back all he has been saying this time....[63]

Tania did not marry Stakhovich, and years later one of Tania's suitors confessed to her mother that he thought Tania and Masha were too unstable for marriage. In 1897, Misha Olsufiev remarked to Countess Tolstoy:

> 'Your daughters are very emotional,' he said, 'and they are interesting and highly gifted—but it would be risky to marry them.'[64]

In her thirties, Tania noted in her diary that she had fallen in love with a married man Mikhail Sukhotin, and her parents were horrified. She resisted this love for awhile, but after the death of his wife, they wed. They were happily married, and she had several babies. However, the first three were stillborn, which depressed her. Finally she had a baby that lived, and she named it Tatiana, showering her with love.[65]

d. Happiness in Adversity, Anna Dostoevsky

> The idea that I would no longer be parted from him, would share in his work, could look after his health and shield him from persistent and irritating people seemed so attractive to me that there were times when I was ready to weep at the realization that all this could not soon come about.
>
> Anna Dostoevsky, *Reminiscences*

Anna Dostoevsky's marriage was also a love match in the mid 19th century. She had read Dostoevsky's writings as a youth, and was delighted to have her first job as a stenographer taking dictation from him. A woman of the 1860s, Anna valued economic independence, which is why she had studied stenography as a profession. Although Dostoevsky did not admire women's independence she still idolized him. He valued her kindness, help, and beauty, and she wanted to devote her life to the "great writer." Although Dostoevsky was twice her age, Anna's mother did not object to their marriage. Nor did her mother remind Anna of Dostoevsky's defects—his epilepsy, emphysema, and indebtedness. Others tried to dissuade her from marrying Dostoevsky, but not her mother. In the mid 19th century, men over 40 were considered "old," but as Anna thought "who indeed could have

Anna Dostoevsky

persuaded me to refuse this great imminent happiness which later, despite the many difficult aspects of our life together, proved to be a real and genuine happiness for both of us?"[66] Looking forward to her marriage, Anna recalled in her *Reminiscences*:

> Our marriage depended chiefly on whether some arrangement could be worked out with the *Russian Messenger*. Fyodor Mikhailovich prepared to go to Moscow over the Christmas holidays to offer the publisher, Katkov, his next novel. He had no doubt that the editorial staff of the magazine would wish to retain him as a contributor in view of the fact that their publication of *Crime and Punishment* in 1866 had made a considerable impact in the literary world and had attracted many new subscribers. The only question was whether the journal would have sufficient resources available for an advance of several thousand rubles, lacking which we could not think of setting up a new household.[67]

Living in St. Petersburg, Anna encountered some problems that Countess Tolstoy did not—interfering relatives. Dostoevsky had a stepson from his unhappy first marriage, and this stepson resolved to live with them and to fleece Dostoevsky when he could. Moreover, Dostoevsky had taken on the debts of his brother who died young, and he was accustomed to helping his sister-in-law, nieces and nephews as well. In Anna's opinion, Dostoevsky was a soft touch, giving away his money to all who asked. Throughout their wedded life, Anna had to deal with intriguing relations while trying to get her new family out of debt. After their marriage, they lived abroad for four years so they could have some calm for Dostoevsky's writing and some time to themselves without bothersome relatives. They eventually succeeded in getting out of debt, but only shortly before Dostoevsky's untimely death in 1881. Despite fourteen years of poverty, she counted her marriage a happy one because they shared genuine love for each other and their children.

While Dostoevsky was insanely jealous of Anna and couldn't bear another man even kissing her hand at a party, he did love her truly, and she him. His jealousy did prevent her returning to work as a stenographer to augment the family finances; but she accepted this as she did his gambling. Moreover, she even helped him in his work, co-publishing with him the journal *Dnevnik pisatelia* (1876-77, and 1880-81). She was able to conclude her *Reminiscences* of their life together in the following words:

> In truth, my husband and I were persons of 'quite different construction, different bent, completely dissimilar views.' But we always remained ourselves, in no way echoing nor currying favor with one another, neither of us trying to meddle with the other's soul, neither I with his psyche nor he with mine. And in this way my good husband and I, both of us, felt ourselves free in spirit.
>
> Fyodor Mikhailovich, who reflected so much and in such solitude on the deepest problems of the human heart, doubtless prized my non-interference in his spiritual and intellectual life. Therefore he would sometimes say to me, 'You are the only woman who ever understood me!' (That was what he valued above all.) He looked on me as a rock on which he felt he could lean, or rather rest. 'And it won't let you fall, and it gives warmth.'
>
> It is this, I believe, which explains the astonishing trust my husband had in me and in all my acts, although nothing I ever did transcended the limits of the ordinary. It was these mutual

attitudes which enabled both of us to live all the fourteen years of our married life in the greatest happiness possible for human beings on earth.[68]

Anna also makes it clear throughout her reminiscences that she and her husband shared a deep Russian Orthodox religious life. Their strong faith and their attitude of gratitude in vexing circumstances strengthened their marriage. Most of all, they seemed to share a belief in redemptive suffering. Their political views, with the exception of the 'woman question,' were also similar. Dostoevsky disliked the nihilist women of the 1860s, and he generally thought women did not persevere or take their work very seriously. Slowly he changed some of his views, and at the end of his life he gave many readings to benefit women's as well as men's higher education. The death of a second child drew Anna and Fyodor Dostoevsky together; whereas the death of their son Ivan eventually drove the Tolstoys further apart.

By the 1890s, the Tolstoys did not share much social and religious harmony, and their differences caused Sofia much grief and anguish. While Anna Dostoevsky found happiness in adversity with her husband, Countess Tolstoy experienced bitterness. In 1885, Anna Dostoevsky was able to advise Countess Tolstoy on a method of publishing her husband's books to financial advantage, and to save Sofia some of the mistakes she herself had initially made.

e. Anna Bek

Another happy marriage amidst adversity was that of Doctor Anna Zhukova Bek just before WWI. While Anna confessed in her memoirs that she was initially drawn to handsome men, she never let herself get too involved with men who did not share her socialist worldview. Observing her youthful behavior, Bek commented in her *Life of a Russian Woman Doctor*:

> My attraction to Sushinsky always seemed absurd to me. I saw his superficiality from his conversations, his frivolous attitude toward life; I understood that we were completely different people. I had not the slightest wish to live with him. Meanwhile, contrary to reason, I yearned for him until disclosure of his baseness destroyed this blind feeling.[69]

In Siberia, she knew she could marry the mining engineer Lovitsky, who loved and courted her. But she rejected that path, musing:

> What sort of prospects did I have in Nerchinsk Zavod? I could marry an engineer. My position obliged me to. Mining engineers received huge salaries. Where could they spend them? Engineers' wives ordered stylish dresses from Paris, held evening card parties at home in turn, competing with one another in the richness of their hospitality, who had the finest fruit liqueurs and wines, and so on. I had a different path before me.[70]

At 30 years of age, Anna met her future husband Dr. E. V. Bek, whom she admired for his dedication to his patients and work. Neither had had a serious relationship before, and after about 6 months of working together in the same hospital, they fell in love. As she recalled in her *Life of a Russian Woman Doctor*:

> Soon he began to come by in the evenings to call on me at home. Our commonality of interests and aspirations led to the growth of friendly relations between us. I will write separately in more detail about our growing closer. Until then, he had lived like a hermit. His need for friendship and love blazed, and our friendship changed into mutual love. I was already thirty and he thirty-four. The past was poor in romantic episodes for us both. For him and for me it was the first serious love, based on profound respect for the individual.[71]

Sharing an interest in scientific research, Anna helped Bek in his work by reading French articles and books for him. Having studied in France for two years, Anna knew French, but neither of them knew German, and they had to read those studies with the help of a dictionary. Dr. Bek also loved music, so they alternated their study with music especially Tchaikovsky's "Autumn Song" and arias from "Carmen." After six months of courting, he asked her to marry him. Anna's father had observed their "friendship," had investigated Dr. Bek's situation, and approved of him as his daughter's suitor. She recorded his proposal thus:

> When the last patient had left the operating room Evgeny Vladimirovich first cleaned up the instruments and then walked up to me, for the first time addressing me as 'thou,' said, Anichka,

I love you, let's get married.' I answered silently with a look, and we kissed.[72]

While neither Anna nor Evgeny liked church rites and rituals, they did marry in the Orthodox Church, but an hour later were at work on his tour of duty to his patients around the district. On his trips, Evgeny always took one box of medications and another box of brochures by the Pirogov Medical Society and famous Russian classical writers including Gorky and Tolstoy.[73] From her memoirs it appears that they had a very happy and devoted marriage. While there were a few instances of jealousy on both sides, they trusted and loved each other. Their happy marriage was cut short by Dr. Bek's untimely death from typhus at the age of 50.

It's hard to tell whether the happy marriages of the Dostoevskys and Beks would have remained happy if they had lasted 40 or 50 years as the Tolstoys'.

e. Ordinary Gentry-Class Marriage and Family

> I will never forget the tens of troikas, one rivaling the other in beauty and speed, the bedecked coachmen wearing multicolored cloaks belted with red sashes, the elegant crowd of guests, the numerous bouquets of flowers, and the solemn church service.
>
> Elena Gorstkina Skrjabina,
> *Coming of Age in the Russian Revolution*

Judging by family photographs and the description of her early family life in her memoir *Coming of Age in the Revolution*, Elena Skrjabina's parents had a contented and happy marriage. Her parents, Alexander and Nadezhda Gorstkin lived on a landed estate near Nizhni Novgorod. When the Parliament or Duma was created after the 1905 Revolution, Alexander Gorstkin served as a Duma deputy in St. Petersburg. Her parents did not always agree, but they usually got along. Elena only remembered one disagreement when her father decided to give a peasant a cow so he could marry, and her mother objected because she thought their family finances a shambles. Although they differed politically, they seemed to live in relative peace and harmony, and amicably celebrated their 25th wedding anniversary. Elena does not report her parents' marriage

*Elena's mother Nadezhda Gorstkina,
Courtesy of University of Iowa Women's Archives*

as unhappy as that of Count and Countess Tolstoy in the same period. The accompanying photos show her mother as a young woman, possibly before her marriage, and in a family photo in the late 19th century.

The family was separated during the Civil War following the 1917 Revolution. One brother, Elena, and her mother stayed in Russia, while another brother and her father fought for the White Army and left Russia during the Civil War. Elena never heard from them again. Her brother who stayed fought for the Red Army, but was killed in the purges in the 1930s. While the Revolution of 1905 did not divide many gentry-class families, the Civil War in which the Bolshevik "Red Army" fought the conservative "White Army" did divide families such as the Gorstkins.

In her memoir, Elena described the in-law problems a new bride might experience upon marriage. Her new aunt Olga was an educated and emancipated woman, while Elena's grandmother, Olga's mother-in-law, detested emancipated women. Whereas Elena found Olga pretty and exciting, her grandmother found her condescending and quarrelsome. Grandmother Gorstkina thought women's

Gorstkin family, Nadezhda second row far left.
Courtesy of University of Iowa Women's Archives

Gorstkin Family Life, early 20th century.
Courtesy of University of Iowa Women's Archives

place was the nursery, pantry, even the kitchen, and that higher education and women's courses were not meant for their minds. Elena liked Olga and thought she brought a new spirit onto the estate. It was Elena's first experience with a young woman who had interests other than the home, and Olga made a great impression on Elena.

Elena recorded the jubilant celebration of Olga's marriage to her Uncle Nikolai especially the wedding dinner:

> I was particularly impressed by the magnificent dinner and the huge table of hors d'oeuvres that was the main attraction for us children.[74]

5. Fictitious Marriages, 1860s and 1870s

> We read books together, and were of one mind with respect to my entering a university.
>
> Vera Figner, *Memoirs*

While these were Vera Figner's words, they characterized Sofia Kovalevskaya's marriage too. In addition to arranged marriages and some love matches, gentry-class Russian women adopted several unusual kinds of marriage. One was "fictitious marriage" or marriage in name only that some intellectuals and politically active women engaged in so they could study and work abroad in the 19th century. This arose out of women's legal need for a male guardian — father or husband — to sign their internal passport, showing they had permission to attend courses in higher education or to travel abroad to study. If a father refused his daughter's request to study, then fictitious marriage appeared as a solution to one's problem. Nikolai Chernyshevsky's path breaking novel *What is to be Done?* (1863) depicts such a marriage with an obliging man so the heroine could study medicine. This novel became the Bible of the intelligentsia in the 19th century, and some young women imitated Chernyshevsky's heroine Vera Pavlova.

Several autobiographies attest to this arrangement. Sofia Kovalevskaya (1850-1891), a mathematical genius, begged her father to allow her to study abroad, but he refused. So, with the help of her sister, she arranged a fictitious marriage in 1869 with an obliging

Y. V. Shteinberg, "Sofia Kovalevskaya," St. P. (Photo Archive)

scholar named Vladimir Kovalevsky. They maintained this arrangement for some time before the marriage was consummated. Only 33 at the time of her husband's suicide, she desired to marry again, but found that while men married successful singers and actresses, they seldom chose intellectuals like herself, because they found educated women threatening.[75] In addition to teaching mathematics at a Swedish University, Sofia also wrote her memoirs and scientific articles in Russian and European journals, so she was a well-known intellect.

Women doctors like Vera Figner and Emilia Pimenova also resorted to such marriages in the 1870s. Figner (1852-1942) described her infatuation with a young lawyer named Aleksey Filippov and their subsequent "fictitious marriage" in her *Memoirs of a Revolutionist*:

> Shortly after this, Aleksey Victorovich was transferred from Kazan to Tetyushy, so that he might have the opportunity of visiting us. He shared my views and sympathized with my plans.

They married in October 1870, and she left for Zurich to study medicine in the spring of 1872. Slowly, Vera and her husband drifted apart when she became more politically radical than he. In 1875 they separated, and she refused any further financial aid from him.[76]

Vera Figner, 1870

A more detailed description of a fictitious marriage occurs in Dr. Pimenova's autobiographical writing "Bygone Days," which reads:

> 'Have you heard about fictitious marriage?' he (Lt. Z.) asked me on another occasion.
> 'Of course I have heard and read about it,' I said.
> 'Well, there you are, you need a fictitious marriage.'
> I stared at him in great astonishment. 'Who would want to marry me in that way?' I exclaimed.
> 'I know a man,' he said. 'I will let you know his name soon.'[77]

After her wedding and completing her entrance exams for medical study in St. Petersburg, Emilia's marriage was consummated. She records her husband's devoted support of her medical studies, but then shows that when they had children, it became more difficult for her to continue her work. This was partly because she was an impoverished gentry-class woman without much of a dowry, and she and her husband were unable to hire enough servants on his meager salary to enable her to study fulltime.[78]

> I was in my third year of the medical courses when my next son was born. This time the birth did not go quite so well. I did

not recover for a long time. Besides this my husband had been appointed to an engineering position in a naval factory in Kolpino. Although we lived in government housing—a small cottage with a garden—deductions for rent were made from his salary, which was very small because officially he was in the military service. Our life became even harder.

I had to travel to lectures all the way from Kolpino. The traveling was time consuming and very tiring. I became depressed and was afraid that I would not have the stamina needed for the courses. I felt all this the more keenly because we were in want, and I did not wish to ask my parents for help and concealed our poverty from them. At such moments I often thought about my friend, lieutenant Z. Only then did I begin to understand what his farewell words meant: 'Watch out for yourself!' He knew that family responsibilities would clip my wings and hold me down. I was too young and inexperienced then to understand what he meant, and he had not wished to be more explicit.[79]

6. Marriage and Women Revolutionaries

During the many years of illegal work I often came across women—wives of revolutionaries—who because of their children, were obliged to play the unenviable role of mother and housewife even though they had all the attributes required to make them real Party workers.

Cecilia Bobrovskaya, Memoirs

In addition to fictitious marriages, Russian society spawned another unusual phenomenon: married women revolutionaries. Social Democrats such as Cecilia Bobrovskaia, (1873-1966), Maria Chekhova (1866-1934), Maria Golubeva (1861-1936), Maria Kostelovskaya, Nadezhda Krupskaya (1869-1939, Lenin's wife), Tatiana Liudvinskaya, and Konkordia Samoilova (1876-1921) all combined marriage and political activity prior to World War One. Yet, most of them found it hard to reconcile motherhood and revolutionary work. Although Chekhova had 5 children and Kostelovskaya and Bobrovskaia at least one child each, they were exceptional.[80]

CHAPTER TWO: MARRIAGE

Nadezhda Krupskaya

Some revolutionaries like Nadezhda Krupskaya (Lenin's wife) had companionate marriages, which made it easier for them to lead active political lives. However, few Bolshevik women like Krupskaya wrote much about marriage. When asked to submit her autobiography to the German Social Democratic Party in the early 1920s, Alexandra Kollontai does not even mention her early marriage or child. Instead, she focused on women's need to be existential subjects rather than sex objects. Indeed, she entitled her very brief memoir *The Autobiography of a Sexually Emancipated Communist Woman*.

Accounts of how unimportant marriage and family life were to some revolutionary workers appears in two memoirs by Social Democrats—Menshevik Eva Broido and Bolshevik Cecilia Bobrovskaya. (In 1903, the Social Democrats, which were an illegal Marxist Party in Russia, divided into two wings: Mensheviks, who were willing to work legally within the Tsarist system and who modeled themselves on European social democratic parties, and Bolsheviks, who believed in more radical ideas of a party-dominated worker socialist revolution.) In *Daughter of Revolution: A Russian Girlhood Remembered*, Vera Broido indicates that underground political work was more important to her father and mother than family life. So while many Russian women considered marriage their whole existence, some politically active women focused on politics, with husbands and children of secondary concern. Vera Broido was initially raised by her grandmother since her parents were in and out of prison and exile. When her mother politically opposed Russia's entrance into WW I, Vera found herself in Siberian exile with her mother and got to know her better then. Her father, who was also a Menshevik revolutionary, did not oppose the war and remained in St. Petersburg with the other three children who were in school, and Vera had her mother to herself for awhile. In many ways this was the "sunniest" time of Vera's childhood, and she enjoyed the spacious house that other exiles had prepared from them in Siberia. However, when her mother later took a full time job to support them, their mother-daughter bond loosened again. Vera didn't think her mother really understood her, especially when her mother tried to provide formal education for her. Vera much preferred educating herself by reading Russian and European literature. She felt no need for the confines of formal schools with nasty classmates and strict regimens.

Most Bolsheviks did not write much about their personal lives in their memoirs, and Cecilia Bobrovskaya was a classic example of this practice. In *Twenty Years in Underground Russia, Memoirs of a Rank-and-File Bolshevik*, Bobrovskaya abruptly mentions on page 90 that she had a husband Vladimir Bobrovsky. Nowhere does she discuss how they met, fell in love, and married. In only a few instances does she mention her husband. Held in Butirsky prison in 1905, Cecilia heard that her husband had been exiled to Siberia and she expected him to stop at the Butirsky prison on his way from the Caucasus to Siberia. When she asked the governor of the prison to permit her to see her husband if he came, the Governor replied haughtily: "Prisoners are forbidden to talk to each other." However, a week later in Moscow she did meet Vladimir because they had both been freed by revolutionary crowds.[81]

Arrested and exiled to Vologda and then Veliky Ustiug in 1910, she wrote in *Twenty Years in Underground Russia*:

> At the time of my journey to the district, called Veliki Ustug (sic), my health was so poor that I had to send for my husband

to take me there. Veliki Ustug is a splendid little town once you get used to it. But when you are ill and shaken by a journey of sixty versts by horse and cart through the winter frost and arrive before dawn, you feel a bit differently. Everything seems dark and desolate. The first person I met in Ustug was a doctor, the second—an architect, Vladimir Kuritsin. Among the Ustug exiles were two rather secluded groups—Social Democrats, the majority of whom were Bolsheviks, and a group of Socialist-Revolutionaries.[82]

While Bobrovskaya shows some concern for her husband, she expresses rather negative attitudes towards children. In one place she writes about the difficulty of staying with a worker family in Kostroma and of the problems of revolutionary minded women with children, saying:

> Further, I did not want to add to the cares of Comrade Stopani's wife, which were heavy enough as it was, by my possible arrest. A true revolutionary in spirit, she had to take care of four young children, although she yearned for active Party work....During the many years of illegal work I often came across women—wives of revolutionaries—who because of their children, were obliged to play the unenviable role of mother and housewife even though they had all the attributes required to make them real Party workers.[83]

After living with her husband in Ustiug in 1910, Bobrovskaya became pregnant and described her distressing situation in the following words:

> ...Perhaps if I had gone to the districts and had got into my old harness of professional district worker, everything would have looked much brighter, but I could not do that because of a purely personal disability. I had a newborn child on my hands, a sick little boy, who unjustly had to pay for my restless life.[84]

Since this child is never mentioned again, one doesn't know if her son survived and was taken care of by her mother-in-law, or what happened to him.

Several gentry-class married women, especially strong-minded, politically active ones, found it impossible to reconcile marriage, motherhood, and revolutionary work. Social Revolutionary Catherine Breshko-Breshkovsky (1844-1934) as well as Social Democrats like Alexandra Kollontai (1872-1952) and Inessa Armand (1874-1920) forsook marriage, motherhood, and philanthropic work in favor of full-time revolutionary work to ameliorate the condition of the lower orders. It broke Breshkovsky's heart to entrust her child to relatives to raise, but she preferred being a fighter for justice to being the mother of a victim of tyranny. And she worked for the Socialist Revolutionary Party among the peasants all her adult life—from 1860-1918.

Kollontai also left her son in the care of her parents to travel to Europe to study socialism in the 1890s. Kollontai reportedly said, "I hate marriage. It's an idiotic and meaningless life...." Kollontai and Armand joined the Social Democratic Party in the 1890s and promoted working class women's issues until the early 1920s. (The Social Democratic Party in 1903 broke into two wings: the Mensheviks and the Bolsheviks, who later took the name Communist Party.) Armand established a Party organization for women called Zhenotdel, but she died of typhoid or cholera in 1920. Kollontai initially served

Alexandra Kollontai

as Minister of Social Welfare, but broke with Lenin in 1921 over his introduction of the New Economic Policy. Then, she was posted abroad as the first woman ambassador in the world. However, this represented less of an honor to Kollontai and more a way of removing her from Party politics.[85]

7. Liberated Women and Marriage

Other marriage models were those of liberated "New Women," and these were found in life and in Russian novels of the late Tsarist period. Artists, revolutionaries, writers, and others often lived together with their beloved instead of marrying. Indeed, Natalia Goncharova lived with fellow artist Larionov for 50 years, from 1905-1955, until they married in exile in Paris. Journalist and Marxist Ekaterina Kuskova (1869-1958) engaged in a companionate marriage in the late 19th century. Marrying her former science teacher in 1885 at the age of 16 enabled Kuskova to escape penury after the death of her parents. Moreover, marriage offered her further education and personal development. Her first husband died, and in the mid 1890s she engaged in a common law marriage with a gentry-class landowner named Sergei Prokopovich. Historian Barbara Norton argues that Prokopovich gave Kuskova complete freedom in their relationship, and she was the dominant person in their partnership. Sharing similar radical and Marxist ideas, they had a long and intellectually fruitful life together working on various publishing and political enterprises. The income from his estates allowed them to live independently and to actively participate in the 1905 and 1917 February Revolutions. Critics of the Bolsheviks, Kuskova and her husband were deported from Russia to Western Europe in 1921.[86]

Another example of common law marriage was the Social Democrat Maria Kostelovskaya. She and her husband worked for the revolutionary cause, and they had a child. During the late Tsarist period, they were not wed in the Orthodox Church, and their illegitimate daughter was not allowed to attend a prestigious gimnaziya.[87]

During World War One, poet Marina Tsvetaeva (1892-1941) embodied another life-style of the 'new woman." She had a lesbian relationship with the poet and literary critic Sofia Parnok (1885-1933) and simultaneously a love affair with Osip Mandelstam while legally married to Sergei Efron.[88]

Writers sometimes depicted artists living unconventional, yet married, lives. They are often portrayed having satisfying careers, but unhappy marriages. Describing the new sexually liberated career woman in somewhat lurid novels, neither Anastasya Verbitskaya in *Keys to Happiness* nor Evdokia Nagrodskaya in *The Wrath of Dionysus* portrayed happily married career women. While their characters' circumstances vary, neither heroine is able to continue her work after marriage. Instead of a "grand love" in marriage, each feels bored and stifled. Both characters represent the New Woman who is educated and has a career as well as lovers, while a happy marriage eludes them.[89]

At one point Nagrodskaya's heroine Tania notices how her stepdaughter has forsaken her music career in caring for her children and husband. In the *Wrath of Dionysus*, the mother says to her son-in-law:

> "You cherish her virtue because it satisfies your needs at the moment. But when your wife's youthfulness begins to fade, you will reproach her for that same virtue. You will decide that you need more unconventional women, primitive passions, frenzied love, and you'll go anywhere, spend anything for it. And you're going to delude yourself into thinking that they love you for your mind, your looks..." [90]

8. Chaste Marriages

A final unusual arrangement was that of chaste marriages where individuals sublimated procreative sexuality to religious and intellectual work. Writers like Zinaida Gippius and her husband Dmitry Merezhkovsky lived in such a marriage for 52 years. The poet Alexander Blok and his wife Liubov' Mendeleeva also entered such a pact around 1900. These writers were influenced by the Russian philosopher Vladimir Soloviev's idea of sublimating erotic love to the Divine. Since Blok suffered from syphilis, he feared infecting his wife and fathering degenerate children. In Gippius's case, a physical deformity made heterosexual love impossible.[91]

9. Divorced, Remarried Women, and Mistresses

> Sergei was the children's father, but their mother, who was not married to him, was a simple peasant woman who lived on their estate in the Novgorod region.
>
> Irina Tidmarsh, Memories

At the time Tolstoy wrote his novel *Anna Karenina* in the 1870s, divorce involved the church courts, was very expensive, time consuming, and rare. However, by 1900, Russian society had changed and some women were able to obtain annulments to unhappy marriages or to more easily obtain divorce and keep their children. In her memoir about her married life from 1908 to 1913, Grand Duchess Maria mentions how bored and unhappy she was. A young woman of 23, she determined to leave her husband Swedish Prince William. With the intercession of her cousin Tsar Nicholas II, she had her marriage annulled. Five years later she fell in love for the first time and married happily during the difficult days of the Bolshevik Revolution.

In an interview about her life during the Russian Revolution, Irina Tidmarsh remarks that when she was born in Moscow in 1903, her mother, a 28 year old gentry-class mathematician, was living alone and separated from her first husband. She was not yet married to Irina's father. So she was born out of wedlock. She doesn't explain how her mother obtained a divorce, but notes in an interview:

> "When things like that happen, according to the old Russian law, you had to be adopted by your father later on, which I was."[92]

Growing up in her mother's gentry-class family, Irina wintered in Moscow and summered at her aunt's country estate Belokolodets. However, life was not always so easy for Irina's mother because her mother-in-law thought she had spoiled her son's life and his career. His family believed that he could have held a higher position if he had not married Irina's mother. Instead, he became a lawyer for foreign firms, earning lots of money, but not necessarily high social status. Indeed, there were distinct divisions between her parents—her mother dedicated herself to educating the workers and the Menshevik Party prior to the Revolution, while her father was apolitical and devoted to making a name for himself as a successful lawyer. The implication is that Irina's was not a child-centered home and that she resented her mother's devotion to worker education when they lived in Moscow in the winter, while she was raised by nannies, maids, and governesses.[93]

Irina's interview throws light on another sort of arrangement—that between a gentry class man and his peasant mistress. She writes about such a couple who had several children. They were raised in the father's well-to-do household, while the low-born mother was only allowed to see them on holidays like Christmas and Easter. Irina had come to live with this family when her brother developed pneumonia and it was thought best to isolate him. Brought up in a liberal family of the intelligentsia, she felt that she had moved into another world when she stayed with her family's Moscow friends. She observed:

> I think that they were really still serf exploiters and proprietors. It was 1915 but they still had all that in them. To me it seemed a dark world, a forbidding world. The family consisted of an elderly brother Sergei Fedorovich, his sister Maria Fedorovna.... They lived in Moscow during the winter. They had carriages, horses and coachmen, a butler and a cook and were far better off than us. They came from the nobility. The poor peasant mother wasn't allowed to be with her children. She couldn't live with them in Moscow and was only allowed to come and see them at Christmas and Easter. She used to come in her peasant clothes, in a large shawl and bringing whatever she had, sweets or something for the children. She sat in the chamber hall on a little chair and that's where the children came to see her. Sergei Fedorovich never saw her, and Maria (the children's aunt) only allowed her to see the children for half an hour or so. Otherwise these poor children were entirely in the hands of Maria.[94]

Irina was shocked that although the aunt educated the children, she also whipped them and the servants. Irina had never experienced anything like that. At the end of two months, she was delighted to return to her happier, more lenient, home.

10. Never Married

There was another small group of gentry-class women who never married. A biography of the composer Modest Mussorgsky suggests that he loved Nadezhda Petrovna Opotchinina, but she refused to marry him. Still, he lived with her and her brother from 1868 until 1875, the year of her death. It's not clear from the biography whether Nadezhda refused to marry him because of his alcoholism, his poverty, or some other reason.[95] Many unmarried gentry-class women, like Nadezhda, were supported by male relatives. In a study of Russian women's autobiographies, Mary Zirin suggests that some Russian women may have wanted to marry but lacked dowries to do so. In the mid 19th-century, Nadezhda Sokhanskaia bewailed her situation where she lacked a dowry and lived in an isolated area where no suitors came to court. Likewise, the late 19th-century writer Anastasia Verbitskaia complained that her widowed mother refused to provide dowries for her and her sister.[96]

Historian Christine Ruane suggests that many gentry-class Russian women chose the career of teaching as an alternative to marriage. Ruane indicates that in 1885, 73% of female rural teachers came from the gentry-class or were the daughters of civil servants. Their high social status may have prevented them from marrying male colleagues of lower rank.[97]

The life and writings of Dr. Maria Pokrovskaya (1852-1921?) suggest that some doctors like herself and perhaps other career women felt a greater need to serve Russian society than to seek personal fulfillment in marriage. Underlying Pokrovskaya's views was a profound sense of female moral superiority. As Rochelle Ruthchild indicates in an article about Pokrovskaya, she genuinely believed that women would ennoble politics since they represented the highest ideals of humankind. Pokrovskaia believed that politics suited women better than men, and that since men degraded women through prostitution, they were less fit to govern or claim the moral high ground. As a doctor, she encountered poor, sick women every day, and she detested the government regulated prostitution of her society. She blamed men for women's woes, and deeply resented the enfranchisement of men, but not women in 1905.[98]

In an autobiographical essay on being a woman doctor, Pokrovskaya wrote: "I was not only a doctor, but also a pioneer for women. I had to serve the people and also prove to society that women could in practice be as good doctors as men."[99] She truly believed that women could have fulfilling lives in their careers and help their society immensely. She never suggested that no one marry, but she herself chose not to. Moreover, the more engulfed Russia became in revolution in 1905 and 1917, the more of a convinced feminist she became.

A final group of never married upper-class women were lesbians. Not so much is known about these women, but scores existed. Some well-known women writers were lesbians. Elena Guro (1877-1943), Sophia Parnok (1885-1933) and Polina S. Solovyova (1867-1924) were three of the most gifted, unmarried lesbian women writers. Zinaida Gippius, Liudmilla Vilkina-Minskaya (1873-1920), and Maria Tsvetaeva had lesbian affairs, but they also married.[100] A poignant poem Parnok penned to Tsvetaeva in 1915 was entitled "You appeared before me like a clumsy little girl," and reads as follows:

...
I remembered, how you dismissed a kiss with a trick,
Remembered those eyes with remarkable pupils...
You entered my home, happy with me, as with something new:
A belt, handfuls of beads or colorful boots, —
"You appeared before me like a clumsy little girl."

But under strokes of love you are malleable gold!
I bowed to your face, pale in the ardent shadow,
Where it is as if death passed over like a snowy feather...
I thank you, my delightful one, because in those days
"You appeared before me like a clumsy little girl."[101]

Marc Chagall, Wedding, 1918

B. Middle Class Women's Marriages

Not all middle-class marriages were as happy as that of Marc Chagall and his wife or as the couple depicted by him above. Some mid 19th century writers and critics depicted wedlock in that stratum as doomed to "softly sighing grief." Even in the early 20th century, Soviet sociologist Anton S. Makarenko described the family life of craftsmen and petty officials as mainly "accumulation." For the lower middle class, capital accumulation was necessary for the children's schooling, daughters' dowries, a peaceful old age, and to enable the family to keep up appearances. A dowry for women in the lower middle classes would include a "wardrobe, a sewing machine, a bed with nickel knobs on it, and dreams of a gramophone." Prior to World War I, young people in the merchant estates sometimes married without seeing each other before the wedding, obeying tyrannical decisions of their fathers.[102]

Yet, by the early 20th century some change had occurred in this class. Painters from well-to-do middle-class families like Vera Popova and Anna Ostroumova Lebedeva arranged love-based marriages, and the painter Boris Kustodiev depicted many happy middle-class marriages in his paintings. Likewise artist Mark Chagall and his wife Bella married for love in their Jewish community in Belarus. Her memoirs *Burning Lights* and some of his art tell of their happiness in the early 20th century.

1. *Praskovia Tatlina*

> I had heard tell of the passion of love, of course, but I did not know how to analyze it. I had never felt it myself, and in others I considered it an illness; a psychological disorder.
>
> Praskovia Tatlina, *Reminiscences*

In the mid-19th century, middle-class wife and mother Praskovia Tatlina described her mid-middle-class married life as virtuous, but unhappy:

> Young people think they will find happiness in marriage but it always brings grief. People in love torment one another out of love....I lived my married life honestly and virtuously, unegotistically and rationally, but it destroyed me nonetheless.[103]
>
> ... He was my husband and that was enough. I was able to find many fine qualities in him, and I would not have permitted anyone to treat him disrespectfully....[104]

Some of Tatlina's marital bitterness was because she and her husband held different views on women's education. Tatlina wanted to educate their eldest daughter to become a self-supporting musician, but her husband thought this unnecessary. Later, the daughter disappointed her mother by falling in love, marrying a poor tutor, and living in penury.

While Tatlina didn't mind her daughters Nadezhda and Masha reading novels by the French writers Hugo, Balzac, and Sue, she thought George Sand's idealization of romantic love unrealistic and dangerous. At one point, she berates her daughters for emulating Sand and rebelling against her and society generally:

> George Sand seduced Natasha....the writings of that woman do not at all present a womanly ideal, but only one of the escape routes from her slavish, senseless situation....I completely fell out with Natasha in my view of the vocation of a woman. I respected 'useful' love; while she was infected with so-called Sandian ideas.[105]

2. *Anna Volkova*

Less resigned than Tatlina, Volkova (1847-1910) experienced a disappointing youthful marriage to a Moscow banker. According to recent articles by Carolyn Marks and Adele Lindenmeyer, Volkova found her youthful marriage boring and lacking in companionship, so she sought stimulation in reading and founding a women's journal. She was dismayed at her husband's narrow attitude towards her, describing one scene early in her marriage as follows:

> I began to speak with my husband about books, about a library, about the desire to read, imagining that he too, my ideal, thought the same as I, and aspired to the same things. And suddenly disillusionment! My husband called me a fool, which greatly astonished me. He wouldn't give me money for books, but ordered me to buy a pillow and embroider it for him for his name day. I obeyed, though I could not possibly understand why it was permissible to embroider a pillow, but not to read.[106]

Volkova never adjusted to her husband's attitude, and confessed in 1888:

> The winter of the past year has been rather hard for me: family troubles have completely worn me out. Every day scandals, scenes, senseless screams, swearing, and then again a lull, and so without end.[107]

Soon after her marriage, she read John Stuart Mill's *On the Subjection of Women* and was drawn into the "woman question." In her journal *Drug Zhenshchin*, she strove to educate readers and prepare them to resist the social norms of women of the middle estate. She rejected the notion of "trophy wife," the trappings of fashion, beauty, and light reading. She rejected the enforced leisure that wealth conferred on many merchant-class women. She felt that women had a moral obligation to serve society, not lead glamorous lives.[108]

3. Nadezhda Khvoshchinskaya

> Well, that's some character you've got! You'd better break that habit, my angel, break it—tone yourself down! You'll have to live with your husband and his family...
>
> Nadezhda Khvoshchinskaya, *The Boarding-School Girl*

Novelist Nadezhda Khvoshchinskaya presents three different attitudes towards marriage in her 1861 novel *The Boarding-School Girl*. The parents of the heroine have a rather traditional provincial marriage. The husband is a minor government functionary, possibly marginal gentry-class or middle class. The mother has internalized the behavior of a wife—trying to please her husband, ignoring his boorish behavior, and yet lording it over their children, especially their teenaged daughter Lolenka. As parents, they secretly arrange a "good marriage" for Lolenka with a handsome, upcoming civil servant named Farforov. They do not consult their daughter about this, but use a matchmaker to intercede for them with Farforov's wealthy mother. Khvoshchinskaya describes the process as follows:

> 'It'll be flattering for her, so young, to marry such a handsome man, concluded the guest, 'and you only have to write to sister Alyona Gavrilovna in Petersburg regarding a bestowal, and then the dowry...'
>
> Mama began to calculate with the guest exactly what and how much was needed for the dowry. The suitor, besides music, requested six silk dresses. Mama was almost prepared to agree to four...[109]

At one point the matchmaker Pelageya realizes that Lolenka has a will of her own, and she tells her: 'Just submit, you have to submit,' she added in a whisper.[110] When Lolenka discovers that her mother and the matchmaker Pelageya have been arranging a marriage for her, she cries; but her mother scolds her:

'And the finest man, with money. I daresay you'll be living like a lady. You have God to thank for sending you such a mate. Who do you think you are? It's shameful even to show you in public: this is the mercy of God watching over you. What's there to howl about? You've begun this too early; let Assumption Day pass, Farforov will get his permanent position and you'll turn sixteen; well now you carry on about it all day long, then. But whether you carry on about it or not, I'm still marrying you off. There now, I'll tell your father, try that if you keep on like this! Your father will be in no mood for jokes; you still don't know him well enough.'[111]

It turns out that the mother does not know her daughter well enough, and Lolenka declares: "Mama, you can kill me right where I stand, but I won't marry Farforov![112]

True to her word, Lolenka runs away from home to her aunt's in St. Petersburg rather than marry the man her parents have chosen for her. In the capital during the time of the Great Reforms—the end of serfdom, military, judicial, and educational reforms, and the beginnings of Russian feminism, Lolenka receives a good education and special training as an artist. Having suffered unrequited love for her neighbor Veretitsyn, Lolenka had vowed to never fall in love again and to live only for her work, not for family life and the role of woman as victim/martyr.

She is astonished when she meets her old love Veretitsyn eight years later to find he is still in love with his "beloved" Sofia, who had succumbed to her mother's persuasion to marry a well-to-do gentry-class man to provide for her mother in her old age. Veretitsyn finds Sofia's sacrificial nature admirable while Lolenka finds it evil. Lolenka thinks Sofia is training her children to be victims and martyrs, which she finds repulsive.[113]

So, in this short novella, we find three different sorts of women: the traditional married woman (Lolenka's mother) who accepts some bullying, and bullies her own children; the rebel against traditional family life (Lolenka); and the martyr/victim—Sofia Aleksandrovna who marries a rich man to provide for her mother.

In his short story "The Christmas Tree and the Wedding," (1848) Feodor Dostoevsky portrays a disgusting, greedy, dowry hunter. The narrator first meets this businessman at a Christmas party, calculating a young girl's dowry. Years later, he goes into a church and recognizes them as the wedding couple. While many Americans have tried to make it rich by playing the stock market in the late 20th and early 21st centuries, some 19th century Russian men and women sought economic gain through the marriage market. While Jane Austen pokes fun at such characters in her novels, English writers such as Charles Dickens and many 19th century Russian writers portray them as callous and immoral.

4. Nicholas Dobroliubov: Women's Plight

> This is a world of suppressed, softly sighing grief, a world of dull, aching pain, a world in which reigns the silence of the prison or the grave, disturbed at rare intervals only by a muffled, impotent complaint, which subsides almost the moment it is uttered....
>
> Dobroliubov, "A Ray of Light in the Kingdom of Darkness," 1859

Writing at mid-century, the radical literary critic Nicholas Dobroliubov found a good deal of deceit in arranged marriages. In Russia, the middle estate was divided into several parts: the highly ranked "honored citizens" (*grazhdanstvo*, about 340,000) included financiers, bankers, and other hauts bourgeois. In this group both patriarchy and matriarchy could be oppressive. Wives, mothers and mothers-in-law as well as husbands, fathers, and fathers-in-law might be despotic.

In the middle merchant rank, the *kupechestvo* (280,000), power relations could also be authoritarian. However, women in these two top groups did have a legal right to property, and widows sometimes ran the family business. Strong autocratic family life also occurred in the lowest ranks of the meshchanstvo, or petty bourgeoisie, which numbered over 13 million. In all three groups *Samodurstvo*, or the desire to dominate others, prevailed. Merchants often forced family members, employees, and others to submit to their will. Success seldom softened them, and they ruled their family and workers with an iron hand.[114]

Describing family life in the lower middle class and the lower clerical estate to which he belonged, Dobroliubov agonized about women's pitiful lives in an article the "Kingdom of Darkness." He thought patriarchal family environment developed base instincts where friends boasted of robbing each other, fathers-in-law tricked sons-in-law out of dowries, bridegrooms cheated matchmakers, and wives deceived their husbands. Nothing was sacred or pure. Everyone was dragged down into the quagmire.

Aleksandra Kobiakova, who was born in the mid 19th century into the lowest merchant estate in Kostroma, echoes many of Dobroliubov's criticisms. Describing her grandmother, she indicates that women in this stratum could be as domineering and mean spirited as men.[115] Merchant family life in Nikolai Ostrovsky's mid 19th century plays also appeared sordid and gloomy. Dobroliubov termed this Kingdom of Darkness "Temnoe Tsarstvo" much as we describe abusive relationships today. He observed:

> These unhappy prisoners are silent; they sit in a state of lethargic stupor, and do not even rattle their chains; they have almost lost the power to realize their tragic situation; nevertheless, they feel the weight of the burden that lies upon them, they have not lost the power to feel their pain....nowhere can they seek relief...over them rages the irresponsible and senseless tyranny represented by various types....who recognize no reasonable rights or demands. Only their savage and revolting shouts disturb this gloomy silence and cause a frightful stir in this melancholy graveyard of human thought and freedom.[116]

While Dobroliubov found women in the merchant class doomed, he thought family life among the peasantry not as oppressive. He believed peasant women's work spinning, weaving, sewing, and knitting left them time to think and dream. Basing his views upon the peasant stories of writer and editor Marko Vovchok (1833-1907), he found inner moral strength among her heroines.

5. *Nicholas Ostrovsky: Actress*

> I'm an actress! But according to you I ought to be some sort of heroine. Yet how can every woman be a heroine? I am an actress...And if I were to marry you I'd soon throw you over and go back to the stage. Even for the smallest salary. Just to be there on the stage. I can't live without the theatre.
>
> Negina in Ostrovsky's "Artistes and Admirers"

By the end of the century, merchant life began to change. While Ostrovsky's mid 19th century plays portrayed marriage negotiations and marriage itself as sordid, one of his works from 1881, *Talanty i Poklonniki* or *Artistes and Admirers* shows a provincial actress choosing a career over offers of marriage or being the mistress of a wealthy Prince. In some ways she represents the New Woman who wants to develop herself. Towards the end of the play Negina tells her fiancé: "You don't understand anything...And don't want to understand...

While her fiancé Melusov confesses that this is new to him, but she counters in *Artistes and Admirers*:

> New! It's only new because up to this minute you haven't known what was in my heart, you haven't understood...You thought I could be a heroine, but I can't...And what's more don't want to be. Why should I live to be a reproach to others? You say I'm like that, but I'm really like *this*. Honestly! And perhaps no-one is to blame at all. Judge for yourself. ...
> While I was making up my mind I was weeping all the time about you... Here you are. I cut off some hair for you. Take it in remembrance of me.[117]

Paintings by Boris Kustodiev show a sunnier, happier married middle class life in the early 20th century. In the case of Russia's middle classes, art and literature present different views. Kustodiev's early 20th century paintings show rather endearing pictures of spouses in this estate, whereas 19th century writings of Dostoevsky,

Boris Kustodiev, Shrovetide, 1916

Dobroliubov, and Goncharov show villainy and deceit. Certainly many changes occurred in the upper middle classes in the late 19th and early 20th centuries. Many families became more open minded about educating their children, and some changed their husband-wife relations.

6. Middle-Class Painters

> He used all his energy to facilitate my work and ensure its success.
>
> Anna Ostroumova Lebedeva, painter

Middle-class families like those of painters Anna Ostroumova Lebedeva and Liubov Popova allowed them to study in the 1890s and even funded their work in Europe in the early 20th century. In her memoirs, Anna O. Lebedeva describes her marriage to her cousin prior to WW I as egalitarian and satisfactory. Before WW I, Anna fell in love with an Italian when she was studying in Italy. However, she decided against marrying him. Eventually, she realized her cousin Sergei Lebedev would be a worthy partner for her life. He had loved Anna a long time, and he divorced his wife to marry Anna. He understood her, and she described him thus:

> He has great spiritual strength and is broad minded, and very purposeful in his work. He taught me not to pay attention to the small things in life, not to spend much energy on them, and instead to look at things in a large way. He never envied me, never felt this male jealousy towards a workingwoman who is asserting her independent place in life.[118]

By the turn of the century, middle-class women began to participate more in marriage negotiations. Economic arrangements were still important, but personal preference also began to carry some weight. The diary of Galina V. Shtange indicates that she was born into a family of engineers in St. Petersburg in 1885, and happily married into this milieu in 1903. Her marriage to engineer Dmitry A. Shtange lasted many years and endured the vicissitudes of the Revolutions of 1917, food shortages in the 1920s, the imprisonment of her husband in 1928, and their busy, yet daunting life of the 1930s.[119]

Andrey Ryabushkin, Peasant Wedding in the Tambov guberniya, 1880

C. Peasant Marriages

With a good wife grief is only half grief, and joy is double.
The peasant's wife is his best friend.

Peasant Proverbs

Both arranged marriages and love matches occurred among the peasantry. Yet, economic considerations always played some role in uniting couples. Marriage was almost universal and took place at

Nikolay Bogdanov-Belsky, Church Wedding, 1904

an early age, 16-18 for girls and 18-19 for boys. In farm life, a man could not survive without a wife, nor a woman without a husband. Both were necessary for a household to survive and flourish. Marriage and religion were deeply intertwined in the 19th century. No weddings could take place during the fasts of Lent or Advent, nor on Wednesday, Friday, nor Sunday evenings. Technically the church did not approve of "forced" weddings, but often young people were not consulted about their feelings before or during the ceremony. In Russian Orthodoxy, marriage was a sacrament, a lifetime commitment, so divorce was very difficult and expensive. Certainly few peasants could afford the appeals to church courts that a divorce required. Indeed, the church granted very few divorces per decade, and Russia had one of the lowest divorce rates in all of Europe before the revolution.

In *Coming of Age in the Russian Revolution*, gentry-class Elena Skrjabina shows that peasant families were concerned to marry their daughters as well as possible. Prior to the revolution, a peasant named Ivan approached her father asking for a cow so he could marry his beloved. Elena's mother opposed the extravagance of giving a good milk cow to a peasant, but her father agreed to help him. Apparently Ivan and his sweetheart had loved each other for some time, but her parents would not let them marry because he was too poor. After Mr. Gorstkin gave him the cow, the girl's parents came to the estate to see the cow. They didn't believe that Ivan was actually getting the animal. Years later, this same peasant, who became a Commissar in the new Bolshevik government, helped Elena get a good job when she needed one.[120]

Until the late 19th century, a peasant woman's strength was often valued more than her beauty. A wife needed energy, vigor and health to perform all the household and farmyard chores and to produce children. As in other estates, matchmakers and in-laws engaged in some deceit. If a family were impoverished and unable to pay for wedding costs, including presents, food, and drink, then young people sometimes resorted to elopement. The abduction of a bride freed the family from the obligation of a wedding, and a few days later the couple returned to the bride's parents to discuss the material aspects of the marriage.[121]

Patriarchal, matriarchal, even egalitarian marriages existed. Russian ethnographers observed villages where women were "splendid,

Prokudin-Gorsky, Mugan Settler's Family, Grafovka, 1905-15

strong, and healthy," and others where they were beaten, unattractive, and worn out. Some peasant proverbs showed women's victimization: "A hen is not a bird and a woman is not a human being;" while others showed their appreciation: "A man without a woman is like a house without a roof." [122] Prokudin-Gorsky's picture above shows family life poor, but not completely downtrodden.

Most peasant girls prepared themselves a dowry of pillows, linens, clothes, and other household items. As industrialization penetrated the countryside, however, the handmade dowry was sometimes replaced by ready-made objects, i.e. clothing, furniture, mirrors, etc. Notions of a proper bride also changed from an emphasis on strength and hard work, to beauty.[123]

As more young men migrated to work in the mines and the cities, peasant culture began to change. By the time of the 1905 Revolution, relations between young people had become more relaxed, and they were often allowed to meet for entertainment in a widow's house in the village. At the end of the evening, the girls would exchange the work they had brought with them for dancing and singing. Boys who had not left the village in search of seasonal work and

Prokudin-Gorsky, Side View of Antique Peasant Dress, 1909

bachelors looking for wives would drop by. Usually the men were not invited into the house but the girls came outside to see them. Eventually, young men began to arrange parties themselves. There were usually two or three houses in the village which became popular meeting places for the young people. The young men would arrange a party with the women in advance.

Each man would pay 10-15 kopeks for himself and for the girl he was courting. The boys brought wood for fuel and kerosene for the lamps. Nuts and candies and apples were brought. During the holidays sweets and baked goods were served. These gatherings were places for matchmaking, and parents were glad to see their children participate. Girls did little work at these events, and men who knew how to play a harmonica created the fun. Young people danced, sang, and played kissing games.

Only after the Revolution were the traditional dances replaced by the waltz, fox trot, and songs from the city. After the Revolution of 1905 revolutionary songs became popular and as always the tra-

Prokudin-Gorsky, Young Girls Posing, 1910

ditional *chastushki* (short songs) were great favorites. Masses and parties were celebrated for lads who left for the mines or recruits leaving for the front during the Russo-Japanese War.[124] Then, as now, some young women yearned to escape parental control and establish their own family, and extended families broke apart when they could afford to do so.

1. Peasant Wedding Laments

> Now, my own, my dear father,
>   Accept my affectionate words,
>   Do not betroth me to an old man,
>   An old husband will be my ruin,
>
>   Lament, *Russian Folklore*

Peasant women's voices can be heard in the laments they sang at the time of their weddings. These songs were meant to honor the bride's family and also to show the "death" of the young bride. Henceforth, she would be a wife and mother serving others, but no longer a girl with a will of her own. The wailing also indicates how brides should behave submissively with their future in-laws. Some of the songs were about leaving their parents, girl friends, carefree youth, the village, forests, and trees. Some described the difficulties of living in an extended family among one's in-laws. Occasionally the whining and weeping were prolonged for a week or longer; likewise the merry making could pass into wild revelry.[125]

Although these girls in Prokudin-Gorsky's photo were too young to marry, from the age of eight they began weaving towels for their dowries and learning wedding chants like the following:

> So young, I am so very young,
> So green, I am so very green,
> A very young girl I am,
> Who has no mind of her own
> Just think, my dear mother,
> How will I live with strangers,
> When I'm so silly, still so very silly
> So young I am, so very young.[126]

Some songs and proverbs were about leaving their family, others about not being married to a young boy or old man. One proverb said:

"One can do little with an old horse, but an old bridegroom is ten times worse."

Another: "A wife is not a psaltery: if you play you must pay."[127]

One young girl wails:

> Now, my own, my dear father,
>> Accept my affectionate words,
>> Affectionate and grateful.
>> Do not betroth me to an old man,
>> An old husband will be my ruin,
>> Misfortune upon my poor little head,
>> My maidenly beauty I shall lose,
> All my freedom and joy[128]

In addition to not wanting to be married off to an old man, young girls also refused to "go for a stroll" or cuddle with a mere boy.

> Don't give, don't give,
>   Don't give me in marriage to a young boy!
>   A young boy, a young boy,
>   To the death will I not love a young boy,
> With a young boy will I not take a stroll![129]

Wedding laments varied according to locale—those in Northern Russia differing from those in Central and Southern Russia. They marked leaving one's youth behind and taking up the responsibilities of adult life. Certain rites and rituals accompanied a wedding. Matchmakers and parents initially consulted about the dowry. As the wedding approached, the bride finished her trousseau, took a ritual bath, had her braid unwound and replaited into two braids signifying her new status as wife, and then she and her girl friends held a farewell party. The next day the church ceremony took place. After the wedding night, they enjoyed a feast at the groom's home.[130]

2. Peasant Memoirs

> First of all, my life was so sad that I kept thinking of suicide, and so I decided to describe all my sufferings, so that after my death people would discover my notebooks and find out what had made me want to kill myself.
>
> <div align=right>Agrippina Korevanova, <i>My Life</i></div>

Few memoirs of peasant women survive, but one by Agrippina Korevanova shows the power of parents to marry children against their will—even if they had to beat them. She recounts how at the age of 17 suitors kept appearing at their door. As soon as she got rid of one, another came knocking. She was in love with a poor peasant lad Vasia that her parents rejected. One day her father told her he had betrothed her to a local cobbler, not to Vasia. Despondent, she remembered in *My Life*:

> I ran out into the yard and stood in the garden for a while. Then I went into the bathhouse and sat down on a bench. ...my

head was spinning. I rested my head in my hands, and just sat there without moving. I don't know how long I was there. At some point my aunt came in and touched me on the shoulder. With a shudder, I looked up at and started crying. Without saying a word, she left. Finally I walked out of the bathhouse and looked up at the hill, hoping to see Vasia.

He was not there! ...

'Papa,' I begged, 'Don't make me marry him [the cobbler]... I don't like him at all.'

'Why don't you like him? He's a handsome fellow and a good cobbler; he makes ladies shoes and sells them for fifteen kopeks a pair. And his family has money!'

'I don't need their money, Daddy! I don't love their son!'

'What do you mean by love? Get married first, and then start thinking about love. You'll be fine—they live well. Your husband will have his own shop, and you'll be your own mistress, not some miserable maid. If you marry a poor man, you'll have to work, too.'

'I'd rather work than marry him!'

'That's enough,' said my father. 'Don't be a fool. It's done.'[131]

Her aunt assured her that it was "woman's lot," and there was nothing she could do. Her beloved Vasia seemed to have vanished. Agrippina remembered that she could tell the priest that she was being married against her will at the time of the wedding, but it was arranged in such a way that the priest never asked her if she was willing. Further indignity awaited her since her father-in-law was a bully trying to seduce her as he had another daughter-in-law. She reports in her memoir *My Life*:

After that my life turned into a nightmare. Almost every day I was beaten and told to follow the example of the other daughter-in-law. Afterward our neighbors told me that she had won the old man's good graces by showing him 'respect.'[132]

Since her life was so miserable that she often thought of suicide, she decided to write down her thoughts.

It is hard to remember now at what point I first started writing. I think it was the year my father-in-law died. I had done some writing before then as well, but not very seriously. I would jot something down on a piece of paper and then lose it. But this time I bought myself a notebook. When I finished it, I started a new one, and so it went.

What made me want to write? I think there were two main reasons.

First of all, my life was so sad that I kept thinking of suicide, and so I decided to describe all my sufferings, so that after my death people would discover my notebooks and find out what had made me want to kill myself.

The second reason was my rage and horror at the unfairness of life; my protest against the oppression of women; my sympathy for the poor; and my hatred for a fat wallet. I wrote about all this in poor literary style but with great bitterness and passion. There was no practical use in it, of course, but at least it provided some relief. ... My husband knew about my notebooks, but neither he nor the old man gave me any trouble over them; in fact, they were even proud that their woman was so educated.

Finally (although this does not really count as a reason), it happened once that having looked through all my notebooks, I put them together and really liked the fact that they resembled a book. For the first time, I had the frightening yet thrilling thought: 'What if all this got printed in a real book—a book that people could read?' It made my head spin just to think of it, and I resumed my work with even greater ardor.[133]

Ethnographer V. U. Krupianskaia gives other examples of unhappy peasant marriages in the Village of Viriatino in the late 19th century. She observed that a bride was usually selected from the same village or from one nearby. Marriages were usually arranged by parents, who were trying to "provide" a good husband to their daughters. Engagements were short, and some couples only met at the altar. Dowries were usually not as important in southern Russia as in the North. Some girls wanted to marry for love, but parents were not sympathetic. One woman told Krupianskaia that she had picked out a suitor, and they were deeply in love. They had agreed that after he returned from the mines he would send the matchmaker to ask for her. But before this happened, her father decided to marry her to another man who would provide well for her.

I cried that I didn't want to marry.... My betrothed sent me letters from the mine but I was illiterate and could not answer them. I cried for him—rivers of tears—but regardless, Father had his way.[134]

While there was a great deal of wife beating and abuse in peasant households, not all peasant women were victims. Some songs told of the drowning, burning, hanging, or abuse of old husbands. One such reads as follows:

Go, old man, go, old man, and pick the flower.'
'I'm afraid, wife, I'm afraid, wife that I'll drown!'
'It's most likely, old man, it's most likely, old man, the devil won't
    grab you.'
The first step, the first step is up to his knees,
The second step, the second step came up to his waist.
The third step, the third step came up to his neck,
He cries: 'Wife,' he cried, 'wife, I'm drowning!'
'Thank God, thank God, you're drowning,
Thank God you're drowning!'[135]

Although there were happy songs sung after the wedding ceremony and family feasts, still the general tone was somber and outsiders sometimes thought weddings resembled funerals. Happier songs marked the birth of children and were often sung as lullabies:

> In Ivanovich's home there was joy,
> There was joy.
> Why in his home
> Was there joy, was there joy?
> His young wife a son
> Has borne, has borne,
> And the sweet Theodosia-darling son
> Has borne, has borne,
> Sweet Petrovna—darling son
> Has borne, has borne.[136]

Some plaints were sung at a child's death. Women certainly needed rites and rituals to help them get through the deaths of their children since about one half of them died before the age of five. Fu-

Prokudin-Gorsky, Spinning Yarn, Iznedovo Village, 1910

neral dirges were sung at the time of death, on the third, sixth, ninth, twelfth, and fortieth days even one year after a child's demise.

Dr. Valentina Dmitrieva described one woman's experience during the famine of 1891 in her writing "After Great Hunger:"

> The scene we met was so extraordinary that I stopped dead in my tracks. The cottage had been tidied and swept; there was a white cloth on the table, and a candle was lit in the icon corner. A bench had been placed below the icons, and something was lying on this, covered by a piece of bleached calico. A woman was sitting at table, her apron over her face, head propped on her hand; she was rocking herself from side to side, and wailing at full volume—keening, in fact. The cottage rang with the melancholy, heart-rending sounds of her lament; people were coming in and out all of the time, but no one made any attempt to approach her or to address her....[137]

Still, being unmarried could be a worse possible disaster. Crippled women, and shrews sometimes remained single. They were often shunned and could barely eke out an existence as matchmakers, funeral mourners, lace makers, or handicraft workers. As wards of their village and economic burdens, they were resented and lacked the respectable status of wife and mother.

Interviewing farmers in the village of Viriatino, ethnographer V. U. Krupianskaia reported some changes in peasant courtship and marriage around 1900. By that time, dancing, singing, and courting had become more relaxed, and marriages were beginning to be made according to the wishes of the bride and groom. Apparently young lads who went off to work in the mines became more independent and resisted their father's efforts to marry them off. They made their own decisions and then asked their father to make the betrothal arrangements. If a young girl married into an extended family, which most did prior to the Revolution of 1917, then the young bride was under the control and supervision of her mother-in-law. Some family traditions such as diet and food remained unchanged. The mother-in-law supervised the cooking and rejected any innovations. Rye flour and bread remained the staple food, along with cabbage soup, milk, meat, potatoes, and kasha. Wealthy Kulak households remained the exceptions to these changes. In these households, property remained an important consideration, and customs and confinement of daughters remained strict.[138]

An observer for the ethnographer Count V. N. Tenishev reported a great deal of marital infidelity resulting from arranged marriages in his village near Smolensk. He commented:

> I know hardly a husband who is faithful to his wife. And I know many women who are unfaithful to their husbands. But if (infidelity) does not go beyond the boundaries of propriety and bring shame to the family, it does not interfere with family accord.[139]

While he is writing of peasant life, he could be describing the aristocracy and the lives of women in Tolstoy's book *Anna Karenina*, which was also set in the late 19th century. The major difference is that peasant infidelity seemed to be more often linked to the absence of husbands due to male out-migration and work in the cities, while that of aristocratic and gentry-class women was due more to personal taste and boredom.

D. Working Class Marriages

1. *Maria Botchkareva*

> Anything seemed preferable to the daily torments of home. If I had sought death to escape my father, why not marry this boorish moujik? And I consented thoughtlessly.
>
> Maria Botchkareva, Yashka, My Life

Fewer pictures, paintings, or songs about working-class women's weddings exist because folklorists in the 19th century concentrated on the peasantry and thought workers' songs vulgar. So, we don't have many working-class women's voices. In Russia as in Europe, many urban workers lived in "common law" marriages, what is called today "living together." Their weddings were simpler than in the village where traditions remained strong. In the 19th century, workers were underpaid, so one suspects their ceremonies were shorter and less festive than those in the countryside. Of course, many workers maintained ties to their village and remained technically in the peasant estate, returning home to marry in the usual village way. Historian Page Herrlinger in her book *Working Souls* indicates that weddings of workers in the late 19th century were constrained by time, money, and lack of family. Dowries and match makers became less important in the city. Weddings could cost from 25-300 Rubles, bankrupting a poor working-class family.[140] Many working-class women were remarkable for their devotion to their families and church while holding full-time, usually exhausting jobs in factory or handicraft production.

An unusual, fascinating account of working-class married life is found in the autobiography of worker-soldier Maria Botchkareva. She wrote her story after she fled the Bolsheviks in 1918. She was semi-literate and told her story to an American, who prepared it for publication. The title of her book *Yashka, My Life as Peasant, Officer, and Exile* is a little misleading. She did become a soldier in the Tsarist army in WW I, and she was an exile after the revolution. However, though technically born into the peasant estate, she may be considered working-class since she spent most of her life living and working in cities. Her parents were born and brought up in the village, but when she was a child her family moved first to Novgorod and then to Tomsk, fairly large cities. She remained legally in the peasant estate, but she spent her life from 8-26 working at a wide variety of jobs in cities and towns. So, she appears more worker than peasant.

In the chapter on her childhood, she recounts her father's drinking and abuse of her mother and herself. At eight years old, Maria contemplated suicide because her life was so painful. By the age of 15, she imagines marriage as an escape from her father's brutal beatings. She meets her first husband at her sister's and then at a friend's home. As she remembered it in *Yashka, My Life*:

> ... we visited some friends of my sister's, where I met a soldier, just returned from the front [of the 1905 Russo-Japanese War]. He was a common moujik [peasant], of rough appearance and vulgar speech, and at least ten years older than myself. He immediately began to court me. His name was Afanasi Botchkarev.
>
> It was not long afterward that I met Botchkarev again in the house of a married sister of his. He invited me to go out for a walk, and then suddenly proposed that I marry him. It caught me so unexpectedly that I had no time for consideration.
>
> My father objected to my marrying since I was not yet sixteen, but without avail. As Botchkarev was penniless, and I had no money, we decided to work together and save. Our marriage was a hasty affair. The impression that I retain is my feeling of relief at escaping from my father's brutal hands. Alas! Little did I then suspect that I was exchanging one form of torture for another."[141]

Not surprisingly, her husband drank and soon began beating her. Eventually, she ran away and attempted suicide. But he pursued her, promising to change. When he returned to drinking and stole all the money she had saved from working, she decided to kill him. Fetching an axe from her parents, she was about to kill him when her father intervened. The police took her husband away, and let her leave the city. Now 18 years old, she traveled to the Siberian city Irkutsk where one of her married sisters lived. There she worked in some lowly paid jobs.

After a series of adventures, Maria met her second husband Yakov Buk. At first all went well for them. They decided on a civil agreement because she could not afford to divorce her first husband. Apparently this was a very common arrangement at that time. While she and Buk lived and worked together happily for a few years, he eventually took to gambling and beating her. He twice tried to kill her, so after several years of marriage to him she ran away and joined the army in 1914.[142]

2. *A Nameless Working Woman*

> I worked hard and made some money, and we lived better in our home. But after that my husband came back and said that he had a right to my business. He used my money for his sprees—till at last I got sick of everything. I decided to try my luck in the town, and went back to Moscow.
>
> Ernest Poole, *The Dark People*

Another brutal account of married life by a peasant/worker is recounted by Ernest Poole, who interviewed a peasant woman shortly after the revolution. She told him her life story, and what a sad story it was. Born a peasant, she received some training as a dressmaker in Moscow before WW I. She was married as a teenager, and her husband turned out to be a philanderer and drunkard. Whenever she accumulated some money or goods, he would seek her out and pawn them for drink. Her life reads as follows in Poole's *The Dark People*:

> So again my life was very bad. He sold my belongings and even my dresses. He would come home drunk... He would go to the cupboard and take out a dress, and I knew that I would soon see it in the second-hand shop in the village, as an advertisement that my husband was a drunkard. The village women blamed it on me because I was a girl from the town.

Due to her hard life with her husband, she lost her first two babies. Once, she started a tea-room, but remarked:

> I was now nineteen years old. In the city, I went to my dressmaker friend and told her a part of my troubles. She said:
> 'Don't think about it too much. I know your village people. How can you blame them for being like wolves, when their lives are so dark? You must leave them behind. To get on, you need education. Here you can go to school at night, while you are working in a shop.'[143]

Even when she moved to Warsaw and made a new life for herself, her husband followed her there, and she felt very conflicted:

> ...Soon he came to Warsaw—and then I had two feelings. One was a wish to keep the life that I had worked so hard for there, and the other was an old deep feeling of my duty as his wife. When he came to my room I did not know how to tell him to go away, so instead I said that the room was not mine...[144]

No matter where she lived, her pernicious husband tracked her down and took her money and dignity. This harassed married woman had a hard life.

E. Conclusion

Looking at Russian women's marital experience in the mid and late 19th century, we can see that economic considerations remained strong in the arrangement of most marriages. Yet sources suggest that by the end of the century, some gentry-class mothers were loathe to marry their daughter to a debauched man. Likewise, parents in peasant families had become more likely to consult their sons about their bridal choice than daughters about a husband. This was partly because sons who worked away from home in the mines or factories were more independent and less likely to accept parental control. Daughters had less opportunity to work away from home. They usually remained under the control of their parents and village.

Since marriage was a sacrament in the Russian Orthodox tradition, divorce was not tolerated and Russia had one of the lowest divorce rates in Europe in 1900. One result of arranged marriages was that many women adjusted to loveless marriages. Of course, some did not. While not all husbands were drunkards, gamblers, or abusers, many were, and in all strata of society. Regardless of social rank, some women also sought love and romance outside of marriage. Educated women writers like Evdokia Rostopchina, Karolina Pavlova, and Avdotya Panaeva took lovers in middle age in order to find romance and happiness. It seems few experienced the romance and joy in marriage that the series "Downton Abbey" portrays among the English, or if they did, few wrote about it.

Russian society sometimes supported women's careers, and sometimes criticized them. Upper class Russian women could combine marriage and career because servants freed them from childcare and housework. Moreover, writing, journalism, teaching, medicine, and the religious life often helped single women survive in the mid and late 19th century.[145]

Most Russian women yearned for the respectability and financial security that marriage offered, and most married at some point. Not marrying could be a disaster for women in any estate. Few peasant women could survive farming alone. Nor could most gentry, middle-class or working-class women. As one gentry-class woman's nanny told her: "Watch out, a girl is like a berry: if a berry's not picked, it'll rot in the rain." Most Russian women were poorly educated and not equipped to support themselves. The next section is about women's work, and about some unusual women who obtained training, higher education, and careers in the late 19th century.

Prokudin-Gorsky, "At Harvest Time, Russian Empire," 1909

Chapter Three

Women's Work in the 19th Century

A. Peasant Women's Work

Russian peasants called farm work *strada* or suffering.

Peasant women worked long hours helping in the fields, maintaining the household, grinding grain, baking bread, preparing food, tending the livestock and kitchen garden, preserving food, spinning wool and flax, weaving cloth, making clothes, knitting gloves and socks for their kin or to sell to increase the family income. In the fields, they weeded, harvested. mowed the hay and grain; stacked it; and bound the sheaves. Their long hours of work in the summer meant that they were away from their babies from sunup till sundown, and high infant mortality resulted. Indeed, half of Russian children died before the age of 5 in the late 19th century. The high death rate was higher among the Russians than in other ethnic groups like the Poles, Ukrainians, Baltic peoples, or even Muslims living along the Volga.[1]

Yet, in spite of all their hard work, relatively few peasant households lived well. In the 1890s 65% were poor—without horses or plows to farm or enough land to till—, 20% were middling, and 15% were wealthy kulaks, who possessed horses and plows to use and lend to poor peasants for farming. Wealthy peasants also employed paid laborers in their farming operations and households. In the late 19th century, Russian farmers generally produced only 11 bushels of rye per acre, whereas Europeans obtained 17-24 bushels.[2]

Nina Berberova remembered both rich and poor peasants coming to her grandfather's study to consult with him. In her memoir *The Italics Are Mine*, she contrasted them as follows:

In Grandfather's study, where Goncharov once sat and, as I imagine it, studied his hero, I now sat. In the mornings, peasants, or, as they were called then, muzhiks, came to consult Grandfather. They were of two kinds, and it seemed to me that they were two completely different breeds. Some muzhiks were demure, well bred, important-looking, with greasy hair, fat paunches, and shiny faces. They were dressed in embroidered shirts and caftans of fine cloth. These were the ones who were later called kulaks. They lived on their own farms, liberated themselves from the village commune, and felled trees for new homes in the thick woods that only recently had been Grandfather's. They walked in the church with collection trays and placed candles before the Saint-Mary-Appease-My-Grief icon. But what kind of grief could they have? The Peasants' Credit Bank gave them credit. In their houses, which I sometimes visited, there were geraniums on the window sills and the smell of rich buns from the ovens. Their sons grew into energetic and ambitious men, began new lives for themselves, and created a new class in embryo for Russia.

The other muzhiks wore bast sandals, dressed in rags, bowed fawningly, never went further than the doors, and had faces that had lost all human expression. These remained in the commune. They were undersized, and often lay in ditches near the state-owned wine shop. Their children did not grow because they were underfed. Their consumptive wives seemed always to be in the final month of pregnancy, the infants were covered with weeping eczema, and in their homes, which I also visited, broken windows were stopped up with rags, and calves and hens were kept in the corners. There was a sour stench. But in the homes of the fat ones, for some reason, agile, cheerful, industrious sons grew up and married healthy, pretty girls. When grandchildren appeared, they were sent off to a technical school in a regional town.[3]

The lives of paid female agricultural workers were also difficult since they received lower wages than men and about two thirds of them were married — a much higher proportion than in Western Europe in the late 19th century. Despite their tough lives, peasants managed to sing songs about their work harvesting the grain. One song recorded by ethnographers goes as follows:

> The little wife Petrochkova
> Went out very early
> Into her harvest field;
> With her she brought out
> Her daughters the swans,
> Her daughters-in-law the quail.
> 'Reap, daughters!
> Daughters the swans,
> Daughters-in-law the quail;
> In the morning very early,
> In the evening very late,
> That we may have wherewith to live;
> Very well, yes, very good.[4]

After the harvest, observers noted that reapers might roll or somersault across the harvest field, pronouncing the following incantations:

> Stubble of the summer grain,
> Give back my strength
> For the long winter
>
> Harvest field, harvest field, give back my strength,
> I have reaped you, I have lost my strength.[5]

In addition to songs, peasants also had proverbs about life's difficulties. One recorded by folklorists says:

> It is not a calamity when there is pig-weed in the rye,
> But it is a calamity if there is neither rye nor pig-weed.
>
> The rye feeds everyone without exception,
> but the wheat makes distinctions.[6]

The tsarist censorship controlled which songs, proverbs, and riddles could be published, and certain ones that were collected remained unpublished.[7]

Since the land was not so productive by the late 19th century, several million peasant women also participated in handicraft work of various kinds to augment family incomes. Some made wooden spoons and bowls, some gloves, clothing, and textiles, others worked in food preparation and trade. They received precious little for their hard work. They earned 4 kopecks per day carding wool, 15 kopecks per day picking berries, but 20-70 kopecks for breaking flax. Local raw materials such as wood and flax undergird household manufacturing. Some girls and women helped make toys, felt boots, baskets, and so forth. Both local and national markets influenced cottage industry. Young girls 12-16 years old constituted a high proportion of those involved in handicraft production, so they were unable to attend school since their families needed them to contribute to their economy. Families with the smallest farms often had the highest proportion of women in cottage industry. Proximity to towns and cities also determined the kind of work performed. Those close to Moscow and St. Petersburg often worked in cigarette manufacture, especially making the papers and filters. Some worked in lace making, bobbin winding, or knitting. Women in cotton weaving earned about 3-4 rubles a month.[8] At the same time that peasants earned so little, Countess Tolstoy's daughter Tania spent 1500 rubles on dresses for a ball season in Moscow.

Gentry-class landowner and ethnographer Alexander Engelgardt found that he could make much more money growing flax than rye. He also discovered that women were willing workers when they realized that he would pay them well, and pay them directly, not their husbands or fathers. He also thought women more willing than men to undertake new kinds of work. However, he found that while men would work collectively on projects, women preferred to work singly and individually.[9]

Indeed, Engelgardt found that peasant women were often greedy for money and would sell their sister, daughter, themselves, or young girls in the village for money. According to Engelgardt, rural women did not look on prostitution as evil, but argued:

"It's not soap, you don't use it up."
"It's not a puddle, something will be left for the husband too."

Engelgardt thought the morals of village women simple: money, a shawl, anonymity made anything possible. While a five or twenty-five ruble note meant nothing for a visitor from St. Petersburg, it was a fortune to poor peasant women.[10]

According to the 1897 census, about 10,000 women served as midwives. Since the census records more midwives in the cities than in the countryside, one can only conclude that the number of peasant midwives was undercounted. This is not surprising because the census mainly listed those trained in special institutes, not those who learned through apprenticeship as most peasants did. Indeed, their secrets were often handed from mother to daughter. While peasant midwives did not directly charge families for the delivery of a baby, gifts were usually made to them. A poor family often gave a towel and a cake of soap. If they had money, then they gave according to their means. In addition, midwives often were given special presents on December 26th and September 8th, the Virgin Mary's birthday.

Midwifery was generally considered an honored, professional craft. Usually it was old and widowed women who worked as midwives. Since they were widows, the men of the village often plowed their land for them, and they were given the best places at baptism and wedding dinners. Peasant midwives were often preferred to the government educated ones, because the village ones would stay on a few days after the birth of a child, helping the new mother with the household chores. This was deeply appreciated by the new mothers, but shunned by the professional midwives. Moreover, the local ones knew the customary religious rituals, which the "modern" ones did not. Since trained midwives had no higher success rates than untrained ones in normal births, peasants felt no need to hire a professional one. If one had to hire a modern midwife, and then pay a doctor if complications arose, the cost was too much for most households. Real change only came when government medical institutions provided feldsher-midwives or physicians' assistant-midwives to work in the provinces.[11]

While some peasant girls trained as midwives, few worked in rural areas because the zemstva (local government) paid for few such positions and peasants preferred the more traditional ones. As a result, trained midwives attended only 2% of rural births in 1900. Of the 10,000 trained midwives, 6,000 were in private practice mostly in the cities. There, they did not have to travel far to deliver babies, and city folk could afford to pay for their services, whereas country folk could not. Although the Russian government wanted to train peasant women to become trained midwives, this proved elusive. Most students at the courses were gentry and middle-class, not peasants, and peasant girls who did the training soon shed their rural background. Generally, midwifery offered employment and upward mobility to peasants, Jews, and townspeople. Whereas gentry and lower-middle-class women predominated among midwife trainees in the 1880s-90s, by 1910 women from the lower middle class surpassed all other groups.[12]

According to Rose Glickman, some peasant women, especially widows, worked as healers or znakharki. They used charms, chants, and herbs to cure the sick. The church sanctioned these healers, especially if they invoked angels, saints, and the Mother of God in their chants. Many peasants interpreted illness as God's punishment for sins, so invoking divine mercy was accepted as a way to improve. A mother often passed on her healing knowledge to her daughter. There was some specialization among the znakharki—some healed bones, others toothache, some were blood letters. These healers were seldom paid in cash, usually in kind— with a loaf of bread, some eggs, a length of cotton or wool. There were significant numbers of these healers in the late 19th century because there was a shortage of doctors, especially in the countryside. Some lingered on until the 1920s, but while the 1897 census recorded about 20,000, they had dwindled considerably by the 1926 census.[13]

B. Working-Class Women's Work

> The work is hard,
> Ah, the work is hard....
> Ah, our poor backs are aching!
>
> Sokolov, *Russian Folklore*, 583

According to the 1897 Russian Census, about one million Russian women workers found employment in domestic service, 500,000 labored as laundresses and about 320,000 in textile production. Relatively few, about 9,000, worked in very hard heavy jobs like mining. Russian factory workers were unusual in that a very high proportion of them were married: about 45%, whereas fewer

Abram E. Arkhipov, "The Washer Women," 1899

in Western Europe were married in the 1890s. Women earned lower wages than men, and usually brought their subordinate, submissive attitudes from rural patriarchal family life to the factory with them.[14] Few songs of women workers were preserved because folklorists in the late 19th century focused mainly on peasants. More of workers' songs and letters from the 1920s and 30s exist because Soviet scholars were more interested in them.

Pictures of servants and workers in many albums show them very shabbily dressed. Indeed, Countess Tolstoy's picture of the servants at Yasnaya Polyana, the Tolstoy estate, shows servants very simply, almost shabbily dressed. Although the Tolstoy family entertained famous artists like Ilia Repin, the sculptor Naum Aronson, and pianists like Wanda Landowska and Sergei Tanayev, life there was not on the same scale as that depicted on the TV series "Downton Abbey." Some princely families like the Dolgorukys, Menshikovs, Sheremetevs and Yusopovs maintained fabulous country and city homes, and presumably their servants were better dressed in some sorts of uniforms, but obviously not many Russian families spent much money on their servants. Nor did merchants or manufacturers spend much on their workers as photographs by Prokudin-Gorsky and Chloe Obolensky testify.[15]

The high number of married women workers meant some factories and plants had midwives on their staffs and some furnished workers with barracks to live in. Socialists saw working women oppressed by both capitalism and family life. Certainly they endured considerable sacrifice, hazards, and hardship in wedded life. They experienced not the sentimental motherhood of the upper classes, but too frequent pregnancy, stillbirths, miscarriages, high infant mortality, poverty, and drudgery.[16]

Working-class girls usually had short childhoods and went to work at young ages. One woman remembered begging her father, who was a carpenter, to let her continue her education, but at age 12 she was sent to work as a nurse maid. Her daughter, Dr. Vera Malakhova in her memoirs "Four Years as a Frontline Physician," recorded her mother saying:

> I cried and got down on my knees. 'Papa, send me to apprentice, to learn to sew.' But he answered: 'You must go out and earn wages.' Mama finished the parish school when she was twelve, and they sent her to be a nanny in a doctor's family. So at twelve she was already a wage earner. That's how it was.[17]

Library of Congress Photo: "Queues for Work"

1. *Maria Botchkareva*

> On the day following our marriage, Afanasi and I went down to the river to hire ourselves as day laborers. We helped to load and unload lumber barges. Hard labor never daunted me...
>
> Maria Botchkareva, *Yashka, My Life*

Maria Botchkareva's memoir also reveals the strada or suffering of peasant women. It shows the young age at which girls went to work; how often they changed jobs to find better pay and working conditions; as well as working on her wedding day. In her autobiography, she explains that her parents first hired her out as a babysitter at the age of eight. Unable to cope with the child's devious tricks and the mother's punishments, Maria wanted to escape by drowning herself. At ten, she lived and worked at a nearby grocery store waiting on customers, running errands, cooking, cleaning, sewing, and scrubbing the floors. For her daily grind, she earned one ruble per month, which was paid to her parents. Slowly, she came to resent her endless toil, her father's drinking up her wages, and as a young teenager she began to yearn for adventure.[18]

During the Russo-Japanese War, officers moved into Tomsk where she and her family lived, and she obtained a job as a domestic for an officer's family, earning seven rubles per month—much more than she had received at the grocery. The officer's family liked Maria, educated her, and taught her good manners. Eventually the brother of the family fell in love with Maria and seduced her. He promised marriage, but went off to war without keeping his vow. Seduced and abandoned, Maria returned home only to encounter beatings from her father for her sexual adventure. She then decided that marriage would liberate her from her beastly father. Little did she realize that she had married a drunk as brutal as her father.[19]

Describing her early-married life in *Yahska, My Life as a Peasant, Officer, and Exile*, Maria wrote that she would have been satisfied, had it only been possible for her to get along with Afanasi. But he also drank, while she didn't; and intoxication brutalized him. He

"Maria Botchkareva (middle, medals on chest) "Commander, Women's Battalion of Death," Aug. 1917 Petrograd, (Photo Archive)

knew of her affair with Lazov, and used it as a pretext for punishing her. They worked laying asphalt, and she rose to the position of assistant foreman. However, her husband resented her success and drank and beat her even more.[20]

After several years of unhappy married life, Maria escaped, joining her sister in Irkutsk. There, she took a job as a dishwasher for nine rubles per month, but left that to work in a laundry. This backbreaking work, which lasted from five in the morning till eight in the evening, proved too much for her, so she reverted to laying asphalt. Again, despite ridicule from male workers, she became an assistant foreman in the business. But she worked so hard she undermined her health.[21]

Upon her release from a hospital, she went to an employment agency and found a job as a domestic servant. However, the employer was really running a brothel and tried to lure Maria into prostitution. Hysterical, Maria ran away, looking for help from the local police. The police officer also tried to seduce her, so she once again decided to commit suicide—this time by drinking essence of vinegar. Saved by a young man who had seen her at the brothel, she eventually married her rescuer. They did this by common consent since she could not afford a lawful divorce from her first husband. She then opened a butcher shop, and life went well until her husband befriended an escaped political prisoner. Then he was arrested, tried, and sent into exile. Maria joined her husband in northern Siberia, and she opened a laundry, bathhouse, and café for political prisoners there. Sadly, the harder she worked, the more her husband gambled and beat her. After he tried to kill her, she decided to escape and volunteered as a soldier in WW I, serving from 1914-1917.[22]

In terms of work, Botchkareva seemed to be a representative of other working-class women, but in terms of escaping an abusive marriage and joining the Tsar's army, she was unique. In the army she encountered ridicule from the male soldiers, but she eventually won their respect. In May, 1917, the Provisional Government asked her to organize the Women's Battalion of Death. Initially, 2,000 women joined in St. Petersburg, but after basic training, only 300 remained. Tired of the war, many men just wanted to go home, were deserting the front, and didn't like the idea of women fighting and carrying on the war.[23]

Maria won two medals for her bravery in the war, and she fought until the Bolsheviks arrested her in the winter of 1917/18. Her gender and social status saved her at this time. Then she escaped Russia with the aid of the British Consul in St. Petersburg. She made her way to the United States where she tried to enlist US support for the continuation of the war. In the US, she had her story recorded and published, and she returned to Russia in 1918, joining the Allied Cause and White Army in Northern Russia. Unwelcome by former Tsarist White commanders, she eventually went to Tomsk where she organized medical supplies for General Kolchak's army. She was captured by the Bolsheviks, and this time she was executed in 1920 at the age of 31.[24]

2. Clothing and Textile Production

> "Reading, the theater, these things aren't for us. We don't have time. Our work day is very long and we're too tired."
>
> Russian working woman, 1910-11

The author of this quote was a working woman interviewed by E. A. Oliunina , a student at the Moscow Higher Women's Courses in1910-11. Using Moscow census data from 1900 and comments of workers themselves, she reported wretched working and living conditions. Rooms, apartments, and company barracks were bleak, crowded, and infested. Many slept at their place of work without beds or covers. This was particularly true for apprentices who often worked without pay for three to five years and lived on the workshop premises.[25]

In addition to atrocious working conditions, Oliunina found that managers abused workers by increasing the tempo of work, swearing at them, and even sexually exploiting them. Women occupied in garment production worked 14-15 hours—for mere pittances. When interviewed, workers complained:

> "It's a hard life." "It's a dog's life, no one should live like this." "It's hard to make it in the village, but it's no easier here. There's nothing but poverty and grief no matter where we are."

Working Women Demonstrating, Petrograd, April, 1917, St. P. (Photo Archive)

"This isn't life, this is just drudgery."[26]

Oliunina also noticed differences in the way women workers dressed:

> "Those who are employed in workshops in the downtown area dress comparatively neatly and have fashionable dresses, hats, and overcoats. The women in subcontracting workshops almost always look untidy. They wear kerchiefs. Many women, especially the older ones, have faded, dirty, and torn dresses. After about the age of twenty-five, these women usually drink wine and smoke."[27]

Some insisted that they did not drink for pleasure, but as a release from the backbreaking grind. Others sought consolation in vodka from a life of toil and hardship.[28] One suspects that those in factory production fared no better than those in the workshops.

These women worked such long hours that they had little time for cultural or political activity. Moreover, trade unions and political parties were outlawed in the 19th century. However, during the Russo Japanese War and World War One, their destitute living and working conditions along with the absence of food and fuel drove them to political participation and revolutionary activity, especially in the Revolution of February, 1917. Although Bolshevik leaders had advised women workers against demonstrating on International Women's Day, the women disregarded the advice and their small demonstration provoked the men into strikes and into fomenting the February Revolution. Later, women were also active in protesting the government in demonstrations in April, 1917.

3. Mining

> There they kill us with hunger,
> Ah, they give us naught but cold water!
> Song of a gold miner

According to the 1897 Russian Census, only 9,000 women were listed in various kinds of mining, with 5,000 in gold and platinum mining. As Prokudin-Gorsky's picture shows, such work was hard and dirty. This picture is shocking because women and children had been banned from mining in England since the 1840s. But in Siberia, men had to sign seven-year contracts and agree to the employment of their wives and children in the gold mines. Women only earned about 90 kopeks per day for surface work. In addition to the hard work and low pay, women and young girls also suffered sexual exploitation. Some managers exercised "seigniorial" rights over all the women at the mine.

In the 1890s the owners and government colluded to employ criminals sentenced to hard labor in the mines. Unfortunately, they wreaked havoc among the workers in the barracks. There were lots of police and supervisors at the mines, so it was difficult for miners to resist company demands. Workers had to buy their food at company stores and they hated the horsemeat sloughed off on them. Often meat and fish were spoiled, but their complaints brought no improvement. Life was hard for men, women, and children. Schools that the company set up were mainly for the children of white-col-

Prokudin-Gorsky, "Women Working at Bakalskii Mine Pit," 1910

lar workers. Children of miners were drafted into menial labor. Women's mortality rate was twice as high as men's. Everyone lived in company barracks, but they were of such poor quality that government inspectors were indignant that such profitable enterprises provided such pitiful conditions for their workers. In 1912, the miners at the Lena gold fields peacefully struck for better housing, food, pay, medical care, reduction in fines, and the eight-hour day. While most strikes had been settled agreeably over the years, the greedy owners and managers called in the troops and 200 miners were killed in the famous Lena Goldfields Massacre of 1912.[29]

In 1936, a Soviet ethnographer recorded the song of an old woman in Sverdlovsk about the exploitation of mineworkers. Part of it reads as follows:

> They set us at the convict labor of the mine,
> Ah, and they do not let us out.

> There they kill us with hunger,
> Ah, they give us naught but cold water![30]

Another folksong collector wrote down a curse on cavalry captain Treschenko, who carried out the 1912 massacre at the gold mines. A former woman mineworker F. K. Druzhinina told it to him, saying:

> Grandsons and great-grandsons
> Will curse the name of Treschenko,
> As for you, you villains,
> You cannot escape destruction,
> If not your children,
> Then your grandsons,
> If not your grandsons, then your great-grandsons,
> Will have to drink
> Of this bitter cup
> Which you have given to drink
> To the workers in the Lena gold fields.[31]

C. Commerce

> The boss will court you, pay you on time, treat you politely and give you presents, until you grow heavy in the waist.
>
> Salesclerk, Odessa, 1905

Prior to World War One, even white collar working women had hard lives. Just as women garment workers were tied to their jobs for long hours and low wages, so too were those in commerce and sales. The Russo Japanese War increased female employment in insurance and commercial positions about 50%. In these jobs, women earned about half what men earned, so it was beneficial for employers to utilize female labor. For a 16-18 hour day, sales clerks earned about 15 rubles per month. Moreover, they were expected to dress attractively, which proved impossible on their wages. This led many to engage in part time prostitution. Unemployment during the "off" season also forced some into prostitution, and 45% of all registered prostitutes in Russia were formerly salesclerks or servants.[32]

Getting a well-paid job in a bank, insurance company, or firm could involve sexual "favors." As one worker explained, the bosses only wanted the young, good-looking girls. Most shop girls were from 17-20 years old. A girl over 30 could seldom be encountered and then never in shops on the main street. Often, the boss would court you and treat you politely until you became pregnant. Then he would drop you and maybe even fire you. After that, you might fall into prostitution, become sick, and wind up in the hospital.[33]

Social investigator A. M. Gudvan in his "Essays on the History of the Movement of Sales-Clerical Workers in Russia" cited a sales clerk's description of her life as follows:

> Work in bakeries begins each day at 5 or 6 o'clock in the morning and ends at 8 or 9 at night. In pastry shops, work starts at 7 or 8 and ends at 10:30 or 11 at night. Year-round, we have to work a 15-16 hour day. We don't get any time off for lunch. We have to eat behind the counter. The wage of a female bakery shop clerk ranges from 6-18 rubles a month; in pastry shops, it ranges from 12-25 rubles. Work this out for yourself—a 15-16 hour workday comes to about 450 to 480 hours a month. This means we earn from 2 and a half to 4 kopecks an hour.[34]

Like other women workers, these young girls sometimes lived with their families, sometimes shared an apartment or room with a friend, or sometimes if they were apprentices lived on the premises, sleeping on the floor without beds or covers. Working, eating, and sleeping in close quarters meant lack of privacy and freedom. Other indignities also bedeviled shop clerks. According to Gudvan, those who worked in clothing stores sometimes had to stand in the street to solicit customers. "If we let anyone go by, the boss swears at us in the choicest language. The customers also swear at us for trying to drag them in by the coat tails."[35] Thus, one can see that women working in commercial positions were subject to the same problems as those who worked in factories and handicraft production: long hours, low pay, poor living conditions, work indignities, age discrimination, and sexual harassment and abuse. The worst situation was probably that of prostitutes, and the 1897 census recorded about 15,000 of them: 10,000 20-39 years old, 4,000 17-19 years old.[36]

Judging from the clothing in the picture below, the lives of telephone operators, though closely supervised, seemed better than those of clerks. About 5,000 women were employed in the Post Office as telegraphers and telephone operators in 1897. Their numbers expanded after the turn of the 20th century, and educational statistics for 1913 show more Russian women studying technical and handicraft courses (42,000) as well as commercial courses (9,000) than studied pedagogy (7,000) medicine (6,000), or the fine arts (4,000).[37]

Those working in government offices may have had slightly different experiences. The memoirs of Bolshevik Cecilia Bobrovskaya reveal that women were sometimes delighted to get an office job. She describes her life in Tver after she was released from prison in 1903 in her memoir *Twenty Years in Underground Russia*:

> ... I quickly obtained a room at a reasonable rent and most important of all, I got employment. Although by that time we had come to the conclusion that it was necessary to provide maintenance for those who were engaged solely with Party work,

"At Work, Central Telephone Station," 1911, St. P., (Photo Archive)

this applied mostly to comrades who were illegal. As soon as a member became legalized, even temporarily, he did not think it proper to take money from the Party funds for his personal needs, particularly as, being under police surveillance; he was not in a position to continue Party work for some time. Therefore I was overjoyed at getting a situation as temporary clerk in the insurance statistics department of the Zemstvo. As the job was only a temporary one, it did not require the Governor's approval.[38]

Perhaps because the job was temporary and because she was a young political activist and married woman, she may not have experienced the exploitation many others did.

During WW I, in the summer of 1917, millions of male soldiers were deserting the front, and a special Women's Battalion of Death was fighting on the Eastern Front. The Provisional Government became so desperate for clerks in the Ministry of War that Alexander Kerensky responded to women's associations which had offered their services by drafting an order for the Conscription of Women for War Work. It was published in *Izvestiia*, No. 93, June 29, 1917, and read:

> In recognition of the fact that the extraordinary conditions through which our country is at the present moment passing, demand a full accounting and mobilization of all forces that are capable of reviving and increasing the physical and spiritual forces of the nation, I consider it timely to proceed to a solution of the problem of utilizing the ability and capacity of Russian women (whose rights have already been recognized in principle), in concrete, direct form to take the place of male labor in all the central administrative offices and auxiliary organizations of the Ministry of War.
>
> To carry out this task, I order:
> 1. A special commission organized, under the Principal Bureau of the General Staff, to examine the possibilities and conditions for the employment of women in the Ministry of War.
> 2. That if the Commission agrees in principle that the conscription of women for work is practicable, it shall at once prepare an appropriate bill for submission to the higher governmental institutions.

3. That representatives of the Union of Women's Democratic Organizations and other women's associations (which have taken the initiative in the matter here discussed), be invited to cooperate with the Commission, as well as representatives of other ministries and public organizations whose participation may be necessary.
4. As the Chairman of the Commission, I designate O. K. Nechaeva.
5. The Commission must complete its work in two weeks and submit its report to me for confirmation,

A. Kerensky,
Minister of War[39]

D. Education and Employment

> Every moment we felt that we were needed, that we were not superfluous. It was this consciousness of one's usefulness that was the magnetic force which drew our Russian youth into the village.
>
> Vera Figner, Physicians Assistant and Revolutionary

Women's higher education and moral sensitivity were deeply intertwined in the 19th century. From the time of the Great Reforms, beginning with the freeing of the serfs in 1861, some Russian women dreamed of becoming doctors, pharmacists, or teachers to help downtrodden peasants. However many others, who lacked university education and only graduated from the highest class of a gimnaziya or secondary school became governesses or schoolteachers in a girls' school. Their work lives were not enviable, and their pay deplorable.

1. Governesses

> "To be sure, sweetheart, the most decent thing is for a woman to be supported by a man, but you have missed all your chances for that, and you have neither house nor home."
>
> Olga Forsh, "Ham's Wife," 1919

Vasily Perov, "The Governess Arriving at the Merchant's House," 1866

In Olga Forsh's story "Ham's Wife," (1919) the main character realizes after the death of her father that she is a spoiled penniless spinster, brought up at home, and without a diploma. She had rejected all her suitors when she was young and attractive, and in middle age her aunt tells her "To be sure, sweetheart, the most decent thing is for a woman to be supported by a man, but you ... have missed all your chances for that, and ... you have neither house nor home..." Her only possibility was to become a governess to support herself, and this was not easy since she had no education.[40] The painting by artist Vasily Perov shows the obsequious position that governesses often had to occupy, and that some women rebelled against.

2. *Gorstkin Family Governesses*

The older and less attractive women did not fare too well. Following a week of uninterrupted visits and considerations, the unanimous choice fell on an attractive and charming young girl from Lyons—Yvette Delacroix. My mother was completely satisfied with her recommendations, while my brothers were pleased by her youth and appearance.

> Elena Skrjabina, *Coming of Age in the Russian Revolution*

Trying to find a position as a governess in Russia was not easy. Young, pretty girls might find it easier than older, plain women. A rather amusing account of how the Alexander Gorstkin family hired a French governess to tutor their daughter is found in Elena Gorstkina Skrjabina's memoir. Elena describes how her brothers tried to influence their mother's choice of governess. She says:

> The summer of 1912 was full of the most interesting experiences. I was supposed to learn French and, as a result of Mother's advertisement, numerous women of all ages came to our home to be interviewed for the position of French governess. This happened every day during the few weeks prior to our departure for the country, and it was a great entertainment not only for me but also for my brothers. Paul and George jumped up at every bell and, hiding behind the door, looked over the candidates. After the departure of each applicant, they would burst into the living room and give Mother all kinds of advice.[41]

A year later, Elena's mother advertised for a new governess to teach Elena German. Since her eldest son had died of a mysterious disease at the age of 20, Mrs. Gorstkina was devastated and did not waste much time choosing a new governess. According to Elena's memoirs:

> At the end of April Mother advertised again, only this time for a German governess. The hiring procedure was now entirely different from what it had been a year ago in Nizhny when everyone had been happy. She chose almost the first young German girl who showed up at our house, a girl named Ingeborg. My brothers were not at all interested and even I was indifferent. Since the death of Vasya, it was as though a cloud had settled over the family. Almost everyone had become apathetic. We went to Obrochnoye [the family country estate] in May. En route I tried to speak with my new governess, but my knowl-

edge of German was extremely weak and there was limited conversation. When we at last arrived home, Paul decided to shine. But instead of saying "Wir sind gekommen" (we have arrived), he said "Wir sind gestorben" (we have died). The German girl not saying a word just looked at him blankly. After the happy, witty Yvette, Ingeborg, despite her rather pretty face, seemed unattractive to us because of her cold tone and voice and her characteristic reserve.[42]

Just as Countess Tolstoy tutored her children before sending them to the gimnaziya, so too Mrs. Gorstkina tutored Elena prior to the outbreak of WW I. Elena remembered studying various subjects with her mother, especially those essential for passing the entry exam for the girls' institute, where her parents were planning to send her.[43]

Elena's memoir is fascinating to read because she records the fun children had as well as the difficulties that family life entailed. She remembered that several families in St. Petersburg joined together and organized private dancing lessons in the large, elegant apartment of Colonel Gladky on Tavrichesky Street. She notes:

> The court ballet master was hired, impressing the parents but not the children. The children did not like this tall, handsome gentleman, who was very strict and angrily ridiculed our awkwardness and mistakes. I personally could not complain about him. He apparently was well-disposed toward me and always chose a good partner for me. My mother, who was able to sew very well, made me a light, charming dress of multicolored chiffon. Thanks to her efforts, I was one of the most elegant girls at the dancing classes.
>
> This time is associated in my memory with my first love. At the classes there were about twenty children between the ages of eight and thirteen. From the first day my attention was drawn to a tall, red-cheeked, well-built boy with luxurious light curls. From his appearance one could have taken him for thirteen. His name was Stepan. The only thing I did not like about him was his name. For some reason, I absolutely wanted his name to be Nikita. This name, connected with the Russian past, seemed to me far more romantic. Stepanovs, however, were everywhere in our village; and here in Petersburg our old janitor was also

named Stepan. I became reconciled with this name since I liked its bearer so much. Stepan did not particularly care for these lessons and at the beginning was even absent rather often. Then our ballet master resorted to a few tricks. Catching sight of Stepan in the vestibule (Stepan was always late), our teacher immediately released me from my partner and glided elegantly across the floor, taking me to my hero. It seems we made a good couple and were often applauded. This of course was very pleasing to both Stepan and me. Gradually we began to find more and more pleasure in each other's company. Stepan began to stop missing lessons. But, if for some reason he was not at Gladky's, I did not hide my despondency and as a rule danced worse on those days, provoking snickers from my teacher.

After a two-hour lesson, tea would be served along with very tasty cakes and other sweets from the best St. Petersburg pastry shops. For a long time I remembered the cake with strawberries. There was always a large group that gathered for tea. Besides the children and the adults watching our lessons, there were usually brothers and sisters who were supposed to take home those children whose parents had not come. My brother George always came to pick me up. ...George was always elegantly attired in his Lycee dress uniform. At tea he never looked at me at all; he was too busy flirting with the pretty girls. I was just as happy to be near Stepan, who would treat me with my favorite delicacies.

Soon after tea everybody would disperse. From the very next day, I would already be impatiently awaiting the coming dance lesson. These dances in Gladky's house, and my puppy love with Stepan were the brightest memories of my life in St. Petersburg.[44]

Mrs. Gorstkina and Countess Tolstoy systematically educated their children, but this was not the case in all gentry-class households. The novel *Nihilist Girl*, by mathematician Sofia Kovalevskaya, depicted a provincial gentry-class family the Barantsovs which was impoverished by the poor management of their estates. Economizing, they dismissed tutors and governesses, and their daughters lacked a coherent education. Since the local gimnaziya was attended by daughters of merchants and minor officials, it was not deemed a proper place to educate the daughter of a countess. In the Barantsov household, the elder daughters were directed to teach their younger sister, but neither teachers nor student were cooperative and little learning occurred. Bored, Vera began reading her nanny's book on the lives of the saints. Reading about a Russian missionary to China, Vera resolved to do likewise. Only after an exiled neighboring professor named Vasiltsev came to tutor Vera did she become educated. He explained to her that martyrs existed not only in the past, but that revolutionaries who propagandized among the people were also martyred when they were exiled to Siberia. So, in a variety of ways radical ideas came to girls in the countryside, and some fell in love with revolutionary ideas and the moral of self sacrifice.[45]

3. Girls' Education

By the late 19th and early 20th centuries, some Russian girls' gimnaziya became better organized, offering more mathematics, physics, chemistry, botany, and other sciences. Traditionally, French, German, and English languages were well taught in gentry-class households by special tutors, but they were also offered in the boarding and day schools of middle-class girls. In addition, girls studied history, geography, music, playing the piano, dancing, and physical education. Most of the elite girls' gimnaziya took girls at the age of 10 as boarding students. The schools were strict, and girls wore uniforms and had a set regimen. About half the students received scholarships provided by the Imperial family and other philanthropic organizations. Often, the school day began with prayers, a light breakfast before classes, then a big lunch with prayers before and after eating, followed by a walk in the school courtyard. There were lessons in the afternoon, and speaking in French and German to the two monitors or governesses in charge of the students outside of class. Despite the bleak dorm life, some girls like Tatiana V. Toporkova had fun at the Catherine Institute prior to WW I in St. Petersburg. The girls put on plays; and older ones attended the ballet and opera, and even hosted an annual ball which was attended by boys from nearby military institutes. Indeed, Toporkova's family was so devoted to the Institute that they sent their daughters there when the family was living in London in 1912. Apparently the daughters didn't mind because they were used to being raised by nannies and governesses and didn't normally interact with their parents very much.[46]

While Tatiana Toporkova had fun at the Catherine Institute in St. Petersburg, some girls suffered in organized education. Attending an Institute for Noble Girls in Irkutsk, Siberia in the 1880s, Anna Zhukova described her miserable first year as follows:

> ... In the beginning it was interesting to live in a three-story stone house. But soon I felt the weight of the strict regime of the monotonous days. Each step was under the supervision of the classroom mistress. We could stroll only in the courtyard, in pairs, with calm steps—running and jumping were forbidden. Looking out the window, I thought, 'Even the prisoners in the mines live better, they are taken to the mountains where they work.'
>
> I was homesick. This was combined with the unpleasant sensation of not getting enough to eat. In the morning one glass of tea with a small white roll. For the second breakfast between classes, they brought a tray with slices of black bread. Each girl was given one slice of bread that she had to eat in the corridor before the beginning of class. Eating coarse, often poorly baked bread without any kind of liquid was unpleasant. Many girls were devious and hid their slice in their pockets so that later, quietly, out of sight of the classroom mistress, they could dry it in the oven. The dried bread seemed to taste better.
>
> The three-course dinner on holidays was more substantial. For supper there was inevitable—potato mixed with herring. In our dormitory, next to me *forshmak* was Anichka Kozlova's bed; at night we dreamed of running away from the institute and discussed our plan of escape, although we were conscious of the futility of the plan, since her home was as far from Irkutsk as mine.
>
> The institute had the program of a high school with two preparatory classes for those with less formal education. In the preparatory classes we began to study French and German right away. I did not know any foreign languages; nonetheless I was assigned to the first class, and I had a very difficult time making up for my insufficient knowledge. I remember how I copied from one of the students the words I didn't understand in the German lesson. Tears ran down my face onto my notebook and made blots. The teacher showed my note-

book to the whole class later, brandishing the dirtiest page with indignation. The girls tittered, and I suffered deeply. In the course of a year I caught up with the class in knowledge of foreign languages.[47]

Yet from the second year on, Anna was at the top of her class, and when a new school inspector took over, he improved the food, the classes, exercise, etc. By the time she graduated, Anna received the gold medal as the best student! However, none of her teachers mentioned the women's courses in higher education that operated in the capitals, and Anna left the institute quite sad, thinking her education ended. She was touched by the director's admonition not to lead an idle life, but she didn't know what to do in her hometown. She started teaching and eventually opened a school in Nerchinsk Zavod for 23 pupils. Eventually she learned of the opening of a Medical School for Women in St. Petersburg, and this inspired her to become a doctor—first studying in France and then in St. Petersburg in the 1890s.[48]

Some Russian girls' schools also offered Latin, which was necessary for medical students. When women's higher education was once again tolerated after the Revolution of 1905, many women were well prepared to study medicine and other scientific studies. By the early 20th century, girls' secondary and higher education became less gentry-class dominated, as more middle-class girls attended; and some lower-class even peasant girls held scholarships. Prior to 1870, most girls' education occurred in private schools, but after educational reforms in the 1870s state gimnaziya for girls also appeared. In late 19th century, women were generally excluded from Russian universities, so a few hundred attended French universities and a few thousand studied in Swiss universities where they did not have to present a school leaving certificate to enroll and where Swiss professors were paid by the number of students in their classes, whether male or female. According to one study, 70% of women students at Zurich came from the Russian gentry-class in the 1870s, but during the 1880s when severe quotas restricted the number of Jews admitted to Russian educational institutions, many more Russian Jews came there to study, and they constituted 60% of the female students. By the 1890s, these two groups were more evenly split with 38% coming from Jewish merchant backgrounds and 35% from the gentry classes.[49] The Russian gentry was composed of two parts, the hereditary usually landed gentry, and the personal nobility whose meritorious service ennobled them for their lifetime, but not their children's.

By 1911, 24% of gimnaziya students were gentry-class, 46% were middle-class, 20% peasant, and 10% other, perhaps working-class or Jewish girls. Girls from Russian Orthodox clerical families often attended special diocesan schools, becoming teachers or priests' wives. By 1911, about half of trained midwives came from the merchant estates, whereas in the late 19th century, gentry-class and middle-class women had each constituted about a third. Of 1400 medical students in 1903, over 200 held scholarships from zemstva and other public organizations, suggesting poorer women from various classes were attending medical courses. Freeing the serfs in the 1860s had impoverished many gentry-class families, so some gentry-class girls could be poor and in need of scholarships too. Before WW I, some daughters in poor families like the famous poet Maria Shkapskaya, teacher-doctor Valentina Dmitrieva, and historian Anna Pankratova respectively received scholarships to girls' gimnaziya in St. Petersburg, Tambov, and Odessa.[50]

World War One changed women's education. High schools became co-educational, and women began to outnumber men in university study in fields like medicine and teaching. By 1914, Russian faculty and their research were on a high level—the equal of many institutions in Western Europe. The main problem was that education for peasants and workers still lagged behind, and illiteracy remained a drag on the economy and society.

4. *Higher Education*

> So began my student life. Attendance at lectures filled my life. I mastered the content of the lectures easily. I acquired some girlfriends among the students. Coming home from classes, I would find a noisy company of students and officials in the dining room.
>
> Anna Bek, Siberian Doctor

Despite social support for women's higher courses at mid century, the Russian government vacillated in its policies regarding

K. Bull, "Professors at Women's Medical Institute," 1913 (Photo Archive)

women's education. During the Great Reforms from 1858-1863, several girls' gimnaziya were established in provincial cities, and Russian women were allowed to attend lectures at the major universities if professors permitted it. Many professors obliged, and scores of women attended university lectures. It was at this time, shortly after the good work of Russian nurses in the Crimean War in the 1850s, that women began taking up professional work, including medicine.

Becoming a doctor and serving the people became a mission for many gentry-class women. Just as some British and American women became missionaries to "aid" the less fortunate in certain parts of the world and enjoyed a certain amount of adventure and autonomy in the 19th century, becoming a doctor and "helping" Muslim, peasant, or worker-class women appealed to idealistic Russians. The photograph above shows several studying to become doctors prior to WW I.

One idealistic influence on women's decisions to become doctors was Nikolai Chernyshevsky's novel *What is to be Done*? published in 1863. In the novel, his heroine Vera Pavlova engaged in a fictitious marriage to get away from her family, and study medicine. This book became the Bible of the intelligentsia, and some young women emulated the liberated Vera as well as the male revolutionary hero Rakhmetev. Other impulses in Russian society also encouraged women to become economically independent. Utopian Socialist ideas became fashionable in the 1860s, and the emphasis on women's emancipation influenced young people. Along with these ideological influences, the literary tradition of the "strong Russian woman," also influenced some young girls. Nadezhda Khvoshchinskaya in her popular novella *The Boarding-School Girl*, depicts a young girl who has become a self-supporting artist by 1860. She tells a former provincial acquaintance that she had been educated at a good boarding school in St. Petersburg, that her teachers had noticed her artistic talent, that she attended art school, and now paints at the Hermitage. She told him:

> I know three foreign languages. I translate and prepare compilations. I earn so much doing this that I can say I'm not an extra burden at home: my aunt isn't rich. ...
>
> 'I'm not obligated to anyone for anything. My aunt, it's true, gave me my education, but since she had the means, she should have done this, and I had the right to accept. But from the time I was able, I've worked for myself. I don't cost her a thing. I even earn enough for my entertainment'...[51]

Besides Khvoshchinskaya, famous novelists like Ivan Turgenev and Ivan Goncharov depicted "strong women" characters and weak superfluous male figures in their writings at mid century. So it was a confluence of all these factors that encouraged Russian women to pursue their own dreams and the professions including medicine in the late 19th century.

Following male student demonstrations in 1863, the government closed University education to all women and men from the lower estates. The only exception to this policy was Varvara Kashevarova-Rudneva who had a scholarship from the Governor of Orenburg to study medicine to help Muslim women, and she graduated in 1868. In the 1870s, the government changed course again, allowing women to study at special evening lecture courses in St. Petersburg and Moscow or to study medicine at the St. Petersburg Army Medical Surgical Academy (1872-82). After the assassination of Alexander II in 1881, the Ministry of Education once more closed higher education to women and demanded that those studying abroad return to Russia. Only the Bestuzhev courses of higher education for women remained open during the reign of Alexander III.

One response to this zigzag educational policy was that some, gentry-class women, went abroad to study. Vera Figner and her sister went to Switzerland to study medicine. Still others travelled to the U.S. and France, where until 1899 they outnumbered French women studying at the universities. Sofia Kovalevskaya and her friend Julia Lermontova went to Germany to study Mathematics and Chemistry respectively. While Kovalevskaya won French medals for her mathematical brilliance, Russian University teaching remained closed to her, and it was only in Sweden that she found employment in 1883. Like most countries, Russian women could teach girls at elementary and secondary level schools, but not at government universities. In 19th century Russia, university professors enjoyed government honors, perquisites, and civil service rank not accorded lower level teachers, women, or Jews.[52]

Scientist Sophie Satina's book on Russian women's education recounts stories of her own experiences studying at a Moscow girls' secondary day school in the 1890s, as well as her scientific education at various Women's Higher Education Courses. She found women of all ages attending the special evening courses established in Moscow and St. Petersburg in the 1870s and some married women participating as well. These two factors set Russian women's higher education apart from that in England in the late 19th and early 20th centuries, when only young, single women attended university.

Prior to World War One, the Bolshevik underground worker Cecilia Bobrovskaya decided to study at the free Shanyavsky University in Moscow. A married older woman, Bobrovskaya decided to study for several reasons: 1) police surveillance made illegal and legal political work almost impossible, 2) she wanted to systematize her education which she had mainly obtained at Party meetings and discussion groups, and 3) the university provided a good place to carry out propaganda work among students and to meet other revolutionaries. As she recalled in her memoirs *Twenty Years in Underground Russia*:

> In the autumn of 1911 I went to the Shanyavsky University where it was not necessary to produce a diploma or a certificate of political good behavior to enter. I was induced to do this

by the illusion that I could systematize the fragments of knowledge I had gained by studying during the involuntary interruptions in my work by arrests and imprisonment. I wanted to make the best use of my legal position in order to get a proper education.[53]

However, Bobrovskaya was disappointed in her bourgeois professors' interpretations of Russian History and political economy. Still, the university proved "an excellent place for accomplishing all sorts of tasks to resuscitate the Moscow organization. Here a number of comrades, intellectuals as well as workers, found refuge. But even here we could not escape the interference of the provocateur."[54] She noted in her memoir:

> It goes without saying that the omnipresent and omniscient secret police were not slaw in penetrating the Shanyavsky University. I often made appointments with two famous provocateurs, Poskrebukhin and Romanov, of course I did not know they were provocateurs then, who would insist that there was no better place in the world to discuss Party matters than the halls of the Shanyavsky University. ...
>
> I had my own corner in a particularly secluded corridor of the Shanyavsky University where from time to time I made appointments with George Romanov who afterwards turned out to be a provocateur. I had met George during my work on the Moscow Regional Committee, he would come to see me on Party business as the representative of the workers in the works of Kolomna. He kept me informed of all the latest news which he received from the Centre abroad, gave me fresh literature received from abroad, informed me of the conditions of the Ivanovo-Voznosensk organization and of other cities in the Moscow Region whenever he chanced to be there. Also he kept me informed about the affairs of the Duma fraction in St. Petersburg. I confess that it did seem strange to me that as insignificant and poorly educated fellow like George could occupy such a responsible position in the Party. But I reminded myself that he had attended the Party school in Capri, where most probably, he had studied a bit and become acquainted with our leaders, that he must have progressed intellectually a little during these last few years. I was impressed by his indefatigable work during those times of depression. Neither Romanov nor

Poskrebukhin were regular students at the University; but they attended periodical courses on co-operation, I believe, merely to have free entry into the place. ...

I was allowed to remain in Moscow without interference and I continued my studies at the Shanyavsky University. There all our Party people used to gather. We used the Students' Mutual Aid Society to the board of which I had been elected, as a screen for our activities.[55]

Another unusual feature of women's higher education in the late 19th and early 20th century was the cooperation and camaraderie, not competition, they enjoyed and practiced. Describing her gimnaziya years, scientist Sophie Satina says in *Education of Women in Pre-Revolutionary Russia*:

"Having spent so many years together, the pupils in each class knew each other very well. There was real close friendship among many of us. I do not remember a single case when the whole class would not stand up in defense of a classmate offended by someone or something. Brighter pupils were always willing to help those who were less able, explaining items that were difficult to understand, coaching those who were left behind, encouraging them and trying to help them. Like in all Russian schools it was considered absolutely inadmissible to inform on one's classmates...."[56]

Later, she refers to this same quality among students in the Moscow "Society of Women Tutors and Teachers." In 1900, those in the physico-mathematical faculty all resigned in protest over the dismissal of two women students. The students found Director V. I. Guerrier's condescending behavior towards them unacceptable. While he had been a pioneer in supporting women's higher education in the 1870s, his views had become outdated a generation later. Like many men of his generation, he thought it was acceptable for women to become teachers, but couldn't imagine women becoming serious scientists. Slowly, the expelled students were readmitted; the resignations of those in the science faculty were ignored; and they all continued their educational work.[57]

A slightly different memoir of girls' education is found in Nina Beberova's book *The Italics Are Mine*. Unlike Satina, Berberova wanted to be a poet, not a scientist. She felt this calling as a young child and was writing poetry from the age of 10. Since her interests were literary, she was not shy about copying her science lessons from friends. Writing about her school and family life in St. Petersburg in *The Italics Are Mine*, she says:

> Early in the spring of 1915, in the Army and Fleet Hall on Liteiny Avenue, a gathering called 'The Poets to the Warriors' took place. This was one of those many charity evenings that the intelligentsia liked to attend. I don't know why it was decided to take me to it. It was a weeknight, and my homework, as always, probably had not been done. I studied in bursts and somehow managed to 'get by,' for I was not squeamish about copying or being prompted, especially in algebra and physics, after too much time had been devoted to the reading and writing of verse till late at night. That evening after dinner my mother announced to me that we were going to 'listen to some poets.'

After listening to several famous poets, Berberova heard Anna Akhmatova recite her verse, describing her as follows:

> Akhmatova wore a white dress, with a Stuart collar (which was then a la mode)—and was slender, beautiful, dark-haired, and elegant. She was then near thirty; this was the heyday of her glory, the glory of her new prosody, her profile, her charm. 'You will receive no more letters from him,...From burned-out Poland...' she intoned, hands folded over her bosom, slowly and tenderly, with the musical seriousness that in her was so captivating.[58]

One of the monitors at Berberova's school introduced her to Akhmatova as "the girl who writes verse," and Berberova was embarrassed and overwhelmed by her own insignificance. She was also introduced to Blok, but he barely acknowledged her. Berberova's outlook was very different than Satina's. Berberova was precocious and had decided to become a poet as a child. She wasn't the serious student Satina was, but appreciated Russian language classes and other student poets.[59]

Prior to the war and Revolution of 1917, Russian women chose a variety of subjects to study. The famous poet Anna Akhmatova initially studied Law in the Women's Higher Courses in Kiev in 1908.

After her marriage to Lev Gumilev in 1910, she studied History and Literature at Rayev's Higher Courses in St. Petersburg. According to Russian statistics, over 5,300 women in Moscow and 5,200 in St. Petersburg studied in university level courses in 1912.

University courses remained the prerogative of the relatively small gentry-class in the late 19th century. About 4,263 noble women had such education. About 1,302 in the middle-classes and 129 women technically from the peasant estate obtained such distinction. Gentry-class women predominated in all levels of study, even in the polytechnic or special schools. Naturally, they prevailed in the preparatory schools or gimnaziya as well.[60] By World War One, however, the middle and lower classes began pursuing professional and commercial education.

As a young working-class girl, future Soviet Historian Anna Pankratova enrolled in the Historical Philosophical Faculty of Odessa's Higher Courses for Women in 1914, and in 1916-17 these courses were merged with Novorossisk University. Working part-time as a teacher in evening courses for workers, Anna Pankratova completed most of her course work, though not her exit exams or thesis because like many students she dedicated herself to the Revolution in 1917. Although she interrupted her studies, she resumed them in the 1920s.[61]

In the late 19th century, some revolutionaries like Lenin were shocked that there were as many priests and nuns as teachers in Russia. While nuns led largely invisible lives, women teachers and doctors were visible. Society found women doctors especially fascinating—the embodiment of the educated, autonomous "New Woman." The low social and economic status of teaching and medicine in Russian society meant these fields were more open to women than law or university teaching. The low ratio of teachers and doctors to the total population showed a great need for their services. This was unlike the situation in Germany and England, where the professions were considered "overcrowded," and no women need apply.

Christian and secular notions that women should dedicate themselves to serving others also made women's professional education in these fields acceptable. Moreover, the urbanization, industrialization, and modernization of Russia in the late 19th century created a need for better educated workers and more career women.

These factors also reduced some of the hostility towards women teachers and doctors.

Three wars, the Crimean War of the 1850s which saw women first serve as nurses, the Russo-Turkish War of the 1870s in which 25-30 women served as doctors, and then the Russo-Japanese War of 1904-5 gained women public support for their good work. Their service culminated in their equal access to medical education in 1913. Since medicine was not held in high esteem in Russia, both Jews and women were tolerated in that profession. This was quite different than the situation in Teutonic countries where men considered career women unwanted competition.

5. *Education for Women in Medicine*

Russian literary critics and novelists also influenced trends in women's higher education as early as the 1850s and 1860s. At the beginning of Alexander II's reforms, radical literary critics like Nicholas Chernyshevsky, Nicholas Dobroliubov, and Dmitri Pisarev all espoused women's right to higher education as well as their duty to "serve" the people as a way of repaying the gentry's debt to the peasantry. Chernyshevsky's influential novel *What is to be Done? Tales of New People* (1863) swayed generations of young people to become doctors and revolutionaries. Some like Lenin and Kollontai became revolutionaries; others like Vera Figner and Vera Zasulich (1849-1919) initially chose the helping professions as ways of serving "the people." Later, these two women forsook their medical careers to become full time revolutionaries and publicists in the Social Revolutionary Party, and Social Democratic Party respectively.

Increasing numbers of Russian gentry-class women studied medicine in the late 19th century. Until the opening of the Women's Medical Institute in St. Petersburg the 1890s, some traveled to Paris or Zurich to study. In her memoir, Vera Figner tells how her father ignored her desire for higher education and refused to sign her passport allowing her to go abroad to study. It was her fictitious marriage to a liberal lawyer who signed her passport that enabled her to travel to Zurich to study.[62]

a. Anna Zhukova Bek

> My aspiration to a medical career was not moving ahead. No one heard anything about the opening of the Medical Institute.
>
> Anna Bek, Siberian Doctor

In her memoirs, Anna Zhukova Bek tells of her uncle intervening for her with her father for permission and support to study at the Women's Higher Courses and then to study medicine in France. Accepted to study in the physical-mathematics department of the Women's Higher Courses in St. Petersburg, Anna found life interesting even joyful with her student friends. As she remembered in her *Life of a Russian Woman Doctor*:

> In work and play the year passed by as though a dream. In the spring (of 1895) I passed all the exams successfully and was promoted to the second year. But here I began to feel dissatisfaction. My aspiration to a medical career was not moving ahead. No one heard anything about the opening of the Medical Institute. On learning that women could get a medical education abroad, I wrote Father a persuasive letter and asked him for permission to go to Paris.[63]

In Paris her application was held up because so many foreign students were crowding out French students, so Anna decided to go to the University of Nancy where she proved an outstanding student thanks to her preparation in science courses in St. Petersburg. Mastering the French language, she began taking notes in French and gave them to her friends to use. However, Anna was eventually drawn back to Russia where the Women's Medical Institute opened in 1897. However, her studies in France more than prepared her for the Women's Medical Institute in St. Petersburg, and she had time on her hands and became involved in revolutionary activity. Participating in student strikes drew the attention of the police and she was suddenly dismissed from the Medical Institute and sent home to Siberia. Her readings in a student circle at this time made her a life-long Marxist.[64]

Who knows what impact the memoirs of women doctors had on the minds and imaginations of young women in the late 19th century? The heroic and selfless service of women teachers and doctors appealed to many. While medicine was a male dominated field in the late 19th century with 16,000 men but only about 1,000 women doctors, by 1911 the number of women doctors had almost doubled. At the turn of the century, there was less resistance to women's medical education in Russian than in Germany or England. Prior to WWI, a special Women's Higher Institute of Medicine trained women as feldshers (physicians' assistants).

In 1914, female medical students outnumbered males 5,636 to 3,702. It is unclear if these medical students were studying to be feldshers or vrach (physician). At six other institutions of higher education, 2,300 women medical students were recorded, but only 1,170 men. During the same period, pedagogy did not become as feminized with 7,800 women and 18,600 men in 351 Teacher Training courses. Still, the number of women teachers increased from about 70,000 in 1897 to 83,000 in 1911.[65]

The autobiographies of women doctors reveal incredible determination, dedication, talent, and hard work. In her memoirs, Varvara Kashevarova-Rudneva, one of the first women doctors, explains many of the obstacles she overcame to become a medical doctor in the 1860s and a Doctor of Medicine (Ph.D.) in the 70s. After a great deal of hard work and struggle, she was admitted to the midwifery courses in St. Petersburg. but then was not allowed to continue her studies to become a doctor. Eventually, she did so, but only after much perseverance and appeal to the highest authorities. She explained in her autobiography that it was her own efforts and talent that enabled her to succeed, not the help of her doctor husband.[66]

b. Vera Figner

> For the peasants, the appearance of an assistant surgeon, 'a she-healer,' as they called me, was a great marvel. The muzhiks went to the priests for an explanation: had I been appointed to attend them all, or only the women?
>
> Vera Figner, *Memoirs of a Revolutionist*

In her *Memoir*, Figner wrote that before going to work in the countryside, she had never spoken to a peasant and wasn't sure how to do this. She soon decided that medical help was a mere palliative and did little to change the plight of the peasantry. Still, she felt her work as a doctor had been useful. She fondly remembered the peasants' first reactions to her:

> For the peasants, the appearance of an assistant surgeon, 'a she-healer,' as they called me, was a great marvel. The muzhiks went to the priests for an explanation: had I been appointed to attend them all, or only the women? After they had been enlightened, I was besieged with patients. The poor country folk flocked to me by the tens and hundreds as though I were a wonder-working ikon; a whole train of wagons surrounded the country doctor's little cottage from morning till night; my fame spread swiftly beyond the boundaries of the three counties which I served, and later, beyond the district itself....Attention, detailed questioning, and intelligent instruction in the use of medicine, were veritable marvels to the people. The first month I received eight hundred patients, and in the course of ten months five thousand, as many as a district physician receives in a city hospital in the course of a year, with several junior surgeons to aid him. ...This immense task, of course, would have been beyond my strength if my sister Evgenia had not shared it with me.[67]

In the evenings after their medical rounds, the Figner sisters taught peasants to read. As Vera noted in her memoirs:

> This life of ours, and the relations between us and these simple folk, who felt that light was near at hand, possessed such a bewitching charm, that even now it is pleasant for me to recall it; every moment we felt that we were needed, that we were not superfluous. It was this consciousness of one's usefulness that was the magnetic force which drew our Russian youth into the village.[68]

After many long weeks of hard work, Vera lost her job due to interfering government authorities and jealous priests. It was then she became a full time revolutionary. Good accounts of her life are in her memoirs and also in Barbara Engle's *Mothers and Daughters*. Engle's book is a collective biography of several Russian women who initially studied to be doctors or teachers but who eventually became revolutionaries.

Deploring the terrible poverty and condition of the peasantry during the famine of 1891, Dr. Valentina Dmitrieva (1859-1947) in "After the Great Hunger," showed her shock in the following excerpt:

> There seemed not to be one healthy person in the whole village; I could see the whole panoply of destruction wrought by chronic hunger: the ulcers, rashes, bleeding gums, paralyzed muscles, and putrefying bones...My head was spinning, there was black before my eyes...With difficulty I struggled back to the street, and began to recover myself only when I was safely back in the sleigh again. The crowd straggled after me, staring at me with a mixture of hope and desperation. And I realized my total impotence: all the medicine I could prescribe, the visits I could make, seemed pointless and ridiculous, reduced to childish games in the face of the rural poverty which was closing in on me from all sides... [69]

Rejecting the post of rural doctor, Dmitrieva wrote: "A quiet haven, a well-fed life, quiet work... No, I couldn't do it. The narcotic atmosphere of cards, vodka, rude backwards flirtation, and vulgar gossip suffocated me..." [70]

While Figner and Zasulich found working in the countryside a radicalizing experience, Dmitrieva became a writer instead of a revolutionary. Some women doctors like Figner and Zasulich abandoned medicine as a palliative and devoted their lives to populist and anarchist political movements instead. The later story of Russian revolutionary women is found in Chapter Four.

c. Ekaterina Slanskaia

> Today forty people showed up. Sometimes there are even more. Incidentally, I should mention that the duma doctor's patients are mostly peasant women and their children.
>
> Ekaterina Slanskaia, Doctor

Educated a decade after Rudneva and Figner, Ekaterina Slanskaia earned her medical degree in the 1880s and worked as a doctor in the slums for the St. Petersburg local duma or government. Her memoir describes the life of the poorly paid woman doctor in the

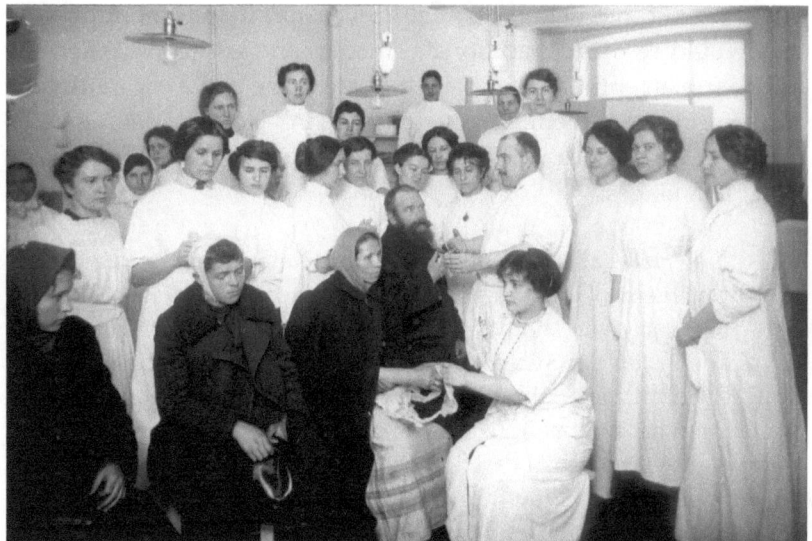

K. Bull, "Russian Women's Medical Institute," 1913, St. P., (Photo Archive)

late 19th century. The photograph above shows the type of patient she treated, and her words describe the situation of welfare doctors.

In her writing "House Calls," Slanskaia remarked:

"My apartment consists of three small rooms, an entryway, and a kitchen. I have set aside one room for seeing patients, but some wait in the entryway, some wait in the kitchen, and occasionally some wait on the stairs....A duma doctor cannot afford to rent a large apartment....

Today forty people showed up. Sometimes there are even more. Incidentally, I should mention that the duma doctor's patients are mostly peasant women and their children. The women bring not only their sick children, but their healthy ones as well if they are very young and there is no one to leave them with at home....Besides, you cannot treat forty people in a hurry. If you are the least bit dedicated to your work, you must devote a great deal of your time to it, attend to a variety of matters, and most of all do a lot of talking." [71]

She also explains the importance of educating her patients regarding hygiene and treatment. To her dismay, many of her patients disregard her instructions. Sometimes, just as they were improving they would resort to traditional remedies and get worse. Then she had to use an entirely new course of medicine and even more time and effort to cure them.[72] In one passage in "House Calls," she displays her impatience with her patients' superstitious belief regarding old bandages:

> Now take all these dirty pieces of cotton and the rags.... Throw them all into the stove and burn them immediately.'
> 'They say you should not burn them,' the patient says. 'The sickness won't go away if you burn all that comes out of it.'
> 'Don't listen to the idle chatter of superstitious people, listen to what I tell you. Don't you see I mean you no harm, that I want to help you? I eased your pain, didn't I?....Then listen to what I tell you. If you throw all these dirty rags on the floor, in the garbage, or in the yard where there are children running around, one of them might step on them with his bare feet, or pick them up and put them in his mouth....What if your little girl gets infected?'
> 'Burn them right away, this minute,' the old man tells the girl. I must admit, I was astonished. Did he agree to burn the rags because he believed what I told him, or was he afraid his daughter might become infected? Or did he simply not want to listen to my admonitions any longer? I frequently have to talk to these people about the superstition that it is wrong to burn rags that have been used to clean wounds. I have never been able to understand where they get this notion. They all say you must not burn them, but no one can tell you why it is so.[73]

d. Nursing during WW I

> As special training courses for nurses had not yet been opened by the various Red Cross societies, it was arranged that I should take my practical work at one of the city hospitals.
>
> Grand Duchess Maria, *The Education of a Princess*

While Slanskaia and many other women became doctors in the late 19th century, WW I drew many aristocratic and upper-class Russian women into nursing. Grand Duchess Maria writes in *Education of a Princess* that she lacked systematic, formal education, but when war came, she sought the Empress's permission to serve as a nurse and threw herself into medical training. She remembered:

> As special training courses for nurses had not yet been opened by the various Red Cross societies, it was arranged that I should take my practical work at one of the city hospitals. I went there every morning, and in the evening attended the lectures of several physicians. As the hospital's only pupil I received individual attention, and learned fast. ...
>
> Princess Helen...offered me the chance to go to the front with this unit and I accepted. Helen's husband was, like Dmitri [her brother], an officer of the Horse Guards. We were to be attached to the sector of the front to which this regiment was assigned. That delighted me. ...
>
> The departure of our unit was set for August 29. I took my final examinations as a nurse. The doctors who interrogated me had known me since childhood; and in spite of my nervousness and the short period of my studies, I was passed. Mlle. Helene [her governess] was never, I think, so proud of me as at that moment when she handed me the certificate authorizing me to wear the Red Cross on the bib of my apron; I also was happy; I felt that I had attained to something real.[74]

Indeed, Maria felt that she was at long last doing something useful. Recently divorced and having no entangling alliances, she was free to serve her country and her fellow man. She writes of this time in the following words:

> ...It seemed to me that the work I had undertaken was nothing out of the ordinary; even if I chanced to lose my life that would certainly be no unusual sacrifice those days. And as to existing values, it seemed to me that I was sacrificing nothing—no home, no dependents, no social life and pleasures of any consequence. I felt, in fact, that I was gaining, at last, an opportunity to apply myself usefully, to find work for which I was really fitted and which I needed, to direct all my energies to one central purpose. Life beckoned to me and I could not pity myself.[75]

Initially, Maria and many other Russian nurses worked close to the front and came at times close to losing their lives. Eventually Marie took charge of a large hospital in Pskov and did an outstanding job. She proved that a Grand Duchess need not be a fragile flower, but a tough, committed, hardworking woman.[76]

Perhaps one additional factor affecting women's decision to become career women was the compatibility of marriage and employment in the Russian Empire. Unlike England and Germany where women were often forced to choose between marriage and career, Russian society tolerated married career women. Moreover, many teachers and doctors came from the gentry-class, were accustomed to having servants tend their homes and children, and thus were free to work. Of course, not all professional women could afford servants.

Like other women workers, many career women had to deal with the burdens of marriage and motherhood, wage discrimination, and sexual harassment. City and provincial authorities paid female teachers and doctors lower wages than men, and this was acceptable at that time. Women doctors during the Russo-Turkish War complained of sexual harassment by army officers, and in her memoirs Pimenova mentions how she dealt with unwanted advances by her male medical colleagues.[77]

Varvara Rudneva in her autobiography tells how after her husband's death, a rejected suitor slandered her openly in a scandalous novel. Her life became so unbearable that she fled St. Petersburg and worked in the countryside instead.[78] Some women berated the lack of support by male doctors and teachers. Although professional women had higher status than factory workers, they also shared several common complaints of their working-class sisters.

6. Writers

> From her earliest years she was forced to place
> Her childish verses at the feet of the crowd...
> To serve as a plaything to cold boredom,
> To be sacrificed for meaningless praise.
> Karolina Pavlova, "Three Souls," 1845

a. Poets

What a magical choir of poets we possess...

Anna Akhmatova

Like nuns, doctors, and teachers, 19th century Russian women writers were exceptional. Some came to terms with their ego, personality and talent quite early. In many ways their lives and work paralleled those of their male counterparts. While there were several important Russian women writers in the middle of the century, as Akhmatova observed there was a remarkable "choir" of poets at the end of the 19th and beginning of the 20th centuries. While these women wrote and published hundreds of poems, I have included some that exemplify their personal lives and longings.

One of the earliest and most famous Russian women writers was Evdokiia Rostopchina. She was part of the group of Romantic poets clustered around Vasily Zhukovsky, Alexander Pushkin, and Mikhail Lermontov in the 1820s and 30s. She was friends with them and critics initially perceived her poems as a continuation of Pushkin's Romanticism. However, Karolina Pavlova replaced Rostopchina as the darling of the literary critics in the 1840s and 50s, and her novel in prose and poetry *The Double Life* became a feminist tract. In mid-century, minor Russian women novelists paralleled the great realistic Russian writers Gogol, Dostoevsky, Tolstoy, and Turgenev. In the late 19th century, Mirra Lokhvitskaya achieved fame, twice winning the Pushkin Prize for poetry, in 1895 and 1905. Lokhvitskaya chose to emulate Pushkin, rather than Baudelaire as some decadent Russian writers did. Certainly, the writings of Rostopchina, Pavlova, Lokhvitskaya, and Gippius paved the way for the two most famous women poets of the early 20th century—Anna Akhmatova and Marina Tsvetaeva.

Despite these women's successes, they had to overcome many obstacles that men did not. Russian society defined women as poetesses, inferior to male poets. Many experienced vicious criticism from male critics and writers who accused them of ignoring their children and husbands to indulge in their writing. In the early 20th century, popular novelist Verbitskaya was accused of pandering to low brow taste! Still, many women writers accommodated and kept writing. In her work *Reinventing Romantic Poetry*, Diana Greene argues that Russian women writers lacked the literary social capital that men enjoyed. They lacked the access to education, mentors, literary gatekeepers and opinion-makers, as well as the social connections needed to make a successful career that men enjoyed. "In such circumstances these women had to resolve the questions of how to find their voice, write about their experience and claim a professional identity as a poet."[79]

Evdokiia Rostopchina

> Yes! A woman's soul must shine in the shadow,
> Like a lamp's light in a marble urn...
> Evdokiia Rostopchina

In the early 19th century, unhappy, arranged marriages took their toll on Rostopchina and Pavlova. In her poem "The Last Flower," Rostopchina complained:

> I am fated to hide under a cloak of silence
> The best of holy dreams,
> To know light in the soul—and to bear darkness in my eyes!
> Little flower of the fields, forgotten, disregarded,
> May I not compare myself to you![80]
> October, 1835

In addition to family problems, Rostopchina also had to deal with Tsar Nicholas I's personal aversion to her after 1846 when she published her poem "Nasilnyi brak," (A Forced Marriage). Some interpreted her poem as a protest against patriarchy; others an allegory about Russia's annexation and oppression of Poland. As a result, Tsar Nicholas I exiled her from court and from St. Petersburg, which was a heavy burden for a writer to bear. Her poem "Chatsky's Return to Moscow" bemoans the stifling censorship of the Russian government under Nicholas I:

> In our country you don't know what to read—
> The only poetry that's any good is what they don't allow.[81]

Rostopchina had to deal with scathing criticism of her life and writing from both conservative Slavophiles and radical Westerners in the 1840s and 50s. Again her poem "Chatsky" laments:

> They will go after you with redoubled malice,
>   They will start to keep tabs on you,
> They will subject your life, opinions, activities,
> Actions, utterances to everyday gossip...
> They're not above lying—
> Their slander will rain down on you
> From all sides like buckshot!
> Oh!...You still don't understand how the spirit of partisanship
> And cliques can avenge itself when it is embittered![82]

Versatile, Rostopchina also wrote about women writers. In her poem "How Women Must Write" (1840), she advises restraint—that the writer not completely give away her best dreams:

> ...
> But women's poetry attracts me with
> Special delight; yet every woman's line of verse
> Troubles my heart, and in the sea of my reflections
> Affects me with anguish and joy.
> Still, I only wish that the modest singer
> Would not completely give away her best dreams,
> That modest, she would keep secret and hide
> The name of the apparition of her unwilling reveries,
> The dear tale of love and sweet tears;
> So that only now and then and in gleams
> She could allude to feelings so tender...
> That the stormy shroud of surmises
> Always should be above the murmur of hopeless doubts,
> Always should she hover mysteriously
> Above the song of golden hope; so that the echo of languid passion
> Would sound trembling under the frame of a modest thought;
> ...
> The inner impulse forged by the imagination,
> Decorum would struggle with enthusiasm,
> And wisdom guard every word,
> Yes! A woman's soul must shine in the shadow,
> Like a lamp's light in a marble urn,

Like the moon at dusk through the cover of storm-clouds;
And warming life, unbeheld, glimmers.[83]

September, 1840

Karolina Pavlova

Grumbling about her fate, Karolina Pavlova complained in her poem "Three Souls," in 1845:

> From her earliest years she was forced to place
>   Her childish verses at the feet of the crowd
>   As a humble tribute to it;
>   To carry her prayers and penances
>   To the social whirl, the marketplace of crowded salons,
>   To serve as a plaything to cold boredom,
>   To be sacrificed for meaningless praise.
>   And so she became acquainted
>   And quite comfortable, with boring banality,
>   Her secret gift became a noisy rattle,
>   The sacred seeds in her were choked.
>   And her blessed days and former prescience
>   She doesn't recall even in her dreams;
>   And she squanders her life in society's noise,
>   Fully content with her fate.

In the same poem, a third voice sadly observes:

> All blessings were bestowed on her,
> A life inwardly dynamic
> And outwardly calm.
> But in her soul, now full-grown,
> A sad question can be heard:
> After half of her life,
> Whatever has she accomplished?
> What about her power of ecstasy?
> What of her soul-filled language?
> What has her love achieved,
> And what has her impulse attained?
>   ...

> It might have been better for her
> To lose her senses in a life of vanity
> Or to fade in the wilderness...[84]
>
> November, 1845

Two years later, Pavlova parodied Rostopchina in an untitled poem, but in one clearly meant for Rostopchina since it referred to her as her contemporary the Countess. Her poem seems a bit envious of Rostopchina's aristocratic, high society life, as the following lines reveal:

> ...
> Byron's glory gave life to us,
> And Pushkin's oral line of verse.
> Yes, it's true, we are the same age,
> But not the same vocation.
>
> You are in Petersburg, in the noisy dale
> You live on without obstacles;
> You move as you wish
> From place to place, from city to city.
>
> Beautiful woman and George-Sandiste,
> You sing not for the Moscow river,
> And for you, a free artiste,
> No one has crossed out a line.
>
> My existence is different; I live at home,
> ...foreign lands are unknown to me.
> As Petersburg is unknown.
>
> In all capitals of various nations
> I have not strolled until now
> I do not demand emancipation
> And self-determined life;
>
> I love the community and frost of Moscow;
> In quiet I accomplish modest work,
> And hand over simply to my husband,
> My poems for a harsh verdict.[85]
>
> 1847, Moscow

Although Pavlova's novel *The Double Life* was well received by Russian critics in 1848, and her poetry was considered stronger than her husband's or Rostopchina's, yet personal life happiness eluded her. After a decade of married life hosting a Moscow literary salon, her profligate husband had squandered her inheritance, had established a second family with Karolina's own cousin, and had humiliated and impoverished her. When Karolina brought charges against her husband for bankrupting her, Russian society sided with her husband, not her. So she fled Moscow in the 1850s. In Dorpat, Estonia, she fell in love with a young law student and wrote a new cycle of love poetry. Later she lived in Germany, surviving through poorly paid translations, dying alone in obscurity and poverty in 1893.

While there were not large numbers of women poets in the late 19th century, they were a significant part of Russian culture and are becoming more widely known as more literary studies and history are being written. In addition to Zinaida Gippius (1869-1945), who was a significant figure in Russian modernism, writers like Lidia Zinoveva-Annibal (1866-1907), Elena Guro (1877-1943), Mirra Lokhvitskaya (1869-1905), her sister Teffi (1872-1952), Sofia Parnok, (1885-1933), and Polina S. Solovyova (1867-1924) are studied and appreciated today.[86]

Zinaida N. Gippius

> I want love—and I am unable to love.
>
> Gippius, "Helplessness"

Some of Gippius' poems written in the Symbolist period reveal her alienation, distrust, and fear of loving. The last stanza of one entitled "I" reads as follows:

"I"
Sometimes I want to curse everyone—
But I can only insult them timidly...
In me, towards me, there is a sick passion.
This self of mine I love...and despise.[87]
1901

Portrait of Zinaida Gippius, Leon Bakst, 1906

As a famous Silver Age poet, Gippius wrote in several genres: poetry, short stories, literary criticism, diaries, and letters, and on many topics: nature, aesthetics, individualism, apocalyptic religion, and loneliness. Believing in a religious revolution, she despised bourgeois culture, which longed for paradise on earth based on material comfort, accumulation of money and concern for private property. She likewise rejected the positivists with their concern for technological progress. Gippius expected the apocalypse to usher in the Kingdom of God on earth, not political reform, and she was gravely disappointed in the Revolutions of 1905 and 1917.[88]

Her poem "Impotence" or "Helplessness" expresses her personal struggles:

> I am not sure whether to rebel or resign.
> I have courage neither to live nor die.
> God is near me—I cannot pray,
> I want love—and I am unable to love.

> To the sun, to the sun I stretch out my arms,
> And I see a curtain of pallid clouds...
> It seems to me that I know the truth—
> And it's just for that I don't know the words.[89]

Still, Gippius managed to influence others including the young writer Marietta Shaginian (1888-1982). Marietta described Gippius' effect on her before WW I as "one of the most important critical episodes in the epoch of my wanderings." She devoured a book of Gippius' poetry in one night, first by kerosene lamp, then by candlelight, finally by match light. Shaginian longed for some connection between public and spiritual life, and Gippius' work offered it in the idea of *sobornost* or community. In 1909, Shaginian moved to St. Petersburg at Gippius' invitation and became part of a group of 'God-seekers,' who sought to combine their revolutionary and religious ideals.[90]

Mirra Lokhvitskaya

Unlike Gippius' intellectual, mystical, abstract poetry, Mirra Lokhvitskaya's was sensual, personal, and erotic. In some ways her life and poetry resembled those of famous men. She married E. E. Zhiber, had five children before the age of 30. She then took a lover, the poet Konstantin Balmont. She enjoyed sex and wrote erotic poetry as the following excerpts indicate:

> Why should I care that your eyes never leave me?
> I feel the torment of a secret fight,
> In the dark of long nights, the long winter nights,
> I want you to love me.
>
> There's a whole world of bliss in your slightest glance,
> So why should a wall lie between us?
> If I could be alone with you, united by pleasure,
> What heavenly excitement we'd feel![91]
>
> Why does your glance, velvety and burning
>   Excite my blood—

Mirra Lokhvitskaya

And waken in my heart, with irresistible force,
    A dormant love?
Meeting it, without my will, I'm drawn to you,
    But I quell my ardor...[92]

"First Kiss"
We stayed together—and the minutes flew...
I waited, without movement, wearying and loving.
I sought ecstasy, sought oblivion,
I loved you, I desired you.[93]

"To My Rival"
Yes, I believe you, she's beautiful,
But—even with heavenly beauty—
She would try in vain
To tarnish my golden crown.

...

> There I am Queen! I reign
> The crown of rhymes, my slaves;
> My verse, like a lash, hangs above her—
> And I am stern and unmerciful.
>
> A ringing dactyl in sultry dance
> Replaces my fiery iamb;
> Past the worried anapest
> I send my trochees, brightly swarming.
>
> And strophes like a resounding wave
> Run lightly and obediently,
> Joining together the fragrant wreaths
> Chosen by me...
>
> So move on! Get out of the road,
> Get it into your weak head:
> The place where gods have raised their altar
> Is not for the likes of an earthly shadow.
>
> Oh, let them call you beautiful,
> But beauty—is an earthly flower—
> It will fade, wan and voiceless,
> Before the resounding lyre![94]
>
> II. 51-2

Later in life, after bouts with tuberculosis, Lokhvitskaya wrote more melancholy poems like the one below entitled "On a White Night:"

> ...
> I look out the window. A dreary, dismal sight.
> Two withered birches and a fence.
> In the distance are fields. My soul hurts, aches,
> And vainly my gaze seeks repose.
>
> But it's not this sight that saddens me now,
> Rather that, while paired, I was often alone,
> The door of wonders so long ago closed,
> And life for me is hollow and cold.

It's sad that a tedious day draws close,
That saplings are not fated to grow stout,
That my venerable wattle fence was mown,
And a dreary light peers through my windowpane.[95]

III.13

Lokhvitskaya's passionate, personal poetry paved the way for the famous 20th century lyric poets Anna Akhmatova and Marina Tsvetaeva. Her erotic poetry may also have made writing about women's right to free love and lesbian love more acceptable. After the turn of the century, Lydia Zinoveva Annibal, Sofia Parnok, Polina S. Solovyova, and Marina Tsvetaeva all wrote about lesbian affairs. Annibal's story about lesbian love "Thirty Three Abominations" was published in 1907.

Marina Tsvetaeva

One of Tsvetaeva's best poems was dedicated to Akhmatova and entitled simply "To A. A.:"

A slender, un-Russian waist—
Above the folios
A shawl from Turkish lands
Fell, like a mantle.

You could be drawn
With one broken black line.
Coldness in gaiety, heat—
In your despondency.

All of your life is a fever,
And how will it culminate?
The clouded—dark—brow
Of a young demon.

To lure astray every earthly creature
Is a trifle for you!
And an unarmed verse
Aims at our heart.

Marina Tsvetaeva, 1911

>At a drowsy morning hour,
>—Quarter part four, I think—
>I fell in love with you,
>Anna Akhamatova.⁹⁶
>
>   1914

Another rather wistful love poem by Tsvetaeva was entitled "No One Has Taken Anything Away." It reads as follows:

>No one has taken anything away—
>   There is even a sweetness for me in being apart.
>I kiss you now across the many
>   Hundreds of miles that separate us.
>
>I know our gifts are unequal, which is
>   Why my voice is—quiet, for the first time.
>What can my untutored verse
>   Matter to you, a young Derzhavin?

> For your terrible flight I give you blessing.
> > Fly, then, young eagle! You
> have stared into the sun without blinking.
> > Can my young gaze be too heavy for you?
>
> No one has ever stared more
> > tenderly or more fixedly after you...
> I kiss you—across the hundreds of
> > separating years.
>
> > > > > > 1916

Another of Tsvetaeva's poignant poems is entitled "To Kiss a Forehead." It reads as follows:

> To kiss a forehead is to erase worry—
> I kiss your forehead.
> To kiss closed eyes is to give sleep—
> I kiss your eyes.
> To kiss lips is to give water—
> I kiss your lips.
> To kiss a forehead is to erase memory—
> I kiss your forehead.[97]
>
> > > > > > 1917

Anna Akhmatova

The King of Heaven has healed my soul with the icy calm of love's absence.

> > > > Anna Akhmatova

Akhmatova wrote about former lovers with intimacy, irony and tenderness:

> Everything gets so repellent—
> > Into my triumphant night
> > Don't come. I don't know you.
> > And how could I help you?
> > I can't cure happiness.[98]
>
> > > > > > 1914

Anna Akhmatova with family, 1916

In a poem entitled "A Drive," she muses:

> The plume brushed on the carriage roof.
> I glanced into his eyes.
> The heart pined, not even knowing
> The causes of its grief.
>   ....
> He has touched my knees anew
> With a hand that is almost not atremble.[99]

Or, her lament about saying good-bye:

> We're no good at saying good-bye.
> We wander around, shoulders touching.
> It's begun to get dark already.
> You look vacant, I say nothing.
>
> We'll stop in this church and see
> Someone buried, or christened, or married.
> We'll leave, avoiding each other's eyes.
> Why does nothing work out for us?

Or we'll go in this graveyard and sit
Where someone has already sat on the snow
And you'll draw with the end of your stick
Dream-chambers where we'll live forever.[100]

1917

b. Prose Writers

Nina Berberova

Like many other Russian writers, Nina Berberova became aware of her love of poetry and ability to write as a child. As a youth, she hated her mother's "protection" and found the psychology of the "nest" loathsome. She was always sympathetic with the one who fled the nest. As she says in *The Italics Are Mine*:

> ... from my earliest years I strove to be alone. Nothing could have been more terrible for me than a whole day, from morning till night, spent with someone else rather than with my own thoughts—not giving an account to anyone for my actions, carrying on dialogues with myself, reading all that I came upon.
> ... I developed a profound aversion to false comfort and coziness. I wanted a hundred-watt light shining on a book in which everything was expressed, everything was said, a clear day, a black night, no ambiguous meanings, no sad improvisations that were covered by veils of glances, sighs, and hints.... Life was gradually becoming a reality from which I had no intention of hiding behind anyone's back.

Berberova preferred Mikhail Lermontov's poetry to the church prayers she was asked to recite. In *The Italics Are Mine*, she confessed:

> So everything that inspired beauty settled in me, and I thought I would no longer 'recite by heart' a 'prayer' but would recite Lermontov himself, with the same feeling of fullness and happiness he had when reciting a prayer by heart. A circle emerged where Lermontov and I were at one, a blessed circle! Later still others appeared.[101]

Nina Berberova

When she was quite young she noticed that the severe rules of social behavior seemed to crush women's liveliness. Berberova never forgave her mother for accepting this socialization. By the age of 9, Nina felt that her mother had already lost her sincerity. "What was left was the outward form of gestures, glances, dress, walk, superstitions and taboos, forced smiles, general opinions, the trappings of a motionless and mute soul."[102]

Berberova began publishing her work when the Russian Revolution occurred. She immediately learned that the Communist Party didn't need her voice. Only those willing to go along with official policy received grants and food rations in the early 1920s. So she left Russia in 1922 with the poet Vladislav Khodasevich, living in Paris during the interwar period, and in the United States in the post war period.

Olga Freidenberg

Like Berberova, the philologist Olga Freidenberg early on recognized her own talent and took herself seriously. When her cousin

Olga Freidenberg

Boris Pasternak fell in love with her, she did not encourage his love, but his friendship. She described herself in her Diary thus:

> "Locked in against the outer world, I spent all my time working on my inner self, and when I opened the door I was different, hardened. There is in me an unusual store of self-confidence and stubbornness....I am as you see, fated to live in myself and for myself, and when I don't do what I want for myself, I take revenge on myself by remembering everything, forgetting nothing."

Despite her strong ego, she suffered bouts of depression like her cousin Boris.[103] Apparently she had only one love, and he died in WW I. Later, Olga devoted herself to Greek philology at the University of Leningrad and to caring for her mother.

While writing was a respectable career for gentry-class Russian women in the 19th century, it seldom provided sufficient emotional, intellectual, social, or financial support. The freeing of the serfs in 1861 impoverished some gentry households and poor management ruined others. The result was that some women of this class had to pursue a career because their family couldn't afford a dowry for marriage or provide for them as unmarried kin. While women were excluded from editing journals, respected journals sometimes paid famous women contributors reasonable amounts. Zinaida Gippius helped support her household from the earnings from her literary criticism as well as her belles letters. Pushkin prize winner Mirra Lokhvitskaya, however, was shocked when she discovered that male poets earned twice as much for their work as she did.[104]

Of course, gentry-class women writers and artists were not necessarily representative of their gender, but their work reflects some of the conflicts educated women experienced in the late 19th and early 20th centuries. Many dealt with "The Woman Question," i.e. about women's situation in love, marriage, the family, education, and employment in a variety of ways. None depicted as positive a heroine or as utopian a solution as Chernyshevsky's character Vera Pavlova in *What is to be Done?* [105] Some modeled the "New Woman" on their own autonomy, careers, and lifestyles. Some married. Some lived with lovers. Some participated in ménages à trois. Some remained single. Some had children, but most had only one or no children.

Some writers like Alexandra Kollontai, who initially suffered rejection by an editor in the 1890s, abandoned a publishing career in favor of fulltime revolutionary work. Others, like Alexandra Kobiakova (1823-92) experienced prejudice, scorn, and ridicule from neighbors, friends, and even a fiancé. Yet she persevered and published some of her work. Still others like Zinaida Gippius (1869-1945) experienced success but felt she had to write in a masculine voice using male verb endings and adjectives in order for her work to be taken seriously. As she explained, she wanted to write, "as a human being, and not only as a woman." According to literary critic Toby Clyman, Anastasia Verbitskaya (1861-1928) became an extremely successful writer, outselling Leo Tolstoy in the early 20th century, but she suffered alienation and never had any women friends except her sister and mother. Despite her popularity, critics scolded her for pandering to the lowest elements in society.[106]

Successful writers shared some common features such as strong-willed, even tyrannical grandmothers and mothers, and most of them received a good education enabling them to write well. Still, some were constrained by social injunctions that women writers were "unnatural" in rejecting the roles of wife and mother. The social norm some internalized was that "A woman must not write." Growing up in this milieu, Nadezhda Sokhanskaia thought writing revealed too much of a woman's innermost being and destroyed her modesty, the most important quality she possessed. She believed that women's inner world was sacred, to be known only by her family. Still, she kept writing. She justified her actions by appealing to a higher law—religion. She felt that writing was a gift from God and was a way of praising God.[107]

Russian utilitarian literary critics, while encouraging women's education and service to "the people," harshly criticized Rostopchina, Pavlova, Bashkirtseva, Gippius, and Verbitskaia for epitomizing "art for art's sake." Some questioned whether Nadezhda Durova actually wrote *The Cavalry Maiden*, believing that Pushkin, who championed it, may have written it. Others wondered if she in fact existed, suggesting her autobiography was a fabrication. As a result, some women like Nadezhda Sokhanskaia and Praskovia Tatlina felt constrained to write their autobiographies only for their families, which were then published posthumously.[108]

Anastasia Verbitskaia

When youthful Marie Bashkirtseva's *Diaries* were published after her death in the 1880s, some condemned her for being egotistical—wanting to be a painter and writer, not a wife. She was considered unnatural since she rejected the traditional roles of wife and mother and service to humanity. Even European society was amazed that a young woman like her sought fame and fortune rather than traditional feminine selflessness. During the Silver Age, 1880-1917, many more Russian women writers believed in art for art's sake and the celebration of the self. They were some of the "New Women" of their day. Prior to WW I, Verbitskaia described such a character Manya in her novel *The Keys to Happiness*. At one point Manya, a dancer, says:

I've two paths before me. ... The first is art, and I say to myself: 'Here! Kneel and contemplate. Study. Create. The joys of art are eternal. Creation lightens life's inevitable sorrows.'[109]

Verbitskaya's male characters also muse about the New Woman's need to subordinate love to work. Manya's lover Baron Mark Steinbach reflects in *The Keys to Happiness*:

> "It's a tragic battle," he thought. "One can create for oneself a new worldview and preach the freedom of love and freedom *from love*... One can believe in that dogma passionately and consider oneself a new woman. But what does one do with the old feelings that have been cultivated for centuries? What does one do with the instinct of Femininity—that fateful instinct slumbering in the most precious depths of the female organism, beyond the dark threshold where thought doesn't penetrate? What does one do with the need to submit and sacrifice a need that has been cultivated in the female psyche for thousands of years?
>
> "To free one's soul from the yoke of passion. To fill that soul with a great striving upward. To rise to a lofty goal, seizing love like rest and joy. To relegate that love to second place in one's life. Those are the keys to happiness...."
>
> "But should he have laid out this testament for women alone? Isn't love the same sort of drama for me? Haven't I put it at the center of my life? Isn't it a kind of cult?"
>
> "You have a feminine soul,' Manya's said that to me several times. Isn't that the secret of my own weakness?"[110]

Later, Manya fell in love with a poet named Harold. She thought she was just trifling with him, but realized passion had seized her, and she found herself again in love's trap:

> "O, how I despise myself! I wanted to laugh at love. And now love is laughing at me."[111]

Having subordinated love to her work as a dancer for several years, Manya suddenly finds herself unable to continue as a New Woman and to resist the passion she feels for Harold. She says:

"I laughed at the desire that others involuntarily experienced. What's desire? I said to myself, laughing. Does it make any difference? If not this one, then that one's fine. And I even have a lover. Consequently, no one scares me. But to love? O, my God! I had something to fill my soul—my child and my creative work. That was my world. Why did it all fall in ruins, Harold: this feeling I have for you brings me no joy, but only suffering. Furthermore, it's my debasement, an unbearable sense of insult. Having proudly challenged life, I am once again vanquished. Once again I'm down in the dust, with no strength to get up and go any farther. I'm not an artist now, but a pitiful puppet. For years I built my castle and considered it indestructible. Then you passed by—and now it's all in ruins. And I don't have the strength to start building anew."[112]

After spending a wonderful night together, Manya and Harold both renounce love in favor of their creative work. Manya calls back Steinbach from Moscow to St. Petersburg, and she tries to rebuild her life by marrying him. Once settled in the country, she again encounters her first love Nelidov, who has unhappily married too. They resolved their dilemma by a dual suicide because love and death meant the same thing to Manya.[113]

c. Diarists

> One should never give anybody one's diary to read, or even read it again oneself or lend it any significance, as one keeps it always in the worst possible, saddest moments, when one feels lonely and has nobody to complain to. Then, if only on paper, one has to unburden oneself of one's sorrowful mood; and it works: at once you feel calmer.
>
> Tatiana Tolstoy, Diary

While many Russian women kept diaries, few were published in their lifetime in the 19th century. Whether all recounted their sorrowful moods is questionable. Certainly Countess Tolstoy and her daughter did. Composing their diaries in the late 19th century, they were only published in the 20th century. Tatiana (Tania) Tolstoy (1864-1948) was the daughter of Count Lev and Countess Sofia Tolstoy and tried publishing her fiction in the 1880s, but was unsuccessful. However, she kept a diary, which was published in the mid 20th century. Her diary gives us glimpses into gentry-class women's lives. Trained as an artist, Tania had a personality and a will of her own, yet reflected influences of both her parents. Like her mother, Tania never renounced private property and loved fine dresses and being the coquette. However, she shared some of her father's ideas about simple living. At times, she criticized herself as an aristocratic sponge using the services of large numbers of people: a carpenter to fix her bedroom door, someone to make her new curtains, another making a frock while she did nothing. She also counted the shoemaker, the dressmaker, the tailor, the watchmaker, the furrier mending her carriage cloak, the glove maker, the goldsmith, the optician, and many others mending and doing for her. All of these did not include the butler, household servants, coachmen, maids, and so forth which their family employed. While she eventually was able to dress herself and dispense with a personal maid, she lacked her father's physical strength, and after helping in the hay harvesting for a half day, had to rest two days to recover! As a young woman, Tatiana kept a diary and asked herself why:

> Why do I keep this diary? I really do not know. More than anything else, in order to know, in many years time what I was like at twenty-one, and also because everything is clearer to your mind when you have written it down, and also because there are times when I simply want to write.[114]

Other times she admitted to herself that writing provided solace:

> Bad, bad. I have a really nasty feeling about myself, and though I know that it won't help to write this, I cannot refrain from doing so. The more so since, whenever I am in this sort of stupid, slothful and at the same time restless and unhappy mood, I always feel I must write my diary. I as it were complain to somebody about my lot, and it takes my time up. Though I have a lot to do, I cannot do anything, and as it's the festive season, at first I thought I simply ought to be gay. To-day I grasped that that is avoidable, and in the morning I walked round to the Tolstoys' and began a portrait of Uncle Sergey. As always, the start has turned out well—if only I don't spoil it as I go on.[115]

After finding and reading her sister Masha's diary in February 1888, Tania felt guilty and insisted that one shouldn't let others read one's diary. Later she relented, allowing two of the men she loved to do so. Her father also read her diary at times. Like her mother, Tania often confided in her diary when depressed:

> Just now I have been weighed down by that sort of sorrow and terror, so that I felt I could not go on, for fear. Yesterday the Tolstoys' former bailiff was killed by a beam, and to-day two little boys were drowned in the river, and we were there, and I scrubbed their sallow, unconscious, dead bodies. It was terribly gruesome, and I could not help thinking all the time that if we had such horrors here, could everything be well at home?[116]

Tania was also a painter, and found that this outlet, in addition to writing in her diary, helped. She remarked in her Diary:

> My painting saves me; I can always be absorbed in it....What should I do without paining? All day long, talking to other people and looking at them, I am saying to myself, 'A bit of cobalt and Neapolitan here. How am I to gat a patch of light here?' and so on.[117]

Musing on the dilemma of whether to marry or dedicate herself to art, Tania writes:

> I do not understand how men whom I do not love can love me, and *vice versa*. Though indeed I can think of no one whom I have loved, who has not returned my love. I must be very conceited, or else it is that I have only loved once, and that in a very childish and superficial manner. Nevertheless, it was a real love, it was extraordinarily pure. I doubt if I could ever again feel like that—nor do I want to....I was thinking to-day that I ought not to wish to get married, but work at my painting, to get something serious done. I recall that Surikov once said to me that 'Art is jealous.' And that is true. You have to surrender yourself entirely to it, or nothing comes of it....[118]

While Tania loved painting, she was unable to discuss it in the "drawing room" manner. Musing on her situation of having so much while the peasants have so little, Tania wondered what to do. She decided:

> Logically, this must lead to selling yourself and beginning to write books or paint pictures for money (the possibility of that is still very far off) or marrying for money. I am much inclined to the first, but fortunately my works are still too poor to be sold, and the second I still cannot understand, but still do think that even I, brought up as I have been by Papa and in good surroundings, might find it possible.[119]

Writing again on her struggle with her art, Tatiana says:

> Today I was more firmly convinced than ever before that talent cannot develop without inborn capability for tremendous and intent work. I have not known one gifted person who did not work at the form of his art at tremendous daily strain. Nearest of all, I have seen Papa re-write a sentence a number of times, one way, another, then back again, and so on, endlessly. Also Repin treating his painting in exactly the same way.
>
> For that reason I do not think I shall ever reach any great height of perfection, since I have not that ability. I lack the something to pay such heed to form. I am often amazed it is so strong in Papa. My explanation is that when we love the content, we long to clothe it in the most perfect form.[120]

Tania does not overtly complain about having to devote her time to her father and copy his manuscripts, but she does mention that one autumn when she was about to register to study at the Moscow Painting Academy, he insisted that she instead return to Yasnaya Polyana to "help" him copy his manuscripts and take care of him. While she never suggests that he was jealous of her talent as a painter, she does indicate that he never approved of her sister Masha's or her own romantic partners. To his credit, her father never suggested that she marry for money. Whether Tania would have become a good or great painter or writer is unknown, but certainly her family circumstances—helping with her younger brothers and sisters and helping her father—prevented her from devoting herself single-mindedly to her craft when she was a young woman.

d. Autobiography

> This is a difficult task which you have set me, writing my autobiography, and, although I have already begun it, I am continually wondering whether I am doing it properly.
>
> Countess Sofia Tolstoy, Autobiography

Women's writings sometimes had strange beginnings. A few years after Count Tolstoy's death, Professor S. A. Vengerov, who was the director of the Russian Library in St. Petersburg, asked Countess Sofia Tolstoy to write her autobiography. He wanted her to tell about her husband's literary creativity and to explain how and when they had become estranged. In July, 1913, Sofia agreed to do this, but then realized that she had no model for an autobiography. Not many women published their life stories in pre-revolutionary Russia. At almost 70 years of age, she took up the task, but was not writing in the prime of life as her husband had. Still, she wrote 35 typed pages, and Vasily Spiridonov, the owner of the journal *Nachala (Beginnings)*, edited and published her manuscript.

In her autobiography she recalled writing to Vengerov:

> The chief thing which I have decided to ask you is to tell me what length my article should be. If, for instance, you take a page of the magazine *Vestnik Europa* as a measure, how many full pages, approximately, ought I to write? To-morrow I shall be sixty-nine years old, a long life; well, what out of that life would be of interest to people? *I have been trying to find some woman's autobiography for a model, but have not found one anywhere.* [Italics added] [121]

She pointed out to Vengerov that the famous writers Gogol, Turgenev, Goncharov, and Lermontov were bachelors, without families, whereas Leo Tolstoy's family life was reflected in his works. She explained that although Tolstoy was a great writer, he did not write easily. He experienced the tortures of creative activity, and wrote with difficulty and slowly, making endless corrections. He doubted his powers, denied his talent, and often said: "Writing is just like childbirth; until the fruit is ripe, it does not come out, and when it does, it comes with pain and labour." She also quoted her husband saying: "The poet takes the best out of his life and puts it into his writings. Hence his writing is beautiful and his life bad." But Sofia insisted that Tolstoy's life was not unhappy in the 1860s and 70s.[122] Indeed, many visitors commented on their happy family life. Many visitors like the writers Ivan Turgenev and Afanasi Fet saw Sofia as a good influence on Tolstoy. Count Sollugub told Tolstoy that he was lucky man to have such a wife as Sofia. He told her:

> "You are, in fact, the nurse of your husband's talent, and go on being that all your life long."[123]

She tried to remember this wise and friendly advice and to follow it as well as she could as she joyfully copied and recopied *War and Peace* in the 1860s. But sometimes life corrected her plans. She lost three children in the 1870s, and this left her depressed and dispirited, unable to finish copying the second half of *Anna Karenina*.

She recollects that Tolstoy began to have inner religious crises in the late 1870s and 1880s. Initially, he became more ardently Orthodox. But, he gradually left that faith, and that was one of the differences between them. Sofia notes that her household tasks and caring for their nine children prevents her from living completely in her husband's intellectual interests. She thinks he began to go further away from family life. Initially, he had studied Greek so he could teach their sons this classical language while Sofia taught them Russian, French, German, and English. Sofia also taught the children church history and the Russian Orthodox liturgy. By the early 1880s, Tolstoy had given up trying to educate their children since he thought they were being taught according to principles and a religion which he considered harmful for them.[124]

In her autobiography, Sofia tried to vindicate herself, stressing that it was not she who changed, but Tolstoy who drifted away from her. At one point she says:

> I and my life remained the same as before. It was *he* who went away, not in his everyday life, but in his writings and his teachings as to how people should live. I felt myself unable to follow his teachings myself. But our personal relations were unaltered: we loved each other just as much, we found it just as difficult to be parted even temporarily…[125]

Sofia Tolstoy with daughter Alexandra, painting by Nikolay Gay, 1886

Both Count and Countess Tolstoy were hot-tempered and jealous. Towards the end of their lives, Sofia realized that her husband's soul, which had been open to her for so many years, had suddenly been closed to her, while it was opened to an outsider, a stranger, the disciple of his beliefs V. G. Chertkov. The complexities of life made Sofia turn towards philosophy, especially the classical writers such as Marcus Aurelius, Seneca, Epictetus, Plato, and among more modern thinkers Spinoza and Schopenhauer. In 1891, Tolstoy decided to divide his property among his children since he had come to believe that property was evil. He gave his wife power of attorney, and she saw to the publication of his books. He refused the copyrights of writings completed after 1881.

In 1895, their youngest son Ivan, or Vanichka died. This event almost unhinged Sofia. Count Tolstoy also grieved and seemed to lose his connection to his family after this. Sofia's chief pleasure thereafter was music, and she especially enjoyed Sergei I. Taneev's compositions and his playing for them in the 1890s.

Various complications arose between them as Tolstoy's followers and Sofia clashed over Tolstoy and the copyrights of his works.

The death of their daughter Masha brought Tolstoy and Sofia together for awhile in 1906. Then again visitors and disciples of Tolstoy made Sofia's life difficult. The final rift came in 1909 when Tolstoy wanted to renounce the copyright to all his writings, even those done before 1881, which Sofia had used to provide for their family. Various wills were made in her absence, and she was prevented from consoling him until he was literally dying. So Sofia's autobiography was an attempt to exonerate herself from being perceived as an hysterical shrew and show how she had been wronged by Tolstoy and his disciples.[126]

Writer Anastasia Verbitskaya wrote a less gloomy autobiography and charmingly describes how the past leaves us a particle of our soul. Mary Zirin quotes Verbitskaya's autobiography: "... the great truth is that we love our past no matter what it gave us ... that the places where we left a particle of our soul, a fragment of our life, are sacred."[127]

7. Artists

> I want to distinguish myself, I have the ability, and I will show them, how a heartless weak female can work.
>
> Anna Ostruomova Lebedeva

A remarkable generation of women artists also emerged in the late 19th and early 20th century. They received good training in Russia and Europe, and many belonged to avant-garde groups prior to the revolutions in 1917. Like writers, women artists were significant contributors to their craft and the outstanding ones were accepted by their male colleagues. Just prior to WW I, there were significant numbers of women studying the fine arts (4,000) compared with teaching(7,000) and medicine (6,000). Some of the most famous artists were Aleksandra Ekster or Exter (1882-1949), Natalia Goncharova (1881-1962), Anna Ostroumova Lebedeva (1871-1955), Liubov Popova (1889-1924), Olga Rozanova (1886-1918), Zinaida Serebriakova (1884-1967), Varvara Stepanova (1894-1958), and Nadezhda Udaltsova (1886-1961).[128]

a. Anna O. Lebedeva

> I myself want to live on after death! I myself!
>
> Anna O. Lebedeva

The Russian Academy of Art opened its doors to women in 1891, and the following year Anna Ostroumova enrolled for training. Like women doctors, however, artists were not allowed to become professors at the academy or hold high civil service rank with all of its perks and privileges. Still, some women felt accepted at the academy and were able to become professional artists. Artists like Alexandra Ekster, Natalia Goncharova, Anna Ostroumova, Liubov Popova, and Zinaida Serebriakova, with the help of their well-to-do parents, were able to continue their art education in Paris. As in the other professions, it was gentry-class women like Goncharova, a descendent of Pushkin's, and well-to-do middle-class women like Ostroumova and Popova who had the money and time to become artists.

Living authentic lives was not easy for these women. Early on, Anna Ostroumova clashed with her mother over women's role

Anna Ostroumova Lebedeva, portrait by Konstantin Somov, 1901

in society. As a young woman, Anna was haunted by the need to leave a legacy behind. In one conversation with her mother, she says,

> The thought that one could die and leave nothing behind fills me with horror. When I talked to my mother about this, she said: 'Get married, have children, then you'll make your mark. The children will fill your place.' 'That's not what I mean! I myself want to live on after death! I myself! How can all of you not understand that!'[129]

Later, Anna clashed with her family over her right to earn money from her work. In the late 19th century, the reigning social ideal in Russia as well as Europe was that "Ladies do not work for pay." Challenging this notion required a lot of energy and commitment. Eventually she prevailed, and prior to WW I her family finally allowed her to sell some of her engravings. They were very popular, and she did well financially.

Anna also clashed with feminists of her generation. Some wanted her to join the League of Women's Equality. She turned down their offer, arguing that her contribution to women's rights was her work and success. Regarding this, she wrote:

> I never call myself a woman, but always a female person, because I stopped being a woman, but turned into some sort of workaholic."[130]

In addition, Anna struggled with her professors in the Art Academy. The famous Russian painter Ilia Repin regarded her as one of his most talented pupils, praising her exceedingly. However, she preferred doing engraving to oil painting and the art community looked down on her making that choice.[131]

Failing to find understanding in her family or artistic community, Anna persuaded her family to let her study in Paris in the late 19th century. She found a place at the American artist Whistler's studio and visited museums, galleries, etc. At the grave of youthful writer and artist Maria Bashkirtseva in France, she was deeply touched by the artist's great talent and early death. In Paris, Anna also met Russian artists Alexander Benois, Konstantin Somov, and Zinaida Serebriakova.

Upon her return to Russia, Anna joined the group and journal *Mir Iskusstva*, the *World of Art* group. This progressive group included Gippius, Merezhkovsky, Diaghilev (director of the Ballet Russe), Zinovieva-Annibal and others. Her alignment with them led to a rupture with Repin, the head of the Art Academy. Anna began publishing in the journal *Mir Iskusstva* and exhibiting her work in St. Petersburg. Before WW I, she again went to Europe to study in Italy. Like Frank Lloyd Wright, Anna was critical of Italian churches. She found many of them tastelessly decorated with stolen antique monuments. Such churches gave her "the creeps."[132]

Eventually, Anna chose marriage and a career, but excluded children, considering her artistic creations her "children." In 1916, colleagues in the Russian Academy of Art suggested Anna become the first woman candidate to receive academic rank. Much discussion ensued, and in January, 1917, the Academy voted to admit her into its ranks. After the 1917 Revolution, Anna was invited to teach at the Academy. Hard times following the revolution meant it was difficult being an art professor: lack of heat, electricity, and food made teaching and learning difficult. Although Anna Lebedeva rebelled against her family and the artistic community in choosing engravings rather than oil painting, she did not belong to the group of women involved in the Avant-Garde (1905-1932). Nor did her contemporary Zinaida Serebriakova.

b. *Zinaida Serebriakova*

> All Serebryakova's art is free, and it is full of a gaiety which reflects the conditions of joyful emotion in which the artist works.
>
> Alexander Benois, Russian Art Critic

Serebriakova's self portrait reveals some of the gaiety, inspiration, and excitement that her uncle, art critic Alexander Benois, noticed in her work. Born into an artistic family in 1884, Serebriakova studied painting with famous Russian artists Ilia Repin and Osip Braz. Her father Yevgeny Lansere (1848-86) was a sculptor, her brother Yevgeny a painter, printmaker, and sculptor, and her brother Nikolai an architect and art historian. Her uncle on her mother's side Alexander Benois was an artist and art critic. Since her father died when Zinaida was only 2 years old, she and her family lived with her uncle while growing up. Living in her uncle's highly cultured environment, Serebriakova went to Italy to study the Viennese masters in 1902-03 and to Paris in 1905 to study Watteau, Fragonard, and the Impressionists, especially Renoir, Monet, and Degas. By 1906, she was a fully fledged artist and joined *Mir Iskusstva*. However, like Anna Lebedeva, she eschewed Art Nouveau, Symbolism, and abstract art that were popular in early 20th century Russia. She remained a critic of non-objective art and an exponent of "cheerful realism."

Her life was satisfying, and she married an engineer in 1905 and had four children. This also set her apart from most of the women artists of her day because many women artists had no children, or only one. Her self portrait painted in 1909 and exhibited in 1910 was the beginning of her successful career in Russia. The Tretiakov Gallery in Moscow bought her self portrait after the exhibition, and brought her into the mainstream of the Russian art world. Her nudes and paintings of Russian peasant women were widely acclaimed. She was expected to be elected the first woman to the Russian Academy of Art in the spring of 1917, but the February Revolution intervened. After the February and October Revolutions, her life took a downward spiral. Her country estate was plundered and burned in 1918; her husband was arrested; then he died of typhus in 1919. A glance of her self portrait done in 1922, compared with that of 1909, shows the lack of gaiety in her life after the revolution.[133]

Public acclaim came with her "Self Portrait: At the Dressing Table" (1909). She retained this style throughout most of her career. Like her self portrait, she depicts women as subjects, not objects. Her women look directly at the viewer and are not sexually objectified. Serebriakova painted pictures on popular themes like the Russian peasants and rural life. She eschewed cubism, futurism, and other avant-garde styles. In 1916, she painted murals on oriental themes for the Kazan Railroad Station in Moscow. She represented each country as a different beautiful woman.

Left with four children and a mother to support in 1919, she went to Petrograd to make her living. There she did charcoal and pencil drawings because she had no money for oil painting. Despite her situation, she refused to paint lucrative portraits of Bolshe-

Zinaida Serebriakova, "Self Portrait: At the Dressing Table," 1909

vik commissars. Following Lenin's death in 1924 and changes in Soviet policy, she accepted a commission to paint a mural in Paris, and didn't return to Russia until the 1960s.

The Soviet government only allowed two of Serebriakova's children to join her in France, and she never saw the other two until the 1960s, during the "Thaw" under Khrushchev. In the late 1920s, she travelled to North Africa, painting landscapes and Arab women. Despite her accomplishments, her art was not exhibited again in the Soviet Union until 1966. Then her work was very popular and she sold millions of albums of her work.

c. Natalia Goncharova

> At the beginning of my development I learned most of all from my French contemporaries.
>
> Natalia Goncharova, "Preface to an Exhibition," 1913

Goncharova like several other female artists broke with traditional representational art. A great niece of the poet Alexander Pushkin (her great aunt was Pushkin's wife) Goncharova came from a well-to-do family. She was able to study and exhibit in Paris (1906) as well as in Moscow, beginning in 1908. Her self-portrait, painted in 1907, shows cubist influence. She experimented with neoprimitivism, cubism, and rayonism in her work prior to WW I. Although influenced by the French Impressionists, she broke with European influences early in her career. Dubbed a "youthful Mother Superior" by Maria Tsvetaeva, Goncharova was a talented, strong, hardworking woman of the early 20th century. In one quote, Tsvetaeva wrote:

> She has the courage of a Mother Superior. A directness of features and views. She rarely smiles but when she does it's delightful. Her gestures are brief and meaningful. Such is Goncharova with her modernity, her innovation, her success, her fame, her glory, her fashion—she has everything to tempt—but no! She did not lead a permanent school, she did not convert a one-time discovery into a method and did not canonize...To sum her up? In short: talent and hard work.[134]

An innovator, Goncharova presented several female nudes in a private exhibition in 1910, and was arrested for pornography, tried, and acquitted. Goncharova's nudes were unusual in that her women were not portrayed as sex objects as many male artists depicted them. According to Jane Sharp's analysis in "Redrawing the Margins of Russian Vanguard Art," Goncharova portrayed her monumental, front-facing nudes as subjects, not objects. However, a newspaper reporter who had crashed the show misinterpreted them, and denounced them as pornographic. The next day the show was shut down. Male critics often misunderstood her work. When she had a show in 1914, one painting depicting a god/goddess was condemned as blasphemous, and her show was closed. Her illus-

Natalia Goncharova, "Self-Portrait," 1907

trations for a book entitled *Mystical Images of War*, 1914, were radically anti-war, and in 1915 she left Russia never returning. Although not active in feminist political circles, Goncharova's art was feminist by our standards. It undermined patriarchal authority and was too avant-garde for the Russian censors.[135]

In the "Preface to a Catalogue of her One Man Exhibition" in 1913, Goncharova turned her back on Western Art, arguing that French artists had stimulated her awareness, but she also realized the significance of the East in art:

> "Hitherto I have studied all that the West could give me, but in fact, my country has created everything that derives from the West. Now I shake the dust from my feet and leave the West, considering its vulgarizing significance trivial and insignificant—my path is toward the source of all arts, the East. The art of my country is incomparably more profound and important than anything I know in the West. (I have true art in mind, not that which is harbored by our established schools and societies). I am opening up the East again, and I am certain that

Natalia Goncharova, "Washerwomen," 1911

many will follow me along this path. We have learned much from Western artists, but where do they draw their inspiration if not from the East? We have not learned the most important thing: not to make stupid imitations and not to seek our individuality, but to create, in the main, works of art and to realize that the source on which the West draws is the East and us. May my example and my words be a good lesson for those who can understand its real meaning."[136]

Goncharova developed neoprimitivism, explaining that the East meant new forms, an extending and deepening of the problems of color. Continuing, she confessed:

"If I extol the art of my country, then it is because I think that it fully deserves this and should occupy a more honorable place than it has done hitherto."[137]

A year earlier, Goncharova had given a speech on cubism at the "Knave of Diamonds" debate in 1912. In a letter that year, she explained her views:

Cubism is a positive phenomenon, but not altogether a new one. The Scythian stone images, the painted wooden dolls sold at fairs are those same cubist works... Contrary to Burliuk (another Russian artist), I maintain that at all times it has mattered and will matter what the artist depicts, although at the same time it is extremely important how he embodies his conception."[138]

It is ironic that in 1915, shortly after denouncing the West, Goncharova and her partner Mikhail Larionov (1881-1964) emigrated there, living in Paris where she had the opportunity to paint authentically and design modern sets and costumes for Diaghilev's Ballet Russe. One of the reasons for their emigration was their split from certain Russian artists and critics; another was Goncharova's political persecution by the Tsarist government and accusations that her renditions of icons was not only irreligious, but anti-religious and pornographic. Perhaps the ultimate irony is that while she and Larionov died in poverty in the 1950s, her paintings in the 21st century fetch millions of dollars at auction! (One of her paintings entitled "Spanish Dancer" is exhibited in the new modern wing of the Art Institute in Chicago.)

While Goncharova was one of the early radicals of the Russian Avant Garde, there were others in her remarkable generation, including Olga Rozanova (1886-1918), Liubov Popova, Vera Stepanova (1894-1958), Nadezhda Udaltsova, and Aleksandra Ekster. All these women came from middle-class families, but some like Popova and Ekster's were well-to-do and funded their studies in Paris as well as in Moscow. All of them practiced cubist and other non-objective forms of art. Several worked in theater design, and most of them also designed book and journal covers, even music scores. All the women artists married, but only Popova and Serebriakova had children.

d. Olga Rozanova

> How does the world reveal itself to us?
> How does our soul reflect the world?
>
> Olga Rozanova

Olga Rozanova, "Self Portrait," 1911

Unlike Lebedeva, Goncharova, and Serebriakova, Rozanova did not study in France. While there were many recognizable elements in Rozanova's early work, i.e. her cubist portrait of her sister "Portrait of a Lady in Pink," her art became non-objective. Constructivist artist Alexander Rodchenko ((1891-1956) described her as "one who wanted to light up the world in cascades of color, one who thought of creating color through light." The critic Nina Gurianova described her art in the following words: "Perhaps, after all, Rozanova was the only suprematist able to combine 'cosmic' disharmony with the human dimension, and the spiritual, mystical and mental with the emotional, intuitive, and sensual."[139]

Rozanova's art moved from cubism in 1911 to abstract by 1917. Writing in 1913, she responded to critics of modern art in an essay entitled "The Bases of the New Creation and the Reasons Why it is Misunderstood." She began by asserting that the world is a piece of raw material—for the unreceptive soul it is the back of a mirror, but for reflective souls it is a mirror of images appearing continually. She explained:

> In this way, nature is a 'Subject' as much as any other subject set for painting *in abstracto* and is the point of departure, the seed, from which a Work of Art develops; the intuitive principle in the process of creation is the first psychological stage of

Olga Rozanova, "Portrait of a Lady in Pink," 1911

this development. How does the artist use the phenomena of nature, and how does he transfer the visible world on the basis of his relationship with it? ...

—Because the artist must be not a passive imitator of nature, but an active spokesman of his relationship with her...

A servile repetition of nature's models can never express all her fullness.

It is time, at long last, to acknowledge this and to declare frankly once and for all, that other ways, other methods of expressing the World are needed. ...

Each moment of the present is unlike the world of the past, and the keys of the future carry inexhaustible possibilities for new revelations.[140]

Rozanova argued that Modern art was no longer a copy of concrete objects; it has set itself on a different plane. It has turned upside down the traditional conception of Art.[141] She thought:

For the majority of the public nurtured by pseudo artists on copies of nature, the conception of beauty rests on the terms 'Familiar' and 'Intelligible.' So when art created on new principles forces the public to awaken from its stagnant, sleepy attitudes crystallized once and for all, the transition to a different state incites protest and hostility since the public is unprepared for it.[142]

She thought critics like Alexander Benois in his essay "Cubism or Ridiculism?" do not help prepare the Russian public for Modern Art. Critics and newspaper reviewers often ignorantly dumped Cubism, Futurism, and other manifestations of art life onto the same heap.[143] Rozanova noted that every new epoch in art differed from the preceding one and introduced new artistic theses into its path of development. It worked out a new code of artistic formulas and then slackened off.

Rozanova saw the pre-war exhibitions of the "World of Art" and "Union of Russian Artists" as examples of cozy imitations of the 19th century Russian school of painters called "The Wanderers." She saw the post impressionists in France developing the use of air, light, dynamism, and planar and surface dimensions in their pictures, and believed that Modern Art developed them further. Discussing nonobjective creativity, Rozanova wrote: "We propose to liberate painting from its subservience to the ready-made forms of reality and to make it first and foremost a creative, not a reproductive art."[144]

Summing up the situation of art in the early 20th century, Rozanova asked: How can one explain the premature spiritual death of the artists of the Old Art, if not by laziness? They end their days as innovators before they are barely thirty, and then turn to rehashing. She thinks artists are seduced by the success of a "steady market," and she contemptuously dismissed "those who hold dear only peaceful sleep and relapses of experience."[145]

Like several other women of the Avant-Garde, Rozanova practiced graphic design as well as easel painting. In 1916, she illustrated her husband Alexei Kruchenych's book *War*. Like Goncharova, Rozanova's illustrations were innovative and anti-war. Rozanova also illustrated Kruchenych's transrational poetic writings. Who knows what sort of artist she might have become had she not died in 1918 from diphtheria.

e. Varvara Stepanova

> In nonobjective creation you will not find anything 'familiar,' anything 'comprehensible,' but don't be put off by this,
>
> Varvara Stepanova

Another avant-garde artist, Varvara Stepanova (1894-1958) came from Kaunas, Lithuania (a part of the Russian Empire prior to WW I), studied art in Kazan, where she met and married the Constructivist artist Alexander Rodchenko, and lived in Moscow 1912-25. She was an artist who did not study in Paris. Writing about nonobjective art in 1919, Stepanova noted:

> If we investigate the process of non-objective creation in painting, we will discover two aspects: the first is a spiritual one—the struggle against subject and 'figurativeness' and for free creation and the proclamation of creativity and invention; the second aspect is the deepening of the professional

Varvara Stepanova and Alexander Rodchenko, 1920s

demands of painting...with regard to texture, craftsmanship, and technique.

All this is new to the spectator, but she urges viewers to persevere:

> In nonobjective creation you will not find anything 'familiar,' anything 'comprehensible,' but don't be put off by this, grow fond of art, understand what it is to 'live art,' and don't just investigate it and analyze it, don't just admire it casually, don't just search for intelligible subjects in it or depictions of themes you like.[146]

She pleads with the viewer to be open to new, nonobjective art. Stepanova alluded to the complexity in the nonobjective art of Goncharova and Larionov's Rayonism and in Rozanova, Ekster, Popova, and Udaltsova's Suprematism. Nonobjective art was more geometric, with squares, rectangles, triangles, arcs, not traditional or sentimental landscapes or portraits. Everywhere on the canvas there is energy, every space is filled up and has meaning. For an example, see below, Liubov' Popova's "Traveling Woman" 1915. Stepanova had an exhibition in 1914, became a secretary in a factory during WW I, and did not feature in the art world until after the Revolution.

f. Liubov Popova

> Most important of all was the spirit of creative progress, of renewal and inquiry.
>
> Liubov Popova

Liubov Popova, another member of the Avant-Garde, was born in 1889 to a wealthy textile manufacturing family. She grew up outside of Moscow, but attended high school in Moscow and studied art there from 1908-1912. Then her parents financed her further study in Paris. Influenced by Picasso and Braque, Popova's art reflected Cubism, Futurism, Suprematism, and Rayonism prior to WW I.

A prolific painter and talented designer, Popova abandoned easel painting not long after the 1917 Revolution. In the early 1920s, she devoted herself instead to mass installations celebrating revolu-

Liubov Popova, "Traveling Woman," 1915

tionary holidays, designing textiles, book covers, as well as theater sets and costumes. She teamed with the famous director Meyerhold in the early 1920s, creating modern sets and costumes. She died at the peak of her popularity in 1924. Her husband had died of typhus in 1919; and while she recovered from typhus, which she had also

Liubov Popova, 1920

caught, she was unable to survive the scarlet fever that claimed her son, dying soon after him. Popova was unusual among women artists in that she had a son, but not unusual in dying from a contagious disease in the early days of the Bolshevik regime when food, fuel, and medicine were in short supply.

g. Aleksandra Ekster

> As far as A. Exter's art is concerned, its polemical period is apparently over: its composition has acquired a positive calmness in spite of an increased complexity.
>
> Ivan Aksenov, "On Contemporary Russian Painting," 1913

Aleksandra Ekster

Aleksandra Ekster or Exter was also part of the remarkable generation of avant-garde painters. Like many of her colleagues, she came from a wealthy upper middle-class home, was well educated, and married early. In 1903, she married Nikolai Ekster, a successful lawyer in Kiev, and they hosted a salon at their home where famous writers like Anna Akhmatova and Osip Mandelstam and dancers and choreographers like Bronislava Nijinska met together. Well supported, Ekster like Ostroumova and Popova studied in Paris. From 1908-1924, she lived in Kiev, St. Petersburg, Paris, Rome, and Moscow.

In Paris, she was a personal friend of Picasso and Braque and in 1914 participated in the Salon des Independants there. The same year she exhibited among the Futurists in Milan. In 1915, she became part of the avant-garde Suprematists in Russia. Like other artists of her generation, Ekster participated in and founded a peasant handicraft cooperative in Kiev from 1918-20. She also helped decorate the streets and squares in Kiev and Odessa for Revolutionary holidays and festivals. She also decorated the agit-trains which toured the country to secure support for the Bolshevik regime. In addition, she designed costumes for Nijinska's ballet. From 1921-4, she participated in the Soviet government's Art Academy in Moscow. In 1924, she and her husband, immigrated to

Paris. There she became a professor at several academies of Modern Art (1924-30).

As early as 1913, Ekster drew high praise for her work from the poet and writer Ivan Aksenov in his essay "On the Problem of the Contemporary State of Russian Painting." Discussing contemporary art, he singled Ekster's out for its complexity and delicacy, saying:

> As far as A. Exter's art is concerned, its polemical period is apparently over: its composition has acquired a positive calmness in spite of an increased complexity; the colors have become lighter, the quality of her painting has achieved a delicacy rarely encountered in the pictures of our artists....Of course, the problems of easel painting demand methods of solution other than the questions that decorative work raises, and when judging an easel artist, we should change our criteria. ...
>
> Our age is obliged by force of circumstance to finish what our predecessors passed on to us. The path of search in this direction is broad, its bends are diverse, its forks numerous; the solutions will be many. Among them, those connected in our art with the name of A. Exter will remain as an example of courage, freedom, and subtlety.[147]

Both Ekster and Serebriakova left the Soviet Union in 1924. Lenin died that year, and some political and cultural changes occurred. It isn't clear exactly why these two women artists left, and Soviet sources never say exactly why they left. Lunacharsky remained Commissar of Enlightenment, not resigning until 1929. Still, as early as 1921 people were arguing for the closing of art museums and the end of traditional, bourgeois art. Indeed, Nikolai Tarabukin's lecture entitled "The Last Picture Has Been Painted," indicates some of the hostility towards easel art. Moreover, Lenin's death marked the end of a certain toleration of radical writers and painters.

4. Conclusion

What sort of conclusions can we come to regarding women's work? Certainly peasant and working class women toiled long hours for low pay, but so did many women doctors and teachers. Still, career women experienced a degree of fulfillment in their work that may have made up for their struggles. Women in all kinds of work encountered sexual harassment. Yet, dedication to their profession meant that most artists, teachers, and doctors continued their work in the 1920s and 30s, although life in the cities was difficult following the Bolshevik Revolution, and still more so during the purges of the 30s.

Natalya Goncharova, *Mystical Images of the War*, Lithograph, 1914

Chapter Four

Politics

> My mother is kind, very kind, but there are eight of us children, and she can barely manage. She doesn't understand me. She keeps shouting: 'If you continue you will end up in a forced labour camp! Think of the disgrace that will bring to our family. Who will marry your sisters, if you become a criminal?'... I feel sorry for her, but what can I do.
>
> Klavdia Kirsanova, Social Democrat

Prior to 1900, the educated Russian public criticized the Tsarist regime, but many gentry, middle, and working-class women as well as most peasants continued supporting the Tsar and relatively few joined any of the illegal political parties. After the February Revolution of 1917, some princesses joined the army of the Provisional Government to protect the Tsar after he abdicated. One princess took military training in the spring of 1917, but was never called upon to protect the Tsar before his death in July, 1918. Another princess, A. M. Shakhovskaia, who was a licensed pilot, served in the Russian military during WW I.

However, in the late 19th century, some educated gentry-class women became politically active and radicalized. Yet, most peasants resisted those who came to the countryside to educate and radicalize them. Some peasants denounced the young nobles to the authorities in the 1860s and 1870s. In those decades the peasants were not ready for insurrection, and the gentry-class activists were inept in working with peasants. By 1878 most of those in the "going to the people" movement, like Catherine Breshko-Breshkovsky, had been imprisoned, tried, and exiled. A few idealists like Vera Figner, Sofia Perovskaya, and Sofia Bardina became even more radical and turned to terrorism as a weapon to fight the Tsarist government. They belonged to a group called "The Peoples' Will." In 1881, they too were rounded up, arrested, tried for their assassination of Alexander II, or languished in prison until their release during the 1917 Revolution. Their heirs split into two groups: the Social Revolutionaries who remained devoted to educating and politicizing the peasants, and a group called Social Democrats who focused on workers in the cities because they thought the peasants too retrograde and resistant to revolution. Two books which give good overviews of the role of 19th century gentry-class women in various radical groups are Vera Broido's *Apostles into Terrorists* and Anna Hillyar and Jane McDermid's *Revolutionary Women in Russia, 1870-1917, a Study in Collective Biography*.[1]

After the 1905 Russo-Japanese War and subsequent Revolution, however, Tsarist support fell. Government troops had fired on peaceful demonstrators in January, 1905, resulting in the Bloody Sunday massacre, in which about 100 workers were killed and 500 wounded. Many workers, peasants, and intelligentsia turned against the Tsar, undermining the legitimacy of the regime. As a result of the Revolution of 1905, the Tsarist government granted some reforms—allowing the election of a Duma (Parliament), legalizing trade unions and political parties, granting some freedom of the press, speech, and religion. During the Revolution, some peasants looted gentry-class manor houses, and in 1906-07 the Tsar sent punitive expeditions to the countryside to hang them. The government also arrested teachers and others belonging to the Social Revolutionary Party. A few years after the 1905 Revolution, the government reneged on its reforms, making it difficult for members of the liberal and leftist parties to be elected to the Duma.

Although many women as well as men initially supported Russia's entry into WW I, loyalty to the Tsar drastically declined as the finest flower of the Russian officer class was killed, wounded and captured. As casualties among the peasant soldiers mounted, peasants found it difficult to defend government war aims, and desertions increased. Moreover, the hardships of the war radicalized many peasant women as their men folk and horses were mobilized for the war, leaving them to carry on the heavy work of farming by themselves. Some peasants and soldiers' wives fled to the cities where they were unprepared for work there. A bourgeois woman Kotliarevskaia described them as underdeveloped and almost unemployable:

> What is awful and painful is that they themselves rarely are conscious of their own lack of development....They apply for jobs as nursemaids, servants, seamstresses, floor sweepers, and laundresses, but they do not know how to do any of these things. They actually do not even know how to do laundry or wash floors. 'I don't know how to cook, I don't know how to look after children, I don't know how to polish things,' is what they are saying. Ninety percent of them are illiterate and have never held a pen in their hands. They are scared of everything new.... They are afraid to leave their children in a shelter....They say, 'When my husband comes back, he will give me hell and ask me why I gave the child away,' or 'When the children grow up, they will upbraid me, (asking) why I kept them in an orphanage.'[2]

Nor were peasant women the only "underdeveloped women" in Russian society. Many gentry and bourgeois women were also "undereducated, unskilled, helpless, fearful, and subject to fierce sexual harassment." While many educated women found jobs as accountants, secretaries, telegraph operators, primary and secondary-school teachers, thousands offered their services as nurses for wounded soldiers. [3]

By December, 1916, some members of the aristocracy were so incensed by the despicable role Rasputin was playing in Russian political affairs that they decided to eliminate him. Many resented the German heritage and political blunders of Tsarina Alexandra. As the economy slowly fell apart due to wartime shortages and difficulties, and as casualties mounted on the battlefield, desertions increased, and support for the Monarchy waned especially in the cities where food and fuel were in short supply. Still, there were a few thousand women who had joined Women's Battalions, and one such group under the command of Yashka Botchkareva participated in frontline battles in Galicia in the summer of 1917.

Disaffection from the Tsarist Regime led to the Revolution of February, 1917, which was supported by people in all classes. Unfortunately, the Provisional or Temporary Government which replaced the Tsar muddled along and was unable to restore the economy, provide food and guns to the soldiers at the front, or to exit the war. While their liberal policies satisfied many Russian feminists, since it granted women the right to vote and civil liberties, it did not gain the support of the peasants or workers because it failed to resolve the "Land Problem" or improve the lives of workers in the cities. Liberals in the Provisional Government wanted a fair distribution of land for landlords and peasants, but the land committees set up in the countryside to resolve this problem took too long to suit most peasants. By 1917, peasants favored the policies of the Social Revolutionaries and Bolsheviks who advocated direct takeover of the land. Their slogan "Rob those who have robbed you" proved popular. Both workers and peasants found the February Revolution an incomplete one, hence many supported the later October 1917 Bolshevik Revolution.

So, let us turn to some of the voices of Russian women in the 19th and early 20th century to see how they described their political ideas and behavior.

A. Gentry and Middle-class Women

A variety of events radicalized Russian women turning some into full-time revolutionaries in the late 19th century. While many gentry-class women remained loyal to the autocracy, scores became critical of the old regime and gave up family life, philanthropic, and professional work to take up political life. In the 1860s, 70s, and 80s, some became champions of the peasantry devoting their lives to the Socialist Revolutionary Party (SR's). Many began as youthful idealists devoted to the cause of uplifting the lives of the peasants and workers. In the 1880s and 90s, some became fearless revolutionaries while still in gimnaziya (high school). Some went on to study Marxism, becoming Social Democrats who were more concerned about workers than peasants.

1. Social Revolutionaries

> I was not the only one called upon to make such a sacrifice. Among the women in the struggle for Russian freedom there were many who chose to be fighters for justice rather than mothers of the victims of tyranny.
>
> Catherine Breshkovsky,
> *Little Grandmother of the Russian Revolution*

Working for a social revolution in Russia for over 50 years, Catherine Breshko-Breshkovsky (1844-1934) was one of the earliest and longest lasting Social Revolutionaries. She early adopted her mother's Christian concern for the poor. As a child she often gave her toys and clothes to less fortunate peasant children. Rebuked by her mother, she responded: "Mamma, you read to us from the gospel that if any one has two garments he should give one to the poor. Why are you angry if I do just what you read to us?"[4] Touched by the plight of the peasants, she remarked about her feelings as a seventeen year old:

> Fired by such ideas, I saw the poor, degraded slaves around me, and longed to set them free. At first I believed that freedom could be reached without a radical change of government. No revolutionary spirit had yet been kindled. It was the first great era of the Liberals. The emancipation of the serfs was soon to take place; so too the introduction of trial by jury; and those promised reforms sent a social impulse sweeping through Russia. I was thrilled by the glad news. Filled with young enthusiasm, I opened a little school near our estate.
> ... The twenty peasants in my school, like the millions in Russia, suspected that the proclamation had been hidden, and often went to the landowners demanding their freedom. At last, the manifesto emancipating the serfs arrived."[5]

When peasants were cheated of their rightful parcels of land, Katerina saw that liberal reform was ineffectual but she did not become a revolutionary right away. She opened a school for rich and poor at her parents' estate, and only slowly realized that liberal reform was not enough. Living among the intelligentsia in St. Petersburg in the early 1860s converted her to populism and doing something to help the peasants. She established another school in 1867 and in 1869 (at the age of 25) married Nikolai Breshko-Breshkovsky, a nearby liberal landowner. Catherine slowly realized that other landowners and the government itself meant to thwart the rightful distribution of land to the peasants and any improvement in their wretched lives. The flogging of countless peasant men, who simply wanted their fair share of land, convinced her of the government's cruel policies and punishments. Threatened persecution of her husband and herself for helping the peasants through a land bank further convinced her that reform was impossible. After her son was born, she reluctantly gave him to her brother and sister-in-law to raise, for she recognized that she had to become a full-time revolutionary. She describes the attitudes of those around her as follows:

> ...I thought of the warning that had been given me when I first spoke of my wish to work for the peasants. While I was still a girl, they said, 'Wait! You will get married, and that will tie you down. Your young blood will be calmed; your running brook will become a quiet lake.' And the time came when I was married, and I was conscious of no change in my spirit. I felt for the people's cause as strongly as ever—even more strongly. And then friends told me, 'Just wait, you will have an estate of your own to care for, and that will take up all your time and thoughts.' But my husband and I bought an estate, and no such result followed; for I could never let one tiny estate outweigh the vast plains of all Russia. My spirit and my convictions remained the same. And with time came new counsel from friends. Now they argued: 'Yes, you have remained unchanged by husband and home, but you will succumb to the command of Nature. With the birth of a child will come the death of your revolutionary ideals. The wings you have used for soaring high in the air among the clouds you will now use to shelter your little one.' And I gave birth to a little one. I felt that in that boy my youth was buried, and that when he was taken from my body, the fire of my spirit had gone out with him. But it was not so. The conflict between my love for the child and my love for the revolution and for the freedom of Russia robbed me of many a night's sleep. I knew that I could not be a mother and still be a revolutionist. Those were not two tasks to which it was possible to give a divided attention. Either the one or the other must

K. Bull: "Catherine Breshko Breshkovsky," St. P. 1917 (Photo Archive)

absorb one's whole being, one's entire devotion. So I gave my child to Vera and my brother, to be brought up as their own.

I was not the only one called upon to make such a sacrifice. Among the women in the struggle for Russian freedom there were many who chose to be fighters for justice rather than mothers of the victims of tyranny.[6]

Like some other gentry-class women of her generation, Breshkovsky was more committed to the revolution than family happiness. In the 1870s, she participated in the "To the People Movement," preaching the overthrow of the Tsarist government, and was arrested in 1874. Kept in solitary confinement from 1874-78, she along with 300 others was sentenced to penal servitude in Siberia for 18 years. Upon her release in 1896, she immediately returned to her propaganda work for the agrarian based Social Revolutionary Party. She went to the U.S. in 1903 to raise funds for further political activity. In 1905, her friends wanted her to remain safely in the US, but she chose to return to Russia during the 1905 Revolution. Arrested again for her participation in the Revolution, she was exiled to Siberia. Altogether she spent 11 years working for the revolution, but 31 years in penal servitude and exile. After the February Revolution of 1917, the new Provisional Government released all political and religious prisoners, and she became a revolutionary icon. But her reign was short lived due to the Bolshevik takeover in October, 1917.

Katerina knew that in the Tsarist time revolutionaries were usually caught after about 3 months activity, but this is the work she had dedicated her life to. After her release and during 1917-18, she worked for the SR Party. The triumph of the Bolsheviks as the dominant political party in 1918 resulted in her exile to Czechoslovakia, where she lived and taught until her death. She was not alone in her class or gender in wanting to improve the situation of the Russian peasants. Scores of other gentry-class women and hundreds of schoolteachers also devoted their lives to the cause of the peasantry and the SR Party, which they thought would provide a better life for the poor.[7]

Catherine Breshkovsky was not alone in dedicating her life to "the people." In the 1860s, many gentry-class women believed in sacrificing themselves to improve their society. Many became career women, believing science, medicine, and teaching were the ways to improve Russia. Still, some like Catherine Breshkovsky, Vera Figner, and Vera Zasulich chose to dedicate themselves to populist causes and radicalizing the peasants. At her trial for wounding the St. Petersburg Police Chief General Trepov in 1878, Vera Zasulich used her defense as a platform to explain why she had turned to terror as a weapon. Although she did not personally know the political prisoner Bogolyubov, who had been flogged for allegedly not doffing his cap at General Trepov, she was outraged at police brutality and decided to respond. She explained:

> I had heard that ... Bogolyubov was flogged until he stopped groaning ... that soldiers broke into the cells and dragged the protesting prisoners into the punishment cells.... Furthermore among those imprisoned at that time in the House of Prelim-

inary Detention many had already been in prison for three or three and a half years, many had become insane or killed themselves.... All this seemed to me to be not punishment but outrage ... it seemed to me that such things should not be suffered to pass without consequences. I decided that even at the price of my own ruin I had to demonstrate that such degradation of human personality should not be allowed to be inflicted with impunity.... I could find no other way of drawing attention to what had happened...It is a terrible thing to lift a hand against a human being, but I felt I had to do it ... I fired without aiming....[8]

In her book *Apostles into Terrorists*, Vera Broido argues that it was the treatment of political prisoner Bogolyubov which turned some peaceful revolutionaries into terrorists, who agreed to kill the Tsar to change the oppressive political system in Russia. After this time, a very small group of about 30 people called "the Executive Committee" decided to engage in terrorist actions, eventually in the murder of Tsar Alexander II in 1881 in their attempts to change and bring down the government. The majority of women revolutionaries however preferred sacrificing their lives to taking anyone else's.

The novel *Nigilistka* or *Nihilist Girl* by the brilliant Russian mathematician Sofia Kovalevskaya showcases a young woman who believed in self sacrifice and who married a condemned revolutionary following the famous trial of 150 Russians arrested in 1875. She married him in order to save him from incarceration and solitary confinement which usually led to death. She decided to follow him to Siberia to support the revolutionary cause in the only way that she could. Though she initially desired to become a Christian martyr, the nihilist character decides to become a martyr for the revolution instead. After being exposed to revolutionary ideas by her tutor, she adopted many of them. She tried to develop and free herself from familial and social constraints. She educated herself in order to help transform Russia. Both nihilists and populists were concerned with direct action and self sacrifice. Many gentry-class women wanted to leave stifling family life and dedicate themselves to a more worthy cause. After the death of her beloved tutor, Vera Barantsova, the heroine in *Nigilistka*, shuns high society and cares only for a "purposeful life." Vera explained that she was little concerned with personal life, but rather with social and political action. She doesn't appreciate mathematics and career women.[9] Her actions are explained to her confidant as follows:

> 'Vera, are you getting married?' I exclaimed, astonished.
>
> 'I already have! My wedding took place at one this afternoon.'
>
> 'But how can that be, Vera? Where's your husband, then?' I asked in confusion.
>
> Vera's face lit up. A blissful, exalted smile played on her lips. 'My husband's in the fortress. I married Pavlenkov.'
>
> 'What? But you didn't even know him before! How did you manage to get acquainted?'
>
> 'We're not acquainted at all. I saw him from afar at the trial, and today, a quarter of an hour before the wedding, we exchanged a few words for the first time.'
>
> 'What? What does this mean, Vera?' I asked, not understanding. 'Did you fall in love with him at first sight, the way Juliet did with Romeo? Maybe while the prosecutor was tearing into him at the trial?'
>
> 'Don't talk nonsense!' Vera interrupted me sternly.
>
> 'There can be no talk of falling in love, neither on my side nor on his. I simply married him, because I *had* to, because it was the only way to save him.!'
>
> I looked inquiringly at Vera in silence. She sat down on a corner of the divan and began telling me her story, without haste or agitation, as if she were speaking about completely simple and ordinary matters.
>
> 'You see, after the trial I had a long talk with the defense lawyers. They were all of the opinion that the situation was far from bad for all the defendants, except Pavlenkov. Of course, the schoolteacher will die in two or three months, but he wouldn't have lasted very long in any case, since he has acute tuberculosis. The others are all being sent to Siberia, but we can count on their returning to Russia, once their sentences are finished, to take up the cause again. That is not what's in store for Pavlenkov, however. His lot is definitely a sorry one, so sorry, that it would almost have been better if they had sentenced him to be shot or hanged. At least everything would be over quickly, but to spend twenty years suffering in hard labor!'

'Well, Vera, it's not as if he's the only one ever sentenced to hard labor!' I remarked timidly.

'Yes, but you see there are different kinds of hard labor. Had he been a common criminal rather than a political one, and if the prosecutor hadn't tried to make such an example of him, it would have been a different matter.... Now, if someone is sent to Siberia, he's not too distressed, knowing that while things will be hard there, in time matters will sort themselves out and he will find like-minded brothers and sisters. He won't be totally cut off and needn't lose hope. And if anyone feels too miserable, with any luck he can flee. After all, more than a few people have escaped from Siberia.[10]

Vera explains that if the government really wants to finish someone off, it sends them to the Alekseev ravelin in the Peter and Paul Fortress in St. Petersburg. There prisoners are subject to hard labor in a pit and to solitary confinement. No visits with other convicts, no letters from friends, and prisoners are forbidden to send out any news about themselves. After a few months or years, prisoners lose their minds, commit suicide, or pass away in some fashion. No one survives longer than three years in the ravelin. And this dungeon was awaiting Pavlenkov. Feeling sorry for prisoner Pavlenkov, Vera discovered that if he were married, his wife could appeal to the Emperor to follow her husband into hard labor. So the Tsar might have mercy and allow the couple to go to a life of hard labor in Siberia.

As soon as Vera heard this, she decided to appeal to the Tsar to marry Pavlenkov. She felt it was her duty to do this to save his life. She appealed to a Count, an old friend of the family and an advisor to the Tsar, to take her request to the Emperor. The Count assumed that Vera was pregnant since she waned to marry such a despicable man, and he thought that to preserve her family honor, he should help her wed the convict. So she married Pavlenkov in the Peter and Paul Fortress chapel. During the ceremony, Vera felt that she was actually espousing her first love Vasiltsev, who had died in custody before they could be united. She thought he would have approved of her action. In a way, she was doing this for him as well as for Pavlenkov and herself.[11]

Kovalevskaya's character Vera Barantsova realized that while she was not suited to go among the people as a propagandist, she could go to Siberia, make a life among the exiles there, comfort them, serve them, and send letters home for them. This is the first real work she has been able to do for the cause, and she was delighted. Pavlenkov had to walk to Siberia with other convicts, but Vera was able to leave by train and meet him in Siberia. Vera was not alone, but was in the company of two other women, going to Siberia to be with their husbands. She went willingly and happily.[12]

In the late 19th century, Russian revolutionaries saw themselves as moral and spiritual as well as political reformers of their society. For example, youthful, gentry-class Vera Figner (1852-1942) struggled whether to serve the peasants by working among them as a doctor, or by preaching revolutionary propaganda. When she finished her medical studies as a doctor's assistant in 1875, she decided to engage in political work upon her return to Russia. In the late 1870s, she combined these two interests working as a feldsher in Samara while also conducting propaganda among the peasants. Disenchanted with her ability to improve the lot of the peasants through medical treatment and harassed by government officials, she joined the Central Executive Committee of The Peoples' Will, a secret, terrorist organization dedicated to bringing down the existing order. After the arrest of many Populists, including Breshkovsky in the 1870s, some women joined secret terrorist organizations like The Peoples' Will. They thought that peaceful propaganda did not work since the peasants often turned them into the government. As a member of the Central Committee, Figner helped plan the assassination of Alexander II in 1880 and 1881. Yet she did not believe in the indiscriminate use of terror and condemned the assassination of American President Garfield, since peaceful, legal tactics for political struggle were available in the United States.

For her part in the assassination, Figner was arrested in 1889 and imprisoned in the Schlusselburg Fortress outside of St. Petersburg. Released in 1904, she lived in Europe in exile, returning to Russia in 1915. She supported feminist goals, joining in women's demonstrations to help women win the franchise and equal rights from the Provisional Government in the spring of 1917. After the Bolshevik Revolution, she did not join the Communist Party, but she did help political prisoners.[13]

While Breshkovsky and Figner were adult women when they became revolutionaries, some girls did so as teenagers during their studies at the gimnaziya or while growing up in politically radical homes. Information about women revolutionaries comes to us in a variety of ways. Some like Breshkovsky wrote their memoirs in emigration, after they had left Russia in 1918. Some women's stories come to us from third parties. An unusual source was the American journalist Marguerite Harrison who was imprisoned in Russia in 1920-21 for entering the Soviet Union illegally. In prison, she met a wide variety of women including many political prisoners—Anarchists, Mensheviks, and SRs. One she chose to write about was the SR Anna Petrovna, with whom she shared a cell in the Moscow prison of the Cheka.

Anna Petrovna resembled the profile of many other radical Russian women—she came from a revolutionary family. Her father was a Nihilist who had been shot for complicity in the assassination of Alexander II. Her mother had been arrested, imprisoned, and died of a broken heart. Anna was raised by a great aunt in the country, near Kharkov. There she grew up, exposed to the plight of the peasantry. At 16 she ran away from home to enter the University of Kharkov. She became a member of a revolutionary student group and later became a Social Revolutionary. She took part in the Revolution of 1905, escaping from Petrograd to Moscow where she hid after the upheavals of "Bloody Sunday." She lived an adventurous life as a revolutionary, but finally settled in Siberia, teaching in Zemstvo schools, after serving several terms in an Irkutsk prison for spreading revolutionary propaganda among the peasants. In Siberia, she also waited patiently for her SR love Ilya. After fifteen years apart, they were finally able to marry, but then the Cheka (forerunner of the KGB) arrested them both in 1921. After many weeks in prison, they were going to Siberia, together. They would have two weeks together in a box car as their honeymoon.[14]

Social Revolutionary Anna Petrovna's story resembles that of some Bolshevik women who became radicalized as teenagers at the gimnaziya. Their stories remind one of some young Muslim men today who are radicalized at university. In the 19th century, many male and female Russian students became politicized while in educational institutions. Some of the same issues moved these young people—vast disparities in wealth between the poor and rich in their societies and the idea of political change as a sacred idea.

2. *Social Democrats*

> One should have a goal in life! Do you understand? What kind of life is it if you don't have a goal?
>
> Tatyana Ludivinskaya, Social Democrat

The Marxist Social Democrats (RSDLP Russian Social Democratic Labor Party) was organized in the 1880s and 1890s. Georgii Plekhanov and Lenin were two of the early leaders. Lenin was exiled to Siberia and subsequently lived in Western Europe where he had more freedom to write and organize. In 1903 the Social Democrats or SD's as they were known split into two factions: Mensheviks and Bolsheviks. Martov led the Mensheviks, advocating a liberal regime modeled on European social democratic ideas. Lenin led the Bolsheviks, espousing proletarian revolution. The Mensheviks did not believe that the workers were ready to transform society through a socialist revolution. They thought a liberal democratic government would have to rule first. However, the Bolsheviks believed that under the leadership of the party and professional revolutionaries the workers could make a successful socialist revolution. Some Mensheviks were elected to and participated in the First Duma in the pre-World War period. The Bolsheviks boycotted it, but allowed delegates to be elected to the Third and Fourth Dumas. After the October Revolution, the Mensheviks found it difficult to compete against the Bolsheviks, and the Menshevik Party was outlawed in 1922. Many fled, some were arrested, some converted to Bolshevism, others died during the Stalinist purges of the 1930s.

Some of the most famous 19th century Social Democrats were Lenin's wife Nadezhda Krupskaya (1869-1939), Alexandra Kollontai (1872-1952), and Inessa Armand (1874-1920). All of them organized study groups for workers, wrote for various journals, and devoted themselves to working women. In 1903, Kollontai initially sided with the Mensheviks, becoming a Bolshevik during WW I when she and Lenin were among the few Russian socialists opposing the war.

a. Konkordia Samoilova

> It was a pleasure to look at her. She looked as if she were always ready to be of service, to plunge into her work heart and soul.
>
> Praskovia Kudelli, describing Samoilova

Among teenagers who became Bolsheviks were Klavdia Kirsanova (1888-1947), Ludmila Stahl (1872-1939) and Konkordia Samoilova (1876-1920), all of whom became politically involved during their studies at the gimnaziya. Konkordia Samoilova's story comes to us from a biography by Party member L. Katasheva in 1934. Ostensibly a hagiography, it may have also been a criticism of Stalinism since she wrote it during the Five Year Plans. She may also have meant to compare the ways of the Old Bolsheviks under Lenin with the Party in the 1930s. Who knows? Samoilova's story differed from Petrovna's in that Samoilova did not come from a revolutionary family, but a priestly one in Irkutsk. In the late 19th century, many idealistic teachers and some revolutionaries came from such families. They often smarted from the injustices they saw in Russian society and vowed to improve the lives of the downtrodden—whether peasants or workers.

While still at the gimnaziya, Samoilova came into contact with a circle of young revolutionaries. After finishing her studies, she went to St. Petersburg to study at the Bestuzhev women's courses. She intended to become a teacher, but in the 1890s revolution was in the air. Samoilova joined like minded students in demonstrations and was arrested. Indignant at the treatment of a woman prisoner, who had reportedly been raped and then burned to death, Samoilova resolved to protest against the Tsarist regime. It was then that Samoilova found her voice as an agitator and moved her comrades to demonstrate against this injustice. In 1901, she was arrested for anti-government agitation and for having a revolver. Like all good revolutionaries, she also had a copy of Chernyshevsky's novel *What is to be done?* in her room when she was arrested.[15]

Imprisoned for three months, Samoilova became an even more convinced revolutionary. In 1902 she went abroad to study and in Paris studied at the Free Russian School of Social Sciences where liberal and radical professors taught. Even Lenin gave lectures there, and she met him. Lenin and other SD's were organizing short courses for training propagandists for worker's circles in Russia, and Samoilova took these classes. She became a professional revolutionary—trained in Marxist thought as well as revolutionary practice.

In 1903, Samoilova returned to Russia to work in the Tver Social Democratic Committee, which had been decimated by arrests. Another Bolshevik Comrade Praskovia Kudelli (1859-1944) was already there. She had joined the SD's in 1903 and described Samoilova as follows:

> She was a young girl, tall, with brilliant, small brown eyes and a glowing, sun-brown complexion. Her features were irregular and the slight slant of her eyebrows gave her something of a Mongolian or Chinese appearance. The general impression was that of a pleasant and likeable person. It was a pleasure to look at her. She looked as if she were always ready to be of service, to plunge into her work heart and soul.[16]

Kudelli was an apt observer, and Samoilova plunged into revolutionary work. She worked tirelessly before and after the 1905 revolution and was arrested several times, spending many months in various prisons. In Tver, her comrades gave her the underground name "Natasha." After a long imprisonment, she was exiled to Nikolaev. She then went on to work in Odessa, and she was there during the strikes and the 1905 mutiny on the Battleship Potemkin, the subject of Eisenstein's famous film. She was disappointed in the behavior of the sailors who did nothing to help the striking workers. The sailors had been influenced by Menshevik doctrine, and Samoilova decided to go to Moscow to get clearer direction on how to work more effectively. She felt that the joint work of the Mensheviks and Bolsheviks in Odessa was counterproductive. She wrote:

> In conclusion, I will say that the very people under whose leadership I have worked for several months, whom I considered till then to be reliable leaders with sound political principles, have turned out to be incapable of coping with the situation....
>
> Cases of such instability of principles have destroyed all my belief in the local leadership and this, in connection with the above-mentioned causes, prompts me to leave the Odessa organization.[17]

Of course, life did not always go according to plan, and before "Natasha" left Odessa, she was arrested along with a long letter she had written. It came to light after the 1917 Revolution when the files of the Tsarist police were opened. After several months in prison, Samoilova was exiled to Vologda in North Russia. She then escaped to Moscow to continue to fight in the 1905 Revolution. In 1912, she worked on the Editorial Board of the Bolshevik Party paper *Pravda*, and also on the women worker's publication *Rabotnitsa*. After the death of her husband from typhus in 1919, Samoilova wanted to get away from St. Petersburg, and she went to propagandize among the oil field workers in Baku. When she encountered the obstructions of the wives of the oil workers, she then decided to raise the consciousness of women to the revolutionary cause. Both before and after the 1917 Revolution, Samoilova worked tirelessly with non-Party women, organizing courses, conferences, working women's congresses, and literacy groups to involve women in political life. Like several other devoted Party members, she died of cholera in 1920.[18]

Ludmila Stahl, another Old Bolshevik who had joined the party before the 1917 revolution, resembled Samoilova in her work and imprisonments. Stahl enthusiastically smuggled the Bolshevik paper *Iskra* from Germany to Russia, announcing: "I will carry it with me, I am not afraid....I am always lucky." Only she was not so lucky one time, when she was arrested by the customs officials and police as she tried to smuggle *Iskra* into Russia in her suitcase.[19] It seems that the worst nightmare for women revolutionaries like Stahl and Samoilova was not arrest, exile, or confinement, miserable as those conditions were, but their inability to change society while imprisoned.

b. Anna Zhukova Bek

> In all of Petersburg at that time the revolutionary mood could be felt; it was reflected as well among students.
>
> Anna Zhukova Bek

Anna Zhukova Bek tells how "revolution was in the air" in the late 1890s, when she was a student at the Women's Medical Institute. Then, she became involved in various student strikes and a

Marxist circle. Writing about her first year of medical studies in Russia, she noted:

> In all of Petersburg at that time the revolutionary mood could be felt; it was reflected as well among students. Shortly after the beginning of classes we organized a strike against the chemistry teacher, Zalessky who had made mistakes from the first lectures and did not please the students. As a result of the strike someone else replaced him.
>
> In organizing a mutual assistance fund, we came into conflict with the director. He wanted to reserve for himself the right to give out assistance. We claimed firmly that only we ourselves could figure out who was the most in need. We knew that the director's choices would be determined by political reliability. ...
>
> I gained a more serious revolutionary temperament in our Transbaikal association. Zemliachestva, associations of people from the same region for the material aid of those in need, were officially permitted in all higher education institutions. Transbaikalians, under the flag of regional association meetings, organized a Marxist circle. Among the organizers were my brothers, Innokenty and Afanasy. The meetings ran according to the following agenda:
> 1) Lecture or chapter reading from Marx's *Capital*
> 2) Discussion, debate
> 3) Tea drinking
> 4) Choral singing
>
> There was never any dancing or drinking. The songs we sang usually had a revolutionary theme...
>
> No matter how the lectures went, after them sympathy for the workers in their struggle with the capitalists stayed in one's soul. The choral singing of revolutionary songs heightened the feeling, and we dispersed after the meeting in a state of excitement. It seemed to me personally that up to that time I had been wandering in some sort of fog; now Marxism gave me solid ground under my feet.[20]

In her fourth year, Anna became involved in a student strike to support students in Kiev. She served on the strike committee, and as a result when she was preparing to take her final exams, she was visited by the police and told to leave St. Petersburg and go home to Siberia. When she complained that she didn't have the money to leave immediately, she was informed that she could pick up a ticket from the gendarme station the following day. All the ringleaders in various institutions were expelled from their studies that spring.[21] A convinced Marxist, Anna Zhukova Bek remained marginally politically active until the 1920s.

c. Maria Golubeva

> I entered the university and engaged in active propaganda work among my comrades, seeking to attract them to revolutionary activities. I was expelled from the university. I then began propagandizing among the soldiers...
>
> Maria Golubeva

Some women teachers like Maria Golubeva and Ludmila Gromozova gave up their teaching posts to become Social Democrats at the turn of the century. Like Samoilova, Golubeva came from a revolutionary family and became further radicalized at the university. She remarked:

> I had an ideal upbringing—in the sense that truth was never hidden from me and that I was taught to love truth from an early age. My father was exiled for defending truth. It was with difficulty that I completed high school because I found the lies and falsehoods there so hateful. I entered the university and engaged in active propaganda work among my comrades, seeking to attract them to revolutionary activities. I was expelled from the university. I then began propagandizing among the soldiers...[22]

Golubeva had one of those marriages where her husband was a liberal, while she was a more radical Marxist. Her husband, who had earlier been exiled to Siberia for his political work, sought peace and quiet, while Maria accepted a life of struggle. He placed his hopes on legal forms of resistance, but she on revolution and the Social Democratic Party. That was how their paths diverged.[23]

Golubeva willingly sacrificed her husband and children to her party work when she felt she had to. In some ways, Golubeva's marriage resembled those of earlier revolutionaries like Breshkovsky and Kollontai.

Others who belonged to and sympathized with the Social Democrats in the late 19th and early 20th centuries included Cecilia Bobrovskaya (1876-1960), Eva Broido (1876-1941), Klavdia Kirsanova, Ludmila Stahl (1872-1939), and Tatiana Ludvinskaia (1887-1976). Women writers who at times supported the Social Democrats included Elizabeth Dmitrieva, Olga Forsh, Marietta Shaginian, Olga Shapir, and Anastasia Verbitskaia. Each woman had a different story, but Kirsanova's break with her mother over her work for the party was especially poignant.

d. Klavdia Kirsanova

At one point, Kirsanova tells a comrade:

> I envy you...It is quite different at my house. My mother is kind, very kind, but there are eight of us children, and she can barely manage. She doesn't understand me. She keeps shouting: 'If you continue you will end up in a forced labour camp! Think of the disgrace that will bring to our family. Who will marry your sisters, if you become a criminal?'... I feel sorry for her, but what can I do....[24]

After arrests in 1906, 1907, and 1908, Klavdia Kirsanova was sentenced to several years exile in Siberia. Her mother grieved at Klavdia's departure in 1913, but finally understood her daughter's political commitment. The day of her departure for Siberia, Klavdia saw her mother from a distance making the sign of the cross over her, and she felt reconciled seeing her mother after four years of imprisonment. With the aid of friends, her mother was able to get a small bundle to Klavdia.[25] This meant a lot to both of them. Although she was doomed to exile, Kirsanova rejoiced to be out of a cell and on a train.

Looking at Russian Criminal Statistics, it is hard to interpret how many women were actually arrested for political crimes. Statistics for the year 1904 suggest that less than 2,000 had been arrested for crimes against government order, presumably a political crime. Ordinary crimes like theft (2,600) exceeded those violating government order. While the total number of women arrested in 1905 seemed to be 36,000, about 5,000 were in prison on January 1st, 1906. The average daily number arrested for all crimes was 4,900. While half of those arrested for stealing were acquitted, only 25% of those arrested for crimes against government order were freed. Of the 75% condemned, most were imprisoned. So the female revolutionaries we read about were frequently arrested, imprisoned, and then escaped. Their numbers may have been small, but still they were a substantial proportion of the total number of women political activists.[26]

e. Ludmila Stahl

In her memoirs, Ludmila Stahl relates another story of revolutionary women—about how hard it was living in exile, away from one's native land and language. She had been expelled from her gimnaziya as a teenager in 1899 and went to France to finish her education. In Paris she studied to be a midwife, but was arrested upon her return to Russia in 1901. Although she escaped, she was rearrested in 1902 and 1906, so fled to France again and lived in exile until the 1917 February Revolution. Her writings tell something of the despair that revolutionaries battled with. At times she grew tired of the struggles against ambushes, fears of arrest, nights at secret hiding places, and fears about jeopardizing those who provided shelter.

In France during WW I, she spoke against the war and workers becoming cannon fodder for the capitalists. At one point, she realized that the police were becoming too interested in her, and she knew that soon she would have to move to another city and another country. After almost 10 years in exile, she was at long last able to return home to her native land in February, 1917. How long she had waited for that hour. In exile she had contributed to the cause more than if she had remained in a Russian prison. Indeed, she had assisted countless Russian political prisoners, sent money for the needs of the revolution, worked on the editorial board of Bolshevik publications, and had given every hour of every day to Russia. So going home was an emotional experience, and years of discipline could not prevent her tears when returning.[27]

f. Tatyana Ludvinskaya

> And you, it turns out, are a coward! You wanted to play at revolution!
>
> Ludvinskaya to a sympathizer

The utter fearlessness of these women revolutionaries is seen in their smuggling political literature into Russia when even gypsies refused to do this difficult task. After the 1905 Revolution, the border guards and customs officials became more brutal. Speaking with a gypsy who had helped hide some Bolshevik literature in the woods, Tatyana Ludvinskaya rebuked him:

> What's wrong then, Yegor? A person decides for himself what path to follow....One should have a goal in life! Do you understand? What kind of life is it if you don't have a goal? ...
>
> Yegor replied: Stop singing the same old song, my pretty one.... We do not know you politicos, so please leave us alone. As it is, I almost got my head cracked open at the gypsy camp when they smelled the kind of work I had agreed to do. Give us the ordinary goods, to smuggle—tobacco, perfume, stockings... Your booklets will only get us hard labour. If they do seize us, no bribe to the customs officials will help. The fools are afraid and don't take bribes.... Customs officials are like wolves: they try to skin three hides off gypsies. They are greater thieves than a vicious bandit. In the case of ordinary goods gypsies can always bribe the customs officials with a gift: please accept it, do not disdain it, patron. ....
>
> But if they find out a gypsy has begun to smuggle booklets—then you'll go to prison without a word. They'll read you some kind of papers and put you in irons. Good-bye freedom! To Siberia with a shaved head! Even money won't help. No, booklets are a hopeless thing and a real gypsy won't take that kind of work, my pretty one.

Then what about you?
The devil has drawn me into this thing! ... I'm too greedy for money![28]

Tatyana understood the gypsy but felt contempt for Russian radicals, who feared retribution from the authorities for helping them. She tells the story of trying to find refuge one night when police agents were on her trail. She went to a dentist she knew, thinking he would help her, but he turned away, saying:

"My dear lady, how could you allow yourself to come looking the way you do? I deeply regret that you have taken advantage of my good will."

Tatyana realized that he was turning her away and thought "so much for a liberal, a so-called sympathizer!" He knew the police were looking for her, and that she would probably be arrested if she returned to the street. So she shouted at him:

"And you, it turns out, are a coward! You wanted to play at revolution!"[29]

Instead of the dentist, it was his poor cook who came to Tatyana's rescue, arguing:

> It's a sin, sir, not to provide refuge, for one's fellow creatures... Anyway, my dear, do not grieve! God will forgive him....Let us go. My sister-in-law lives in the basement. They are simple folk and will take you in. You will be able to warm yourself, drink some tea, and dry out your clothes. You could catch pneumonia this way![30]

Describing a Bolshevik Party meeting in Finland in 1907, Ludvinskaya tells about the intrigue and subterfuge that party members engaged in to arrive on different trains and in different coaches of the same train. At this meeting, she met her old friend from the Odessa underground, Rosalia Zemliachka. It had been dangerous to meet in St. Petersburg because there were too many spies and police snooping around. Ludvinskaia also managed to inject some humor into her memoirs by recounting her meeting with Lenin. He did not make himself known to her, but let her think he was simply another comrade.[31]

g. Cecilia Bobrovskaya

> We carried on propaganda in workers' circles, executed all the technical duties of printing leaflets, hiding and distributing literature, obtaining headquarters for secret meetings.
>
> Cecilia Bobrovskaya

One of the most thorough accounts of underground political activity comes from Old Bolshevik Cecilia Bobrovskaya (1876-1960) who joined the SD's in the 1890s. From Vitebsk, Cecilia decided to become a revolutionary in 1894 after reading Chernyshevsky's *What is to be Done*? In Warsaw, Cecilia worked and tried unsuccessfully to organize her shop mates. She was drawn into underground revolutionary work, and then she went to Vienna in 1896 to study midwifery so that she could work in Russia proper and conduct underground work. While a student in Vienna, Cecilia went to Switzerland on a holiday with a friend, and there she met SD leaders Plekhanov, Zasulich, Axelrod, Bebel, Kautsky, and Bernstein. Eventually, Cecilia decided to go to Kharkov to work. As a midwife, her passport no longer read "valid only where Jews are permitted to live," i.e. the Pale of Settlement along the border regions. Her new one said "Jewish midwife, so and so, has the right to live in any part of Russia."[32]

In Kharkov, Cecilia devoted herself more to political work than to studying to take her exam n midwifery. Joining the RSDLP in 1898, she was such a true believer that she almost starved to death serving it. As she noted in her book *Twenty Years in Underground Russia*:

> The local organization was a well-knit nucleus of revolutionary workers, although it had not yet assumed definite organizational shape and did not even have a definite name. We carried on propaganda in workers' circles, executed all the technical duties of printing leaflets, hiding and distributing literature, obtaining headquarters for secret meetings. We organized illegal gatherings at which reports and lectures on political and economic themes were made. We arranged concerts, plays and other lucrative undertakings from which we obtained the funds to run our organization as well as to support strikers or comrades who had been arrested.

It never occurred to us that we ought to help not only arrested comrades, but also the comrades who were busy all day with organizational affairs and who were literally starving. Many of us, having no definite occupation and receiving no regular help from home, suffered very severely. I can say for myself that in Warsaw and partly in Vienna I had become quite an adept at going short. But trained as I was, what I endured in Kharkov, proved more than I could bear. There were many days when I had nothing but a drink of water. I had no money with which to buy a piece of bread, let alone buy a dinner. All day long I would go about the necessary business; my legs would give way under me, my head would spin. On such days it was particularly distressing to be looking for an apartment for secret meeting purposes or in which to hide illegal literature....During those times of intense hunger I would be in utter despair. I would rather die than give up Party work and daily intercourse with the comrades; yet if I looked for employment it would mean that I would have to give up my Party work and become occupied with something that I neither knew nor liked. I hated midwifery. In all my future life I never helped a single infant to come into the world.

Sickness rescued me from this systematic starvation. The doctor stated that my illness was due to starvation. This diagnosis startled my comrades. When I recovered, work was immediately found for me in a Zemstvo library. The work was very simple and I was paid by the day—two rubles a day. Besides, I soon found out that the Zemstvo library could be used for revolutionary purposes, so that my spirits completely recovered.[33]

Unbeknownst to Cecilia, she had been spied on the entire summer of 1900, and along with 200 other party workers she was arrested and imprisoned in Kharkov. After four months, many of the arrested were let go, but the organizers like Cecilia were detained. Protesting, Cecilia decided to conduct a hunger strike, and after 3 days the prison authorities let her leave because they did not want the other prisoners to learn of her strike and wage one too. About this period, she wrote:

> Thus I paid for a full year's work in Kharkov with less than a full year's imprisonment, which was considered a very cheap price at that time.[34]

While in solitary confinement, Cecilia had decided to become a professional Party worker. Not waiting for her sentence to be pronounced in her home town where she had been exiled, she decided to escape abroad and live illegally. Abroad, she met others who had escaped from a prison in Kiev. Altogether there had been 64 persons—51 men and 13 women, a common gender ratio in the revolutionary movement. After a few months in exile, Cecilia couldn't resist the desire to return to Russia to work in the underground in Kostroma. Spied upon there, Cecilia decided to go to St. Petersburg and ask for a replacement worker. But she was arrested and imprisoned in St. Petersburg. Still, compared with her time in Kharkov prison, her detention in St. Petersburg was much easier. She had a bath and a comfortable bed to sleep on, polished floors, a neat little room, and women warders who grumbled occasionally but who were not brutes like those in Kharkov. Released from prison pending sentencing, Cecilia chose Tver as her temporary residence. There she worked as a clerk in a Zemstvo insurance department. In Tver, Cecelia arranged for a printing press and worked among the 25,000 workers and their circles in the Morozov textile mills. Eventually, the Tver police became suspicious of Cecilia and her place was raided. Not wanting to be imprisoned again, Cecilia and some others went abroad once again to study and find out about the break between the Mensheviks and Bolsheviks that they had heard about.[35]

Cecilia's greatest disappointment in her underground work seemed to be that just when she organized an area and got a printing press set up, it would be discovered and they would have to dismantle it and take it to other places, thus interrupting the work of printing leaflets and newspapers. Describing one such incident, she wrote:

> I cannot recollect just what we managed to print but I can only say that the printshop did not last very long. Shortly after it was established the comrades who worked there noticed that they were being followed, and we had to dismantle our printshop which we had set up with so much trouble....Thus we struggled all summer—packing and unpacking, printing in snatches when fortune smiled.[36]

This happened over and over again. It was quite dispiriting. At times Cecilia was able to set up a book store to sell "legal" materials, but even these would soon attract the attention of the police and be closed as she notes:

> The closing of the book store was a big blow to all of us, and to me in particular. My work as secretary became doubly hard—I had to search for premises for every meeting, consultation, etc. In other words I had to appeal to the so-called sympathizers— a task which I always disliked. Our second apartment, the textile union, was also subjected to frequent raids by the police. Besides, the Cossacks became more truculent and broke up our meetings. To crown it all, spies began to follow us Party workers. I was so persistently shadowed that it became impossible for me to carry on any further work in Kostroma, and I could not even leave the city without being observed.[37]

She was excited about the revolutionary events of 1905, and she and her husband were both freed from prison by workers. However, the joy did not last long because the Tsarist government began cracking down on legal trade unions and political parties in 1907, and workers and revolutionaries became dispirited by 1910-1911. Initially hopeful of a general strike in Ivanovo-Voznesensk in 1907 due to the horrendous exploitation of the workers, she was disappointed when the Party called off the strike fearing that it would not succeed since those in nearby towns had failed. In all areas, the textile workers were overworked, underpaid, and subject to cruel fines. The workers desired an 8 hour day, higher wages, and an abolition of fines. But the vigilant police and Cossacks made even a May Day demonstration impossible. While planning the May Day event, she and other Party members and workers were attacked in the woods, beaten and robbed by the Cossacks.[38]

Arrested again in 1908, Cecilia noticed that the prisons had improved considerably since the Revolution. She recalled that they were "so free in prison that we hated to remain there. Life was so boring that one day the prisoners created a disturbance, broke windows, and swore at the officials. The result was that we were taken to different prisons."[39] Once again she was sentenced to exile in Vologda. After 2 years she was released and decided to go to Moscow. The Party organization in Moscow was a shambles in 1911, and everyone depressed. She had a sickly son, and Party work seemed impossible so she decided to attend Shanyavsky University to meet comrades and obtain a proper education. Cecilia was unimpressed by her "bourgeois" professors who criticized Marxist ideas, but she thought the university a good place to conduct propaganda. Soon her circle was infiltrated with spies and provocateurs, and many of the plans they made came to naught since the police arrested the Party leaders. So ended her memoir on the eve of WW I, the February and October Revolutions.

h. Vera Broido

> Among political exiles in Siberia the grapevine worked perfectly: they always knew whom to expect and when and even what the newcomers would be bringing by way of books and journals, and letters from friends and relatives. And each time there was an air of celebration.
>
> Vera Broido, Siberian Exile

A rather charming account of life in exile during WW I comes to us from the daughter of Menshevik Eva Broido (1876-1941). Eva and her husband Mark had been exiled to Siberia in 1901, and Eva was exiled again for opposing World War One. She and two of her children were exiled to Krasnoyarsk and then to Minusinsk. Treatment of political prisoners had improved under the Tsarist system, and Eva and her two children were allowed to travel in an ordinary train instead of a prison van. They had to pay for their own tickets, but it was a vast improvement over the long walk that prisoners made by foot in the mid 19th century. Eva Broido and her two youngest children Vera and Danya traveled in a compartment of the Trans-Siberian Railroad. The children enjoyed looking out the windows, seeing the Ural mountains, and the hubbub of the station rests. As Vera remembered it:

> It took three weeks to Krasnoyarsk and the end of our journey. On the platform a number of men and women, immediately recognizable as political exiles, were waiting for the new arrivals. Newly arriving exiles were always eagerly awaited and warmly welcomed....Now we in our turn were at once surrounded and helped and escorted to the home of one of the

exiles, where (it had already been decided) we were to lodge. Among political exiles in Siberia the grapevine worked perfectly: they always knew whom to expect and when and even what the newcomers would be bringing by way of books and journals, and letters from friends and relatives. And each time there was an air of celebration.

Krasnoyarsk was the residence of the governor of western Siberia and it was at his discretion that the place of exile in his region was allocated. After several days of waiting Mother was told that she was being sent to Kuragino, a village in the district of Minusinsk, not far from the village where Lenin had lived some fourteen years earlier. Both Lenin and we were lucky to be sent to that area, for it had an excellent climate. Had we been sent northwards we might well have landed, like so many exiles, in the terrible swamps of Turukhansk. That is what happened to Martov and it ruined his health.

We boarded a river steamer for Minusinsk, to spend five days and nights on the Yenisey River, so wide that at times when we were hugging one shore we could not see the other....

At the quay in Minusinsk there were again friends and comrades to welcome Mother; too many for me to know one from the other. And a few days later we were off again, in a horse-drawn carriage, for a day's drive to the village of Kuragino. There was only one political exile here but he had been warned to expect us and to rent a house for us. We entered the village through a barrier and found ourselves in a wide street. This was our first view of a Siberian village—prosperous, clean, wide-spaced. The houses were all of the same pattern: broad-fronted *izby* (long cabins) with large, ornately carved and gaily painted window frames and pots of bright red geraniums on the windows sills. The houses were separated from each other by wide, tall, solid wooden gates. And most of the houses had wooden benches in front.[40]

The Broido family were provided a house of their own, furnished with simple, solid furniture. The kitchen was equipped and there was a bath-house and several outhouses and barns and sheds. Recalling their situation, Vera wrote:

> In most respects it was like any other Russian peasant kitchen, only cleaner and lighter. But then we had never before

lived in a peasant house, so it was rather thrilling to have one of our own.... Thus when the oven was lit, it not only served to cook and to bake but also to heat the kitchen and even the next room. It was particularly cosy on top of the *pech'* where the old and the sick and the very young habitually slept. ...

There was no lack of space in the house. We each had the luxury of a separate room and Mother had a large table for her study. The young man helped us to distribute our belongings and then showed us around. It turned out that my brother and I had overlooked the most delightful feature of the house; a trap door from the larder next to the kitchen led, down a steep ladder, into a large, very cold stone cellar with many shelves.[41]

Luckily for them, their landlord provided them some food and even invited them to dinner the first day. Recalling this time later, Vera described it in the following words:

I remember the summer in Kuragino as nearly idyllic. Mother was always there, either sharing our domestic chores and meals or working at her desk. She was translating a book (or was it articles?) by John Maynard Keynes and rushing to finish it, to be paid. This was indeed vital, as there was no way of earning anything in Kuragino and the state allowance for political prisoners was not enough to cover our rent.[42]

However, this idyll lasted only a year because Eva Broido found it difficult to find work in Kuragino. She and her family then moved to the nearby town of Minusinsk, where Eva found work in a dispensary. As Vera remembered it:

Minusinsk was a small market town, dwarfed by the vast River Yenisey on which it stood. But it was a thriving little place. The administrative centre of an enormous region, it was equipped with banks, commercial offices, hospitals and schools. Political exiles were able to find jobs in all of these. And political exiles were numerous, in fact they formed a large and colourful colony. Political disagreements faded in exile, to be replaced by solidarity and mutual respect. All ages and all shades of dissent were represented, from Anarchists and Social Revolutionaries to Bolsheviks and Mensheviks. Some were exiled for life, others for many years, others again had already many years of exile behind them.

Mother often took me to visit the most celebrated of all the exiles Yekaterina Breshko-Breshkovskaya. A living legend, she was venerated far beyond her own *Narodniki* (Populist) Party. She had been born into a family of prosperous landed gentry and had married into the same class. In the 1860s, she and her husband had enthusiastically supported the government-sponsored movement for rural development; but tiring of the slow and frustrating work of founding and running village schools, hospitals, and dispensaries, she had left her husband to join the clandestine revolutionary movement. Repeatedly arrested, she became the first woman to be sentenced to hard labour in the Siberian gold mines. Now she was once again in Siberian exile. When I met her she was a grey-haired old lady with humorous eyes and a spirit as indomitable as ever. In 1917 she was to be hailed as 'the grandmother of the Revolution.'[43]

The Broidos' exile ended with the February Revolution, and they all returned to Petrograd to participate in the new, freer life.

B. Feminists

> Woman would never again forfeit her rights to education, to her own life, to her own heart, to choose the time when SHE wants to have children, to make her life according to her own plans, and not by the plans of men. And soon the world would see which was truly higher man, with his rude and vulgar mind and dark soul, or woman, with her sensitivity, humanity and emotion.
>
> Nina Krylova, Novelist & Feminist

Another politically active group of Russian women who are not as well known as the revolutionaries, are the feminists. An especially good account of them is found in Rachelle Goldberg Ruthchild's *Equality and Revolution: Women's Rights in the Russian Empire 1905-1917*. Ruthchild argues that Russian feminists achieved their goal of suffrage in 12 short years of struggle, a remarkable achievement compared to the 70 year fight that British and American women needed to gain the vote.

After the Russian Revolution of 1905, Russian feminists founded societies such as The Union of Equal Rights of Women (1905-08), the Women's Progressive Party (1907-18), the Russian League of Equal Rights for Women (1907-18), St. Petersburg Women's Club, Union of Russian women (1907-18), First All Russian Congress for Women's Education, and a variety of feminist journals. Women from all the leading political parties as well as philanthropists and others joined feminist groups.

Some of the most active in these organizations and journals included Maria Chekhova (1866-1934 Educator and Feminist Editor), Liubov Gurevich (1866-1940 Writer and Publicist), Countess Sofia V. Panina (1871-1956 Philanthropist, Social Reformer, and Constitutional Democrat), Dr. Maria I. Pokrovskaia (1852-1921 Feminist Publisher and Physician), Anna N. Shabanova (1848-1932 Philanthropist), Anna Filosofova (1837-1912 Philanthropist), and Ariadna V. Tyrkova (1869-1962 Constitutional Democrat Party). Pokrovskaia published the woman's journal *Women's Herald* and lead the Women's Progressive Party. Liberal feminist writers included Olga Shapir (1850-1916), who belonged to the Russian Women's Mutual Philanthropic Society, a moderate feminist group founded in the 1890s; liberal Kadet Party supporter after the 1905 Revolution Ariadna Tyrkova; and socialist feminists like Maria Chekhova and Liubov Gurevich, who published articles and pamphlets supporting civil liberties and women's rights after the 1905 Revolution. Most feminists supported charitable works, social welfare and divorce reform since political parties were not legal until after the 1905 Revolution.[44]

Many feminist writings show long term commitment to women's rights. Anna Filosofova remarked at the time of the Women's Congress of 1908:

> In my youth I had the pleasure of witnessing the emancipation of the serfs, and now, in the twilight of my life, I am witness to the liberation of women.[45]

Feminists generally sought equality and dignity as the following quotation of Filosofova shows:

Superficially, feminism seems narrow, professional, as if women were egotistically busy with their personal affairs, competing with men. But that, of course, is not so. The real issue is the dignity of the individual, about her right to self-determination, about the manifestation of her inherent abilities and talents.[46]

There were socialist feminists as well as liberal ones. In 1910, the Populist Vera Levandovskaya Belokonskaya appealed to Russian men to grant women the right to vote and equal rights generally. She touchingly pleaded:

Brothers, fathers, comrades
When you sit at the noisy table
On the holiday of freedom
Proudly lifting your glasses high—
Remember us, and look around you!
Can your celebration be truly complete
If next to you the chains are clanking
If next to you, under the yoke of injustice
Silent, and with bitter tears your sisters stand![47]

Expressing her surprise at male prejudice and intransigence at granting women equal rights after the 1905 Revolution, but before the February 1917 Revolution, Ariadna Tyrkova recalled in her memoirs:

I never suspected that the time was near when I would give many speeches, lecture, write articles, advocate women's rights: political, economic, simply human. At that moment I believed so in my equality with men that it never occurred to me to prove it. Later when I really came into contact with politicians, I saw with amazement and indignation that much still needed to be proven.[48]

Solidarity among women occurred between mothers and daughters as well as among friends. Feminist organizations in the early 20th century drew university students as well as wives and mothers into their ranks. Ekaterina Chekhova tells about working for women's rights with her journalist/feminist mother Maria Chekhova. In her unpublished memoirs, she writes:

... as a fourteen year old girl I participated in a marvelous event: the organization of the Russian Union. I was in the very laboratory of that work. I had the thrilling feeling that we, my mother and I, had touched the wheels of history. I say we because I was my mother's ardent helper in this work.[49]

Politically, feminism made some strange bedfellows. Some Bolsheviks like Lenin's sister Elizabeta Ulianova and Alexandra Kollontai, who usually inveighed against feminism, still insisted on women's fundamental equal rights. Remarking on the right of women to vote in the spring of 1917, Ulianova maintained that woman

> ... needs the right to participate equally with men in elections, the right to be elected to the Constituent Assembly, to city councils and to district and rural organizations. She needs the right to study and hold all government positions for which she is qualified, and to receive equal pay.[50]

Echoing the contribution of women workers a month earlier, Kollontai asked in the Bolshevik paper *Pravda* in March, 1917,

> Weren't we women first out on the streets? Why now...does the freedom won by the heroic proletariat of both sexes, by the soldiers and soldiers wives, ignore half the population of liberated Russia?[51]

Most feminist goals had been reached in the spring and summer of 1917 when the Provisional Government extended the franchise to women and removed judicial and legal restrictions against them. Women had precipitated the February Revolution in celebrating International Women's Day in February and had persuaded their male colleagues and co-workers to join with them in huge marches which brought down the monarchy. Lacking a clear answer to the question of women's right to vote and civil equality, Feminists organized another demonstration March 19, 1917, to grant them equal pay and perks in the civil service as well as the same titles as men. As the summer wore on, many of them became fiercely patriotic and supported the continued war effort of the Provisional Government. These patriotic feminists were interesting in that many began as pacifists during the Russo-Japanese War, but became more bellicose during WW I as men began deserting the front and the Women's Battalion of Death was organized. Examples of feminists who changed from pacifism to patriotic support of the war effort were Dr. Maria Pokrovskaia and Ariadna Tyrkova.

Doctor Poliksena Shishkina-Iavein, head of the League for Women's Equality, appealed to Russian women to patriotically support the war effort. She argued:

> We women have to unite: and each of us, forgetting personal misfortune and suffering, must come out of the narrow confines of the family and devote all our energy, intellect, and knowledge to our country. This is our obligation to the fatherland, and this will give us the right to participate as the equals of men in the new life of a victorious Russia.[52]

Women of all classes responded to this clarion call. Gentry-class women, who knew how to ride or to fly joined the Russian cavalry and air force. Most served as nurses. Some drove ambulances.[53]

Elena Iost overflowed with sentimental patriotism, begging the Tsar to let her join the army. She invoked the historical precedent of Nadezhda Durova, writing:

> I pray to Your Imperial Majesty to allow me to join the ranks of the troops with the same kind of noble and radiant outburst for the MOTHERLAND, with which the heart of Durova was filled and with which my own soul, filled with courage and fearlessness and unwomanly boldness, burns...When I hear soldiers' song or see troops (the cavalry, I so, so love horses), I am transformed, everything inside brightens and rejoices, and at the sight of dashing soldiers my soul wants to leap out of my body, and I want to be among them and also be a defender of the Motherland, the sacred, dear, and unceasingly loved Motherland.[54]

A good description of feminist response to the war in the summer of 1917 is found in Laurie Stoff's *They Fought for the Motherland: Russia's Women Soldiers in World War I and the Revolution*. She argues that many middle-class women volunteered to serve in special women's battalions because they thought it would provide an "opportunity to prove themselves worthy of greater rights and responsibilities in public life by demonstrating their self-sacrifice to the nation." Their entrance into combat would be a "great advancement in the struggle for sexual equality, allowing them to enter a realm previously impenetrable by their sex." Feminist and soldier Nina Krylova's views are presented in a historical novel thus:

> Those of us who possessed knowledge of culture, began to feel more clearly that we women had already begun to withstand an unexpected historical test, and that even in the military sphere, the centuries-old prerogative of the male sex, we cannot be inferior. If not in physical force, then in organizational and spiritual strength....And indeed, what of male objectives? Haven't they kept us from studying, from advancing, haven't they kept us only as mothers, housekeepers, and dependent slaves? How is it possible to advance to enrich one's mind and one's spirit, when it is normal for a girl to be forced at eighteen to marry and reproduce—to have a child every year and a half?...But the revolution had already occurred—woman had won for herself the rights of which she had been derived during the course of millennia—THE RIGHTS OF AN EQUAL MEMBER OF SOCIETY.[55]

Generally, what Krylova and other feminists were arguing was women's moral superiority. They wanted to supplant and shame the soldiers at the front who were deserting their duty. Many feminists agreed with some of the leaders of the Provisional Government that the only way to win the war was to encourage the male troops into fighting harder. General Brusilov created special shock units to lead the regular troops into battle. He wanted to bring units from the rear, involving civilian volunteers. A Women's Volunteer Committee organized "women's war-work detachments." To employ women in auxiliary military functions, as telephonists, drivers, clerks, topographers, and medics. They believed that women had a special role in the effort to revitalize the army and that they had a great moral influence that men felt. One appeal read as follows:

> Women citizens, all to whom the freedom and happiness of Russia is dear, hurry into our ranks—hurry while it is still not too late to stop the collapse of our dear motherland. By directly participating in military activity, we women citizens must raise the spirit of the army and carry out educational-agitational work in its ranks, so as to convey a logical understanding of the duty of free citizens to the homeland.[56]

Several feminist groups became involved in these activities and lobbied the government to create a Women's War Work Commission within the Ministry of War. Publications of Russian heroines of the past and of Nadezhda Durova's memoir about her life as an officer in the Napoleonic War appeared in bookstores all over the country to raise women's patriotic fervor. It was a short step in the spring of 1917 to the creation of a Women's Battalion of Death under the leadership of Maria Botchkareva to shame men into continued fighting against the Germans.[57]

A poem urging women near Novgorod to join the women's battalions echoed similar views in May, 1917:

> Arise brave women!
> Take the bayonets from the hands of men,
> And show them quickly
> How life must be given for the children.
> The country has forgotten the honor of soldiers,
> They run in the blood of the homeland
> They take up places in the huts at the washtubs
> Behind our women's backs.
> They are cowards, they are afraid
> To defend us with their bayonets.
> They have already made peace with the enemy,
> To become his hired hands.
> Arise then for your freedom,
> While it is not too late to fight.
> You can bring happiness to the people,
> Let the men do the washing.[58]

Some Russian women were patriotic, but didn't belong to any political party. Poet Marina Tsvetaeva remarked in a questionnaire that she did not belong to any political movement. Like the artist Anna Ostruomova Lebedeva, Tsvetaeva eschewed political parties, even openly feminist ones at the time of the 1917 revolutions. Two other artists Natalya Goncharova and Olga Rozanova also shunned feminist politics, but depicted anti-war scenes in their woodcuts executed during WW I. Goncharova returned from France when WW I began, and during the war she made lithographs for a book entitled *Mystical Images of War*. Both Goncharova's and Rozanova's pictures of WW I mark them as patriots, but anti-war. Rozanova's anti-war graphics appeared in Alexei Kruchenykh's *War*, 1916.

Soldiers at the front opposed shock troops—male and female—and did not welcome the Women's Battalion of Death. So, the Provisional Government's war policies failed, and when the Bolsheviks took over, they dismissed the women's units. After the Bolsheviks took over in 1917-18, many feminists left Russia because the new

Natalya Goncharova, *Mystical Images of the War*, Lithograph, 1914

Natalya Goncharova, Mystical Images of the War, Lithograph, 1914

government excluded bourgeois, gentry-class, and priestly families from voting, being elected, or pursuing higher education.[59]

C. Peasant Political Activity

> The smashing and looting of estates began, accompanied by fires; and one of the first estates attacked was that of our neighbor, Priklonsky. They were looking for him and apparently wanted to kill him. Only ashes were left of his house.
>
> Elena Skrjabina, *Coming of Age in the Revolution*

According to revolutionary Catherine Breshkovsky, beginning in the 1860s, Russian peasants began to believe that the land was theirs since they farmed it. They waited impatiently for the Emancipation Proclamation of 1861, but when it came they thought something had been withheld from them when they only received meager plots of land instead of all the land they had traditionally farmed. The government appointed arbiters to persuade the peasants that the land they were given was all they were entitled to, but the peasants didn't believe them. According to Breshkovsky who then lived in the countryside, when the arbiters failed, troops were sent in. As she describes it:

> Then troops were quartered in their huts, families were starved, old people were beaten by drunkards, daughters were raped. The peasants grew more wild and then began the flogging. In a village near ours, where they refused to leave their plots, they were driven into line on the village street; every tenth man was called out and flogged with the knout; some died. Two weeks later, as they still held out, every fifth man was flogged. The poor ignorant creatures still held desperately to what they thought their rights; again the line, and now every man was dragged forward to the flogging. This process went on for five years all over Russia, until at last, bleeding and exhausted; the peasants gave in.
>
> I heard heartrending stories in my little schoolhouse, and many more through my father, the arbiter of our district. The peasants thronged to our house day and night. Many were carried in, crippled by the knout. Sobbing wives told of husbands killed before their eyes. Often the poor wretch literally groveled clasping my father's knees, begging him to read the manifesto again and find it was a mistake, beseeching him to search for help in that mysterious region, the law court. From such interviews he came to me worn and haggard.
>
> I now saw how ineffectual were my attempts; I felt that tremendous economic and political changes must be made; but I was still a Liberal and thought only of reform, not revolution.[60]

After decades of such treatment by the government and society, Russia's peasants rose up in the revolutions of 1905 and 1917. Russian peasant women became more politically active during the Russo-Japanese War of 1905-6 and again during the Revolutions of 1917. Losses at the front, agricultural strikes, and the take over of manor houses in the countryside in 1905 increased their political awareness. To protect themselves, peasant men often urged their women to form the vanguard of attacks against the gentry-class estates in seizing food, wood, and clothing. Great poverty and land hunger drove both men and women to take matters into their own hands. While the peasants constituted 85% of the population, they owned only one third of the land. Both men and women believed that land belonged to those who tilled it. In 1905, the Peasant Union declared:

> "Land was created by the Holy Spirit, and therefore should not be bought and sold...it is not necessary to pay compensation to anyone." It did not matter how the Tsar and landlords had obtained the land; it was their right to have it and to take it. Their slogan often became "Land to those who work it."

Even in the late 19th century, there were some altercations between parish priests and peasants about the use and ownership of land. Villagers asserted that land was "lent" to the parish priest for his use, but really belonged to the commune. The church hierarchy and government however, usually supported the priest's legal right to the land even if he did not farm it. By 1905, the Peasant Union endorsed the take over of church and monastery land, as well as landlord and crown land.[61]

The Social Democrat Kollontai observed peasant women's activity during the Russo Japanese War and noted:

> This political awakening of women was, moreover, not limited to the urban poor. For the first time in Russia, the Russian peasant woman also raised her voice persistently and resolutely. The end of 1904 and the whole of 1905 is a period of continuous 'petticoat rebellions', sparked off by the war against Japan. All the horrors and deprivations, all the social and economic ills that stemmed from this ill-fated war, weighed down on the peasant woman, wife and mother. The conscription of reserves placed a double burden of work and worry on her already overloaded shoulders, and forced her, hitherto dependent and fearful of everything that lay beyond the circle of her domestic interests, to meet face to face previously unsuspected hostile forces, and to become consciously aware of all her humiliation and deprivation, drain to the last drop the whole bitter cup of unmerited wrongs....The total lack of rights that was the peasant's lot, the lies and injustice of the existing social order, stood in all their naked ugliness before the bewildered peasant women....In the summer of 1905 a whole se-

ries of 'petticoat rebellions' broke out in the south. Filled with anger and with boldness surprising for women, the peasant women attacked military and police headquarters where the army recruits were stationed, seized their menfolk and took them home. Armed with rakes, pitchforks and brooms, peasant women drove the armed guards from the villages. They are protesting in their own way against the intolerable burden of war. They are, of course, arrested, tried, and given severe punishments, but the 'petticoat rebellions' continue. In this protest, defense of peasant interests and of purely 'female' interests are so closely interwoven that there are no grounds for dividing them and classing the 'petticoat rebellions' as part of the 'feminist movement'.[62]

Following the political demonstrations, they turned to agricultural strikes. Women sometimes initiated these disturbances, drawing the men after them. Downtrodden peasant women became one of the central figures in the political drama. In November, 1905, peasant women in Voronezh province sent two of their own deputies to the peasant congress to demand political rights and freedom for women on an equal basis with men.[63]

When peasant men, but not women, were enfranchised following the 1905 Revolution, many peasant women felt dismay. One voiced her unhappiness in a letter to the Duma:

> Our husbands and boyfriends have a good time with us, but when it comes to talks such as the ones which are going on now about the land and the new laws, they won't have anything to do with us. At least before, though they beat us sometimes, we decided things together. But now we women and young girls must sit silently on the sidelines and have no say about decisions affecting our lives.[64]

A 1908 survey by the Socialist Revolutionaries showed that the richest and poorest peasant women supported the reactionary, anti-Semitic Black Hundreds, while the middle peasants backed the populist agrarian SR party. In 1906-07, rural political upheaval had been checked by the army and police through hangings, imprisonment, and exile. The revolution in the countryside died down but casualties during WW I disenchanted the peasantry and fanned the flames of revolution once again. Moreover, many women resented the enfranchisement of men in 1906, but not themselves. They felt their former equality with men had been titled in men's favor. Many also desired the split up of the extended family where the daughter-in-law was under the control of her in-laws. Many women wanted land for their own nuclear family, and 10,000,000 new families emerged from the Revolution of 1917. In debt to local kulak and gentry landowners, peasants responded happily to the SR and Communist slogans of Peace, Land, and Bread. In 1917-18, peasants burned manor houses, killed some gentry, and chased others away so that they could not return as they had done in 1906.

Elena Skrjabina recorded some of the changes among the peasants on her family estate in Central Russia near the Volga River during WW I. She wrote:

> The summer of 1916 was not calm. The pleasant attitude of the local peasants changed, and various small disorders began to occur on the estate. Every Sunday boards from the fence separating the estate from the highway were broken. This highway led from Baev, the neighboring village, to the church in Obrochnoye. In the villages on the other side of the estate there was not one church for a distance of five versts; and therefore, the peasants from these villages had to go past our estate. The summer was hot; the sun baked everything from early morning on. Of course it was more pleasant to walk along the dense birch path and not along the dusty road in the blazing sun. These trips through the park had formerly been forbidden by the manager, and no one had violated his edicts. Now, however, not only the youth but even older people took advantage of this break in the fence and went in whole crowds to the Obrochnoye church. No longer was anything effective. To my mother's great irritation, my father asked that we not interfere. He himself conversed with the elder of the church. For a time it appeared as though order had been reestablished—but not for long. Everything soon began again and with new force. The boards from the fence disappeared; the break kept growing larger, and the birch path was so trampled down that it looked as though a whole head of cows had passed this way.[65]

Sometimes Mensheviks and other strangers appeared and spoke to her father. They were interested in the mood of the peasants. Although her father conversed quietly with them, he was upset and after they left he would speak with his wife about the matter.

Elena observed:

> The longer this went on the more tense became the mood. Already there were suspicious persons in the country, making almost no attempt to hide and appearing at peasant gatherings. They would speak and arouse the peasants with their speeches. Sometimes they would fall into the hands of the police and were taken away, so it was said, to the Nizhny jail. For the most part, however, everything went smoothly for them; and they were left alone.[66]

A friend of Elena's wrote her from Nizhny Novgorod to say things were not calm there. Both she and her friend were on the side of the insurgents. Rasputin was on everyone's lips. It was interesting that even her father had ceased defending the Tsarist family unconditionally, as he had formerly done. His hatred for Kerensky in the Provisional Government continued, and he would curse him.[67]

The February Revolution had little impact on the peasants on their estate, and September and October, 1917, passed uneventfully. However, by the time of the October Revolution life changed. She noted:

> The smashing and looting of estates began, accompanied by fires; and one of the first estates attacked was that of our neighbor, Priklonsky. They were looking for him and apparently wanted to kill him. However, he and his family had long since left the area. Only ashes were left of his house. The estate of the Filosophous (sic), about five versts from us, was also burned.
>
> The most alarming rumors were coming from everywhere. My teacher Zinaida, frightened to death, requested that we let her go; and at the first opportunity she went to Murom. My father refused to move anywhere, convinced that no one would touch him. In this conviction he was supported by the Obrochnoye peasantry and especially by the older ones. Their relationship with Father was unusually good. So many times the man-

ager, and even Mother, had reproached Father for his kindness and wastefulness. My father would always joke and say that he had enough for his lifetime and that of his sons, and that he would give his daughter in marriage to a rich man so that she would need no dowry.[68]

While the Gorstkin family was not harmed, strange peasants began roaming around the area, especially in the direction of his late mother's nearby estate. Servants were living there, but fled. As Elena remembered it:

The frightened girls ran to us, telling us how the crowd had smashed in the doors and shutters. A complete pillaging of the house was taking place. Indeed, soon the shouts and sounds of smashing glass were carried to our house. A delegation of peasants, headed by the village elders, called for my father. They advised us all to leave our house, promising to guard it and the estate from destruction. They said that the pillaging of the old house had been done not by our Obrochnoye peasants but by peasants from other villages, and they could not, of course, guarantee anything in that regard. My father would under no circumstances agree to leave our estate, but he did decide to send the women and us girls away.[69]

Servants helped them pack, but her father insisted on staying ten more days. Her mother stayed behind with her husband, but they eventually decided to go to nearby Lukoyanov, where most of the local gentry had gathered. In Lukoyanov, they heard rumors of pogroms, fires, and even murders. All their horses and cattle were taken the night their grandmother's estate was pillaged. On November 12, they left Obrochnoye forever.[70]

While some peasant women participated in the looting of the estates of landlords, marauding Cossacks and military units often insulted them in the summer of 1917. According to a village letter writer to *Izvestiia* in August 1917, the Cossacks who lived in Podolskaia guberniia, "steal from the land holders and peasants and insult the women. They do not even respect the church. In one village the store of the Consumers' Society was looted…" At the end of his letter, the writer complains that "the military unit which was sent here to protect, robs the people of their cattle, fowl, and bread, and insults the women..."[71] One wonders if the term "insults" is a euphemism for raping peasant women, and if so that it was one more burden of war that the peasant women bore.

D. Working Class Political Activity

> Women deputies representing women workers are not allowed onto the commission under your chairmanship. We believe such a decision to be unjust. Women workers predominate in the factories and mills of St. Petersburg.
>
> Alexandra Kollontai, "Women and Revolution,"

Writing about women workers, Kollontai initially observed that they were oppressed by a 12 hour working day and low wages, terrified by poverty and starvation, so they avoided politics and revolutionary struggle. The number of working-class women involved in the revolutionary movement was small. Indeed, women of the intelligentsia predominated in the Social Democratic Party. Most working-class women still believed that their lot was the oven, the wash-tub, and the cradle. However, the shooting of unarmed workers on Bloody Sunday, January, 1905, galvanized them as well as male workers. Women workers, young girls, working wives were among the mass victims of the Bloody Sunday demonstration. The slogan "General Strike" flew from workshop to workshop and was embraced by women workers who had lacked class consciousness and who began walking out of their factories.[72]

Female and as well as male workers were outraged at the shooting of peaceful marchers who were carrying icons in a sort of political pilgrimage to petition the Tsar for better working conditions in January, 1905. Some labeled the shooting "government banditry." Many lost their faith in the government, and many also lost their faith in the Church when priests were forbidden to bury the dead in consecrated ground. An Orthodox funeral was important to workers, and without that rite, they felt abandoned by the church, which had long been controlled by the state. According to Page Herrlinger in *Working Souls*, worker A. T. Tomasova experienced the disintegration of her religious world view that day. "Belief in God, in the

Russian Revolution, 1905

Church, in God's servant the Tsar, (our) loving Father was strong among workers at the time. We all believed that the tsar would help (us), (and) our mood (on the march) was even joyous, happy festive..." She recorded that "no one thought that they would shoot at people with icons."[73] The deaths of several hundred workers on Bloody Sunday convinced many that political activity, not church rites and rituals would henceforth aid the workers.

Writing about the impact of Bloody Sunday on the worker movement, Kollontai saw that women in the provinces did not lag behind their comrades in the capital. She noticed:

> In the October days, exhausted by work and their harsh existence on the edge of starvation, women leave the factories and, in the name of the common cause, courageously deprive their children of their last piece of bread...With simple moving words the woman worker appeals to her male comrades, suggesting that they too leave their work; she keeps up the spirits of those on strike, breathing energy into those who waver...The woman worker struggled tirelessly, protested courageously, sacrificed herself heroically for the common cause, and the more active she became, the more rapidly was the pro-

cess of her mental awakening achieved. The woman worker began to take note of the world around her, of the injustices stemming from the capitalist system. She became more painfully and acutely aware of the bitterness of all her sufferings and sorrows. Alongside common proletarian demands one can hear ever more distinctly the voices of the women of the working class recalling the needs and requirements of women workers. At the time of the elections to the Shidlovsky commission in March 1905, the refusal to admit women as worker delegates provoked murmurs of discontent among women: the sufferings and sacrifices that they had only recently passed through had brought the men and women of the working class closer together, put them on an equal footing.[74]

When the Shidlovsky commission refused to accept women chosen as delegates from the Sampsionevsky textile works, women workers decided to present the commission a protest declaration:

> Women deputies representing women workers are not allowed onto the commission under your chairmanship. We believe such a decision to be unjust. Women workers predominate in the factories and mills of St. Petersburg. The number of women employed in spinning and weaving mills is increasing every year because the men are moving to factories that offer better pay. We, the women workers, bear a heavier burden of work. Because of our helplessness and lack of rights, we are kept down more by our comrades, and paid less. When this commission was announced, our hearts filled with hope; at last the time is coming—we thought—when the woman worker in St. Petersburg will be able to speak out to the whole of Russia in the name of all her sister workers about the oppression, wrongs and humiliations of which the male worker can know nothing. And then, when we had already chosen our deputies, we were informed that only men can be deputies. However, we hope that this is not your final decision.[75]

Women workers also protested the election in 1906 of Duma delegates where women were excluded. They broke up meetings and protested against the way the elections were being conducted. Women workers contributed to the 40,000 signatures protesting women's exclusion from the voting process. Kollontai and other socialists believed that civic equality for women would not come from the bourgeois feminist movement, but only through a socialist revolution.[76]

One of the biggest surprises of the 1905 Revolution was the formation of unions by domestic servants, laundresses, cooks, and maids. Some participated in mass strikes, others in street demonstrations. Servants demanded an 8 hour day, a minimum wage, better living conditions including a separate room, polite treatment by their employers, and so forth. Their actions especially surprised their bourgeois, feminist mistresses.[77] While these demands were not met, they resurfaced during the Bolshevik Revolution a decade later.

Worker dissatisfactions led women to participate in the Revolutions of 1905 and 1917. A poem by a Russian working woman shows some of their feelings of exploitation:

> ... I would fly to the clear and all-powerful sun...
> ... toward freedom, toward the expanse.
> I would toss my chains away, the slave's shameful chains
> That shackle my body...
> Give me wings! Swift, light wings...
> I would revel in the freedom of flight.[78]

During the Russo-Japanese War, factory workers were prone to mass action and spontaneous political activity. Women textile workers in Moscow, St. Petersburg, and Ivanovo-Voznesensk participated in strikes and formed workers' soviets or councils. They demanded the 8 hour day, a minimum wage, better working conditions, freedom of speech, and the right to strike. A large proportion of working women were married, so they had domestic as well as work duties, and few participated in organized political life. In 1915, women in Ivanovo-Voznesensk demonstrated against the war, and the police killed and wounded forty people. In February 1917, Bolshevik Party leaders provided working women with information for celebrating International Women's Day (February 25th), but told them that the time was not ripe for revolution. Contrary to these directives, women textile workers and disgruntled soldiers' wives organized massive demonstrations in Petrograd (as St. Petersburg was called during WW I), protesting food shortages, the war, and the Tsarist regime. They drew the male metal workers into their demonstration, and soon students, government employees, and soldiers joined the protests against the regime. Thus, the women workers proved more revolutionary than their party leaders. Later a revolutionary named Nikolai Sukhanov remarked:

"No one led the February Revolution, the people made it themselves."

E. Women Soldiers

It's difficult to know where to place women soldiers, but since war is sometimes defined as an extreme form of politics, it may do to discuss their roles here. Certainly women's extreme patriotism was a political feeling and activating force. During WW I, Russian women soldiers came from all classes.

In 1914, 12 young girls from the same Moscow school ran away and joined the army because they wanted to "kill the Germans." Interviewed by reporters from the Russian newspaper *Novoe Vremya* in 1916, the leader of the group, Zoya Smirnov, told reporters that she and her friends wanted to join the army during mobilization in July 1914.

> We decided to run away to the war at all costs, said Zoya. It was impossible to run away from Moscow because we might have been stopped at the station. It was therefore necessary to hire izvozchiks and ride out to one of the suburban stations through which the military echelons were continually passing. We left home early in the morning without saying a word to our parents and departed. It was a bit terrible at first; we were very sorry for our fathers and mothers, but the desire to see the war and ourselves kill the Germans overcame all other sentiments.[79]

Male soldiers protected them and gave them uniforms to wear. Taught to shoot, they fought on the Austrian front. Several of the girls were wounded when the Germans brought heavy artillery to the Carpathian Mountains. One girl, Zina Morozov was killed and buried where she fell. Several were wounded. All were frightened by the German artillery, and the men soldiers were frightened too.

Zoya Smirnov was knocked unconscious and seriously wounded twice. After being wounded a second time, Zoya couldn't find her unit or her friends, so she was then persuaded to work as a nurse at the Austrian Front. All the girl soldiers behaved bravely, and Zoya received the St. George's Cross for her courageous reconnaissance work. The other soldiers respected her.[80]

Mrs. Crosley, the wife of an American attaché stationed in Petrograd in 1917-18, observed better behavior among female than male soldiers in 1917. She saw the men looting and shooting, but she doesn't report female soldiers engaged in such behavior. She met Yashka Botchkareva, the head of the Petrograd Women's Battalion of Death, but was skeptical of women soldiers being able to do much at the front when the male soldiers were deserting in such huge numbers. She thought the male soldiers absolute loafers. She also wondered if the Women's Battalion would really be able to shame the men into fighting on the Eastern Front, when the men were war weary and had suffered from 3 years of inadequate food, guns, and boots. She reported that in the winter of 1917-18, the male soldiers robbed wealthy apartments and loafed around, but forced middle and upper-class civilians to clear the streets of snow and ice.[81] Writing in a letter in August, 1917, Crosley noted:

> The activities of the women soldiers increase, but their successes do not. Their original intention to shame the men soldiers has failed utterly. We hear remarkable stories of Cossacks being placed on guard to protect the women soldiers from the remainder of the Russian Army.[82]

Many of the male soldiers resented the women soldiers' efforts to continue the war when they were war weary and wanted to defect. Some soldiers even killed their officers and apparently wanted to kill Yashka as well. In a letter in September, 1917, Crosley observed:

> The women soldiers have been more than ever in evidence; they now sing as they march about the city, a custom among

Russian troops. They claim to be strong for Kerensky; I trust them to remain honest in their convictions more than I trust any of the men soldiers![83]

The women soldiers in Petrograd—not the Women's Battalion of Death which was at the Galician front under the command of Botchkareva—defended the Provisional Government and President Kerensky in October, 1917. Only a portion of the battalion was distributed to defend the government at the Winter Palace, and some were shot during the Bolshevik take over. While the American Mrs. Crosley thought some of these women soldiers were arrested and raped, a later historian disputes this, as does Yashka Botchkareva.[84] Yashka Botchkareva and her battalion were at the front, and she does not report any rapes. In her memoirs, Yashka does report being arrested and imprisoned, but she was released. All we can deduce is that the women soldiers behaved honorably during the war, supported Kerensky's Provisional Government, and were disbanded by the Bolsheviks after the October Revolution. During the Civil War, about 50,000 women joined the Red Army, and behaved bravely. Out of a total army of 5,000,000, they were a very small percentage.

F. Conclusion

Women of all classes slowly became politically radicalized and active by the time of the First World War. They participated directly and indirectly in the Revolutions of 1905 and February 1917. The Bolshevik Revolution of October, 1917, did not involve so many women since it was more of a coup d'état than a widespread revolution. However, the Civil War, which followed and lasted for three years, did involve several thousand women.

The Revolution of February, 1917, surprised professional revolutionaries like Lenin, Trotsky, and Kollontai who were in exile. After the Tsar abdicated, and a Temporary or Provisional Government was formed in March, it freed political and religious prisoners, and generally adopted a liberal program. Members of the

Provisional Government included Conservatives, Social Revolutionaries, Social Democrats, and some feminist sympathizers. Its downfall lay in remaining in the war, which was unpopular, and trying to settle the land problem by committee when the peasants wanted land immediately.

During the summer of 1917, both the Social Revolutionaries and the Bolsheviks advocated peasant seizure of land. Their slogan was "Rob those who have robbed you." This policy attracted the peasants more than the time-consuming land committees that the Provisional Government appointed throughout the Empire. The peasants had been waiting for more land since their emancipation in the 1860s. Now was the time for them to seize it. They had no patience for democratic deliberations with landowners. They chose direct action, often burning down manor houses so gentry-class landowners could never return as they did after the 1905 Revolution. When the Bolsheviks took control of the government in 1918, the new Soviet Government allowed peasants to farm the land they customarily did and to take what they could of nearby estates. However, the government owned the land, but allowed the peasants to use it. This was agreeable to most peasants, especially peasant women, who were now able to form households of their own instead of living with their sometimes tyrannical mothers and fathers-in-law. In fact ten million new peasant households emerged during the first decade of Soviet rule.

Once political power was granted to women in the summer of 1917, their voter turnout was about 70%, even among peasant women. During the summer and fall of 1917, women appeared on the slates of all the major political parties, including Feminists, Constitutional Democrats, Social Revolutionaries, Mensheviks, and Bolsheviks. However, only 10 out of 767 delegates elected to the democratic Constitutional Assembly were women. These included 4 Bolsheviks: Alexandra Kollontai, Evgeniia Bosh, Elena Rozmirovich, and Varvara Iakovlina. The Social Revolutionaries elected were Catherine Breshkovsky, Vera Figner, Maria Spirodonovna, M. D. Perveeva, O. A. Marveevskaya, and Anastasia Sletova.[85]

After a peaceful opening ceremony to the newly elected Parliamentary Assembly, many Russian women's hopes were dashed as

Bolshevik sailors used force to evict the new assembly. The story of women after the 1917 Revolutions continues in a later volume. Their voices and art cover women's religious, social, educational, work, and political lives in the 1920s and 1930s.

Notes

Notes to Chapter One

1. See, Brenda Meehan, *Holy Women of Russia, The Lives of Five Orthodox Women Offer Spiritual Guidance for Today* (San Francisco: Harpers, 1993).

2. See *Obshchii Svod...pervoi vseobshchei perepisi naseleniia Rossiskoi Imperii 1897 g.* Vol. II: 1, 4, 254-5, and 256-57. (Hereafter cited as *1897 Perepis', 1897 Census*) Several million in the Russian Empire were Muslims, Jews, Catholics, and Lutherans. The age breakdown of beggars, wanderers, and pilgrims was interesting: 16,000 were aged 20-39; 42,000 were 40-59; and 66,000 over 60 years old.

3. See, Brenda Meehan-Walters, "To Save Oneself: Russian Peasant Women and the Development of Women's Religious communities in Prerevolutionary Russia," in *Russian Peasant Women,* Ed. Beatrice Farnsworth & Lynne Viola, (New York: Oxford University Press, 1992), 122.

4. Brenda Meehan-Walters, "To Save Oneself: Russian Peasant Women and the Development of Women's Religious communities in Prerevolutionary Russia," 121-133; William Wagner, "The Transformation of Female Orthodox Monasticism in Nizhni Novgorod Diocese, 1764-1929, in Comparative Perspective," *Journal of Modern History,* 78 (2006), 793-845, especially, 834; and Chris Chulos, *Converging Worlds Religion and Community in Peasant Russia 1863-1917* (DeKalb: Northern Illinois University Press, 2003), 19-20.

5. See, William G. Wagner, "Female Orthodox Monasticism in 18th Century Imperial Russia: The Experience of Nizhnii Novgorod," in *Women in Russian Culture and Society, 1700-1825,* Edited by Wendy Rosslyn and Alessandra Tosi (New York: Palgrave Macmillan, 2007) 191-210; *1897 Perepis'* Table XX, Vol. I, 217.

6. Sophia Tolstoy, *The Diary of Tolstoy's Wife 1860-1891,* Trans. Alexander Werth, (New York: Payson and Clarke Ltd., 1928), 226 and Grand Duchess Marie, *The Education of a Princess, A Memoir,* (New York: Blue Ribbon Books, 1930), 129-130.

7. See Diana Greene, *Reinventing Romantic Poetry Russian Women Poets of the Mid-Nineteenth Century,* (Madison: University of Wisconsin Press, 2004), 256.

8. Meehan-Waters, "To Save Oneself," 105 and Sophie Satina, *Education of Women in Pre Revolutionary Russia,* Translated by A. F. Poustchine, (New York: 1966), 24. Satina perceived peasants in late 19th century Russia not wanting their daughters obtaining education because in their minds, only nuns were educated and they didn't want their daughters becoming nuns.

See also Russian ethnographer N. Dobrotvortskii as quoted in Brenda Meehan-Waters, "To Save Oneself:" 122-131.

9. Page Herrlinger, *Working Souls Russian Orthodoxy and Factory Labor in St. Petersburg, 1881-1917*, (Bloomington: Slavica, 2007), 76-77, 99, 103, 133.

10. As quoted by peasant Nikolai Ivanovich Kuznetsov, an informant for the Russian Ethnographer Count V. N. Tenishev. found in Rose L. Glickman, "'Unusual Circumstances' in the Peasant Village," *Russian History*, Vol. 23, Nos. 1-4, Spring-Winter, 225.

11. Quoted by N. I. Kuznetsov, in Glickman, "Unusual Circumstances," *Russian History*, 226.

12. As quoted by Romy Taylor, "Pavlova's Dvojnaia zhizn': An Icon Turns the Plot," in *Essays on Karolina Pavlova*, Ed. Susanne Fusso and Alexander Lehrman, (Evanston: Northwestern University Press), 85, 74. Information about the icon corner and shelf from Chris J. Chulos, *Converging Worlds Religion and Community in Peasant Russia*, 17.

13. See, Krista Tippett, *Speaking of Faith* (New York, Viking, 2007), 222.

14. Herrlinger, *Working Souls*, 60-62, 78, 82, 99,

15. Anna Dostoevsky, *Dostoevsky Reminiscences*, Trans. and Ed. Beatrice Stillman, (New York: Liveright, 1975), 10.

16. Chulos, *Converging Worlds*, 47-52.

17. Nadezhda Sokhanskaia, "An Autobiography," Trans. by Valentina Baslyk in Toby Clyman and Judith Vowles', *Russia Through Women's Eyes: Autobiographies from Tsarist Russia*, (New Haven: Yale University Press, 1996), 49

18. Sofia Khvoshchinskaia, "Reminiscences of Institute Life," Trans. by Baslyk, *Russia through Women's Eyes*, 101.

19. See L. Zinovyeva-Annibal, "The Wolves" from *The Great Menagerie* as quoted in *Women Writers in Russian Modernism*, Translated and Edited by Temira Pachmuss, (Urbana: University of Illinois Press, 1978), 228-229.)

20. See, Diana Greene, *Reinventing Romantic Poetry*, 158 regarding Pavlova's stern and harsh depictions of God and translation of this stanza of Pavlova's poem.

21. For the second quotation, see, K. Pavlova, "Dvoinaia Zhizn" in *Polnoe Sobranie Stikhotvorenii*, (Moscow: Sovetskii Pisatel', 1964), 276; *A Double Life*, Trans B. H. Monter, 97-98.

22. Karolina Pavlova, "We Shall Not Overcome our Sorrows," *Treasury of Russian Verse*, Edited by Avrahm Yarmolinsky, (New York: Macmillan, 1949), 100.

23. Anna Akhamatova, "Prayer," Translated by Babette Deutsch and Avrahm Yarmolinsky in *Modern Russian Poetry An Anthology* (New York: Harcourt, Brace and Company, 1921), 154.

24. Maria Botchkareva, *Yashka My Life as Peasant, Officer and Exile* as set down by Isaac Don Levine (New York: Frederick A. Stokes Pub., 1919) 72, 84, 98, 116.
25. Botchkareva, *Yashka My Life*, 189-191.
26. Laurie S. Stoff, *They Fought for the Motherland, Russia's Women Soldiers in World War I and the Revolution* (Lawrence, Kansas: University Press of Kansas, 2006), 126-128.
27. Botchkareva, *Yashka*, 303-04.
28. For the role of village peasants in church life, see, Glennys Young, "Into Church Matters": Lay Identity, Rural Parish Life, and Popular Politics in Late Imperial and Early Soviet Russia, 1864-1928," *Russian History*, Vol. 23, Nos. 1-4, (Sp.-Winter 1996), 367-84, especially page 381.
29. Anna Dostoevsky, *Dostoevsky Reminiscences*, Trans. and Ed. Beatrice Stillman, (New York, Liveright: 1975), 8.
30. See interview with Russian woman in Ernest Poole, *The Dark People, Russia's Crisis* (New York: Macmillan Co., 1918), 207-08.
31. Nadezhda Durova, *The Cavalry Maiden Journals of a Russian Officer in the Napoleonic Wars*, Translation, Introduction, and Notes by Mary F. Zirin (Bloomington: Indiana University Press, 1988), 11-12.
32. Durova, 13
33. Nadezhda Sokhanskaya, "A Conversation After Dinner," in *Russian Women's Shorter Fiction An Anthology 1835-1860*, Trans. and Introduced by Joe Andrew (Oxford: Clarendon Press, 1996), 404-5.
34. Nadezhda Khvoshchinskaya, *The Boarding-School Girl*, Trans. Karen Rosneck, (Evanston, Illinois: Northwestern University Press, 2000), 73-5.
35. Khvoshchinskaya, *Ibid.*, 97-99.
36. Khvoshchinskaya, *Ibid.*, 79-80.
37. Khvoshchinskaya, *Ibid.*, 102-3.
38. Nadeshda Sokhanskaya, "A Conversation After Diner, in *Russian Women's Shorter Fiction An Anthology*, 436-7.
39. Sokhanskaya, *Ibid.*, 445.
40. Sokhanskaya, *Ibid.*, 446-9.
41. Anna Bek, *The Life of a Russian Woman Doctor A Siberian Memoir, 1869-1954* Trans. & Ed. Anne D. Rassweiler and Adele M. Lindenmeyr (Bloomington: Indiana University Press, 2004) 74-75.
42. For wedding description, see, governess Rhoda Power, *Under the Bolshevik Reign of Terror*, (New York, McBride, Nast, and Co., 1919), 16-17.
43. S. Tolstoy, *Diary, 1860-91*, 46, 50.
44. Anna G. Snitkina Dostoevskaya, *Dostoevsky Reminiscences*, Trans. Ed. Bea-

trice Stillman, (New York: Liveright: 1975), 74.

45. See, T. A. Listova, "Russian Rituals, Customs, and Beliefs Associated with the Midwife (1850-1930) in *Russkie semeinyi I obshchestvennyi* (Moscow: Nauka Pub., 1898) cited in *Russian Traditional Culture Religion, Gender, and Customary Law*, Ed. Marjorie M. Balzer (Armonk, New York: M. E. Sharpe, 1992), 122-145, especially 125-26, 139.

46. See, Listova, *Ibid.*, 127, 130-31.136, 142 and Samuel C. Ramer, "Childbirth and Culture: Midwifery in the 19th Century Russian Countryside," in *Russian Peasant Women*, Ed. B. Farnsworth, New York: Oxford University Press, 1992, 107-120.

47. Sophia Tolstoy, *The Diary of Tolstoy's Wife, 1860-1891*, 248, Dec. 31, 1890.

48. Sophia Tolstoy, *Diary*, 245, December, 28, 1890.

49. See, Praskovia Tatlina, "Reminiscences," in Clyman and Vowles, *Russia Through Women's Eyes*, 247-8.

50. Irina S. Tidmarsh, *Memories of Revolution Russian Women Remember*, Ed. Anna Horsbrugh-Porter, Interviews by Elena Snow and Frances Welch (London: Routledge, 1993), 54.

51. See, Liubov Nikulina-Kositskaia, "Notes," in *Russia through Women's Eyes*, 121.

52. Herrlinger, *Working Souls*, 67-69,133, 187.

53. S. Tolstoy, *Diary*, 1860-91, 14.

54. S. Tolstoy, *Diary*, 1860-91, 14-15.

55. S. Tolstoy, *Diary, 1891-97, 78*; and *Autobiography*, 81-82. The philosophical book which referred to God as element was entitled *La Vie Eternelle*.

56. See, Meehan, *Holy Women of Russia*, 63-5 and Anna Dostoevsky, *Reminiscences*, 284.

57. See, Kositskaia, "Notes" Trans. by Mary Zirin in *Russia through Women's Eyes*, 128-9. Regarding parental power, see Marie Zebrikoff, "Russia," in Theodore Stanton, *The Woman Question in Europe*, (London: Sampson, Low, Marston, 1884), 394-6..

58. V. Iu. Leshchenko, "The Position of Women in the Light of Religious-Domestic Taboos Among the East Slavic Peoples in the Nineteenth and early Twentieth Centuries," *Soviet Anthropolgy and Archeology*, Winter 1978-79: 23-31.

59. Michael Melancon, *The Lena Goldfields Massacre* (College Station: Texas A & M U. Press, 2006) 39 and Aksakov as quoted by T. A. Bernshtam, "Russian Folk Culture and Folk Religion," in *Russian Traditional Culture Religion, Gender, and Customary Law*, Ed. M. M. Balzer, 47.

60. For information about workers and religion, see, Mark D. Steinberg, "Workers on the Cross: Religious Imagination in the Writings of Russian

Workers, 1910-1924," *Russian Review*, Vol. 53, Ap. 1994, 213-39, especially page 218. Most of the writings he cites are those of male workers, and so are not included here.

61. Rose L. Glickman, "The Peasant Woman as Healer," in *Russia's Women, Accommodation, Resistance, Transformation*, Ed. Clements, Engel, & Worobec, (Berkeley: University of California, 1991), 154-56.

62. Olga Shapir, "The Settlement," (1892) Trans. in Catriona Kelly, *An Anthology of Russian Women's Writing, 1777-1992* (New York: Oxford University Press, 1994), 126.

63. Khvoshchinskaya, *The Boarding-School Girl*, 54.

64. Khvoshchinskaya, *Ibid.*, 66.

65. Nadia Kizenko, A Prodigal Saint, *Father John of Kronstadt and the Russian People*, (University Park: Pennsylvania State University Press, 2000), 108

66. Kizenko, *Fr. John*, 111.

67. Kizenko, *Fr. John*, 118.

68. Kizenko, *Fr. John*, 119-20.

69. Kizenko, *Fr. John*, 120.

70. Kizenko, *Fr. John*, 118-19.

71. S. Tolstoy, *Diary, 1891-97*, 20.

72. Mirra Lokhvitskaya, "O, We the Sorrowful," as trans. by Temira Pachmuss in *Women Writers in Russian Modernism, An Anthology* (Urbana, University of Illinois Press, 1978), 111-112.

73. Lokhvitskaya, "A Prayer for those who are Perishing," as trans. by Temira Pachmuss in *Women Writers in Russian Modernism*, 109-110.

74. See, Poliksena Solovyova, "In the Crypt," Trans. by Temira Pachmuss in *Women Writers in Russian Modernism*, 185.

75. Herrlinger, *Working Souls, 132-38, 206-07.,*

76. Nina Berberova, *The Italics Are Mine*, Trans. Philippe Radley (New York: Vintage Books, 1993), 17

77. Berberova, *Ibid.*, 39.

78. Nina Berberova, *The Book of Happiness*, Trans. Miriam Schwartz (New York: New Directions, 1999), 70.

79. Anna Bek, *Life of a Russian Woman Doctor*, 24-25.

80. "Magdalene" in Mariya Shkapskaya, *The Mother and The Stern Master Selected Poems*, Trans. and Introduced by Sandra Shaw Bennett (Nottingham: Astra Press, 1998), 75

81. Regarding peasant women and religion, see Marie Zebrikoff, "Russia," 404-5 and Laura Englestein, "Rebels of the Soul: Peasant Self-fashion-

ing in a Religious Key," *Russian History*, Vol. 23, Nos. 1-4, Spring-Winter, 197-213.
82. Sonia Tolstoy, *Diary, 1891-97*, 126.
83. S. Tolstoy, *Diary, 1891-97*, January, 1897, 142.
84. S. Tolstoy, *Diary, 191-97*, July, 1897, 179; August, 1897, 203-04.
85. Elena Skrjabina, *Coming of Age in the Russian Revolution*, Tans. & Ed. Norman Luxenburg, (New Brunswick: Transaction Books, 1985) 26.
86. Russian intellectuals, writers, and artists often flirted with the occult, while sects like the khlysty and Skoptsy flourished more among the peasants and urban population. The khlysty and Skoptsy were charismatic sects that celebrated their faith in whirling dances and singing, somewhat akin to the Shakers in America. Stundists arose from the Germanic influences of Lutheranism and the Mennonites in South Russia and Ukraine. Baptists also flourished in the late 19th century.
87. H. P. Blavatsky, *The Secret Doctrine The Synthesis of Science, Religion, and Philosophy, Vol. I. Cosmogenesis*, (Madras, India: Theosophical Pub. House, 1938), 82-83.
88. See, Maria Carlson, "Spiritualism," in *The Occult in Russian and Soviet Culture*, Edited by Bernice G. Rosenthal (Ithaca: Cornell University Press, 1997), 135-152.

N. Aksakov, V. Soloviev, A. Bely, V. Ivanov, V. Kandinsky, A. Scriabin, N. Berdiaev, and P. D. Uspensky were among those flirting with the occult and mysticism in the late 19th and early 20th centuries. Carlson found more than 30 Russian journals and 800 non-fiction books published on the occult from 1881-1918.(152) See also, J. W. Monroe, *Laboratories of Faith, Mesmerism, Spiritism, and Occultism in Modern France* (Ithaca: Cornell University Press, 2008) 235-9; also www.blavatskyarchives.com/longseal.htm and www.theosophy.ru/kamensky.htm .

In the 1930s, Marie Avinov and others shared their Theosophical leanings in Soviet prison cells. See, Marie Avinov, *Pilgrimage Through Hell, An Autobiography*. Told by Paul Chavchavadze. (Englewood Cliffs, New Jersey: Prentice Hall, 1968), 290. Various critiques and exposes of Blavatsky's works were published in the late 19th century. One of the most famous was Vsevolod S. Solovyoff's *A Modern Priestess of Isis* Abridged and Trans. by Walter Leaf (New York: Arno Press, 1976. Soloviev was initially "taken in" by Blavatsky, but later denounced her spiritualist phenomena as fraudulent and her writings as plagiarized. See Solovyoff, especially, 259, Appendix B and C, 322-366.

89. As quoted by Temira Pachmuss, *Zinaida Hippius An Intellectual Profile* (Carbondale: Southern Illinois University Press, 1971), 109-110.
90. As quoted and translated by Evelyn Bristol, *A History of Russian Poetry*,

(Urbana: University of Illinois, 1991) 182-3.

91. Zinaida Gippius, "Monotony," as Translated by Christine Borowec, in "Zinaida Gippius," *Russian Women Writers Vol. 2*, Ed. Christine D. Tomei (New York: Garland Pub., 1999), 692.

92. Zinaida Gippius, "Monotony," as Translated by Borowec, in *Russian Women Writers Vol. 2*, 692-3.

93. Zinaida Gippius, "Psyche," in *Modern Russian Poetry*, Trans. Duetsch & Yarmolinsky, 70.

94. See Mikhail Epstein, "Daniil Andreev and the Mysticism of Femininity," in *The Occult in Russian and Soviet Culture*, Ed. Bernice G. Rosenthal (Ithaca: Cornell University Press, 1997) 325-55, especially 327 and Berdiaev, 332. For Gippius, see, Victor Chernov, "Zinaida Hippius, Chortova Kukla," *Russkaya Mysl'*, No. 1-3 (1911) 318 as quoted by Pachmuss, *Ibid.*, 55 also 104-5.

95. See, Pachmuss, *Zinaida Hippius*, 123-5, 173, 188.

96. As quoted by Clyman in *Russia through Women's Eyes*, 23-24.

Notes to Chapter Two

1. Maria Zhukova, "Baron Reichman," in *Russian Women's Shorter Fiction An Anthology 1835-1860*, Trans. & Introduced by Joe Andrew (Oxford: Clarendon Press, 1996), 156.

2. Zhukova, 169, 166-67.

3. Zhukova, 167.

4. Zhukova, "The Ideal," in *Russian Women's Shorter Fiction An Anthology 1835-1860*, 22.

5. Evkokia Rostopchina, "Rank and Money," Trans. Helena Goscilo in *Russian and Polish Women's Fiction* (Knoxville: The University of Tennessee Press, 1985), 65.

6. Rostopchina, "Rank and Money," 65.

7. Rostopchina, "Rank and Money," 77, 82.

8. Rostopchina, "Winter Evening," as translated by Laura Jo McCullough, in "Evdokiia Rostopchina," *Russian Women Writers, Vol. I*, 94.

9. See E. Rostopchina, "Song of Return," ("Pesnia Vozvrata,") in *Stati o russkoi poezii*, ed. V. F. Khodasevich, (Petrograd, Epokha, 1922), 37, my translation, and "Chiny I Dengi," (Rank and Money") in *Sochineniia*, Tom vtorai, 1-38. For good accounts of her life, see, Helena Goscilo, *Russian and Polish Women's Fiction*, (Knoxville: University of Tennessee Press, 1984), 44-84;

Laura Jo McCullough, "Evdokiia Rostopchina," in *Russian Women Writers, Vol. I,* 89-100; Diana Green's article about Russian criticism of Rostopchina in the 1850s in *Women Writers in Russian Literature,* Ed. Toby Clyman and Diana Greene (Westport, Connecticut: Praeger, 1994); Hutton, *Ibid.,* 12-13, and Diana Greene, *Reinventing Romantic Poetry.*

10. Karolina Pavlova, "Yes, there were many of us young girl friends," in Pamela Perkins and Albert Cook in *The Burden of Sufferance Women Poets of Russia,* (New York: Garland Publishing, Inc., 1993), 31.

11. See K. Pavlova, "Dvoinaia Zhizn" in *Polnoe Sobranie Stikhotvorenii,* 276; *A Double Life,* Trans B. H. Monter, 58, 65-66; 97-98; Barbara Heldt, *A Terrible Perfection, Women and Russian Literature,* (Bloomington: Indiana University Press, Garland, 1987); and Diana Greene, "Karolina Pavlova's 'At the Tea Table,' and the Politics of Class and Gender," *The Russian Review,* 53:281-82.

12. Pavlova, *A Double Life,* Trans. Monter, 97-8.

13. Pavlova, *A Double Life,* Trans. Monter, 103-05.

14. Elena Gan, "Society's Judgement," as Trans. by Joe Andrew in *Russian Women's Shorter Fiction An Anthology,* 110.

15. Gan, "Society's Judgement," 110-12.

16. See, Durova, *The Calvary Maiden,* ix-xxxiii, 32-33.

17. Durova, *Ibid.,* 224-5.

18. Grand Duchess Marie, *Education of a Princess,* 91.

19. Grand Duchess Marie, *Education of a Princess,* 93-94.

20. Marie, *Education,* 94-5.

21. Marie, *Education,* 97.

22. Marie, *Education,* 104, 116, 158.

23. Marie, *Education,* 318.

24. Anna Akhmatova, *Selected Poems,* Trans. D. M. Thomas, (New York: Penguin Books, 1985) 16.

25. See, Nina Berberova, *The Italics Are Mine,* 13.

26. Berberova, *The Italics Are Mine,* 10.

27. "Lidiia Zinov'eva-Annibal," by Jane Costlow, in *Russian Women Writers,* Vol. I, 443

28. For this interpretation of Verbitskaia's story Vavochka, see Rosalind Marsh, "Realist Prose Writers, 1881-1929," *A History of Women's Writing in Russia,* Ed. Adele M. Barker and Jehanne M. Gheith (Cambridge: Cambridge University Press, 2002), 186.

29. A. Verbitskaya, *The Mirage,* Translated by T. Pachmuss in *Women Writers in Russian Modernism,* 140, 154-55.

30. Pauline Gray, *The Grand Duke's Woman, The story of the morganatic marriage of Michael Romanoff, the Tsar Nicholas II's brother, and Nathalia Cheremetevskaya*, (London: Macdonald and Jane's, 1976.) 8-11.
31. Gray, *The Grand Duke's Woman*, 12.
32. Gray, *The Grand Duke's Woman*, 19, 22, 24-5, 39, 85-105, 108-112.
33. Gray, *The Grand Duke's Woman*, 27.
34. Gray, *The Grand Duke's Woman*, 25-6.
35. Sophia Tolstoy, *Autobiography of Countess Tolstoy*, Trans. S. S. Koteliansky and Leonard Woolf, (New York: B. W. Huebsch, Inc. 1922), 38.
36. S. Tolstoy, *Autobiography*, 43.
37. S. Tolstoy, *Autobiography*, 61-2.
38. S. Tolstoy, *Autobiography*, 62-65.
39. Sophia Tolstoy, *The Diary of Tolstoy's Wife 1860-1891*, (1928), 225-6, Nov. 1890.
40. S. Tolstoy, *Diary, 1860-91*, 246, Dec. 1890.
41. S. Tolstoy, *Diary, 1860-91*, 237-8, Dec. 1890.
42. Sophia Tolstoy, *The Countess Tolstoy's Later Diary 1891-1897*, Trans. Alexander Werth, (Freeport, New York: Books for Libraries Press, 1971 (first published 1929), 198, Aug., 1897.
43. S. Tolstoy, *Diary, 1891-1897*, 178-9.
44. S. Tolstoy, *Diary, 1891-1897*, 154, June, 1897.
45. S. Tolstoy, *Diary, 1891-97*, "Vanichka's Death," 252.
46. S. Tolstoy, *Diary, 1891-97*, "Vanichka's Death," 247.
47. S. Tolstoy, *Diary, 1891-97*, "Vanichka's Death," 252.
48. S. Tolstoy, *Diary, 1860-91*, 249.
49. S. Tolstoy, *Diary, 1860-91*, 153-4.
50. S. Tolstoy, *Diary, 1860-91*, 262.
51. S. Tolstoy, *Diary, 1891-97*, 117. January, 1895.
52. S. Tolstoy, *Diary, 1891-97*, 196, Aug. 1897.
53. S. Tolstoy, *Diary, 1891-97*, 201, Aug. 1897.
54. S. Tolstoy, *Diary, 1891-97*, 202-03.
55. S. Tolstoy, *Diary, 1891-97*, 239, Nov., 1897.
56. S. Tolstoy, *Diary, 1891-97*, 218.
57. S. Tolstoy, *Diary, 1891-97*, 221, 149.
58. S. Tolstoy, *Diary, 1891-97*, 221.
59. S. Tolstoy, *Diary, 1891-97*, 231.

60. S. Tolstoy, *Diary, 1891-97*, 231.
61. S. Tolstoy, *Diary, 1891-97*, 166.
62. Tatiana Tolstoy, *The Tolstoy Home, Diaries of Tatiana Sukhotin-Tolstoy*, Trans. Alec Brown, (New York: AMS Press, Inc., 1966), 167, 170.
63. T. Tolstoy, *Diaries*, Feb. 1891, 173-4.
64. T. Tolstoy, *Diaries*, 241, Nov. 1897.
65. T. Tolstoy, *Diaries*, 267ff.
66. Anna Dostoevsky, *Reminiscences*, 48.
67. A. Dostoevsky, *Reminiscences*, 68.
68. A. Dostoevsky, *Reminiscences*, 384.
69. Anna Bek, *Life of a Russian Woman Doctor*, 63.
70. Bek, *Life of a Russian Woman Doctor*, 57.
71. Bek, *Life of a Russian Woman Doctor*, 69.
72. Bek, *Life of a Russian Woman Doctor*, 74.
73. Bek, *Life of a Russian Woman Doctor*, 75.
74. Skrjabina, *Coming of Age*, 8.
75. As quoted in Anna Carolotta Leffler, *Biography of Sofia Kovalevskaia*, Trans. A. M. Clive Bayley. (New York: Century, 1895), 266-68.
76. Vera Figner, *Memoirs of a Revolutionist* Authorized, Translation from the Russian (New York: International Publishers, 1927), 39-48.
77. See, Emilia Pimenova, "Bygone Days," in *Russia Through Women's Eyes*, 318-19ff.
78. Pimenova, *Ibid.*, 325ff.
79. Pimenova, *Ibid.*, 332
80. For an excellent analysis of Chekhova's life, see Rochelle Goldberg Ruthchild, "Writing for Their Rights: Four Feminist Journalists: Mariia Chekhova, Liubov Gurevich, Mariia Pokrovskaia, and Ariadna Tyrkova," in *An Improper Profession*, Ed. Barbara Norton and Jehanne Gheith, (Durham: Duke University Press, 2001), 167-186.
81. Cecilia Bobrovskaya, *Twenty Years in Underground Russia Memoirs of a Rank-and-File Bolshevik* (New York: International Publishers, 1934), 117-18.
82. Bobrovskaya, *Twenty Years*, 210-211.
83. Bobrovskaya, *Twenty Years*, 150.
84. Bobrovskaya, *Twenty Years*, 214-15.
85. As quoted by Barbara Clements in *Bolshevik Feminist: The Life of Aleksandra Kollontai* (Bloomington: University of Indiana Press, 1979), 16, Hutton, 37, 126-7, Katherine Breshko-Breshkovskaia, *Hidden Springs of the Russian Rev-*

olution, (Stanford: Stanford University Press, 1931), 8-30 and *Little Grandmother of the Russian Revolution,* Ed. Alice Stone Blackwell, (New York: Little and Brown, 1917),1-31

86. Barbara Norton, "Journalism as a Means of Empowerment, The Early Career of Ekaterina Kuksova, in *An Improper Profession,* 224-237.
87. Information personally communicated to me in Iowa City, Iowa, by her grandson Vladimir Kostelovsky in the early 1980s.
88. For information about Tsvetaeva's affairs with Parnok and Mandelstam, see Diana Lewis Burgin, "Laid Out in Lavender," in *Sexuality and the Body in Russian Culture,* Ed. Jane T. Costlow et al (Stanford: Stanford University Press, 1993), 198-99 and her marriage described in J. Marin King's Introduction to *Marina Tsvetaeva A Captive Spirit: Selected Prose,* (Tiptree, Essex: Virago Press, 1983), 5.
89. See, Anastasya Verbitskaya, *Keys to Happiness* Trans. & Ed. Beth Holmgren & Helena Goscilo (Bloomington: Indiana Univ. Press, 1999) and Evdokia Nagrodskaia, *The Wrath of Dionysus* Trans. & Ed. Louise McReynolds (Bloomington: Indiana University Press, 1997)
90. Nagrodskaia, *Ibid.,* 141.
91. Olga Matich, *Erotic Utopia,* 204-11.
92. Irina Tidmarsh, *Memories of Revolution, Russian Women Remember,* 47.
93. Tidmarsh, *Memories,* 55-56.
94. Tidmarsh, *Memories,* 57.
95. Oskar von Riesemann, *Moussorgsky,* (New York: Dover, 1971), 139-41.
96. Mary Zirin, "A particle of our soul": prerevolutionary autobiography by Russian women writers," in *A History of Women's Writing in Russia,* 104, 109.
97. Christine Ruane, "Gender," 22, 66
98. See, Rochelle Goldberg Ruthchild, "Writing for their Rights, Four Feminist Journalists: Mariia Chekhova, Liubov Gurevich, Mariia Pokrovskaia, and Ariadna Tyrkova," in *An Improper Profession,* 178.
99. Maria Pokrovskaia, *How I was a Doctor for the City Poor,* as quoted by Ruthchild, "Writing for their Rights, Four Feminist Journalists: Mariia Chekhova, Liubov Gurevich, Mariia Pokrovskaia, and Ariadna Tyrkova," in *An Improper Profession,*
100. Diana Lewis Burgin, "Laid Out in Lavender," in *Sexuality and the Human Body,* Ed. Jane Costlow, 177-203.
101. S. Parnok, "You appeared before me...," Trans. in *The Burden of Suffrance,* by Pamela Perkins and Albert Cook, (New York: Garland Pub., Co., 1993), 146.

102. Anton S. Makarenko, *The Collective Family: A Handbook for Russian Parents*, (originally pub. 1937) Introduction U. Bronfenbrenner, Trans. Robert Daglish (New York: Garden City, Doubleday & Com, Inc., 1967)

103. Tatlina, "Reminiscences," in Clyman and Vowles, *Russia Through Women's Eyes*, 256

104. Tatlina, *Ibid.*, 253

105. Tatlina's memoirs as quoted by Miranda Beaven Remnek, in "A Larger Portion of the Public Female Readers, Fiction and the Periodical Press in the Reign of Nicholas I," in *An Improper Profession*, 43-44.

106. As quoted by Adele Lindenseyer in "Anna Volkova From Merchant Wife to Feminist Journalist," in *An Improper Profession*, Ed. Norton and Gheith, 123.

107. As quoted by Adele Lindenseyer in "Anna Volkova From Merchant Wife to Feminist Journalist," in *An Improper Profession*, Ed. Norton and Gheith, 137.

108. See, Carolyn Marks, "Providing Amusement for the Ladies, The Rise of the Russian Women's Magazine in the 1880s," in *An Improper Profession*, Ed. Norton and Gheith, 105-107.

109. Nadezhda Khvoshchinskaya, *The Boarding-School Girl*, 79-80.

110. Khvoshchinskaya, *Ibid.*, 115.

111. Khvoshchinskaya, *Ibid.*, 118.

112. Khvoshchinskaya, *Ibid.*, 119.

113. Khvoshchinskaya, *Ibid.*, 131-35.

114. See, Hutton, 23-4; also, Nikolai Leskov, *Lady Macbeth of Mtsensk* (1866) which tells of a woman killing her abusive husband and father-in-law, running the family business and living with a lover until discovered and sent into exile in Siberia. In 1934, composer Dmitri Shostakovich made an opera of this story, but Stalin forbade its production.

115. See, Aleksandra Kobiakova, "An Autobiography," Trans. By Lucy Vogel, in *Russia Through Women's Eyes*, 61-74.

116. N. I. Dobroliubov, "Realm of Darkness," Trans. By J. Fineberg, *Selected Philosophical Essays*, (Moscow: Foreign Languages Publishing House, 1948) , 244-45; Dobroliubov, "Temnoe Tsarstvo," 1859 and "Luch sveta v temnon tsarstve," 1860, *Sochinenii*, Tom III, 244-47, (Moscow, 1962), 495-520; and Hutton, *Russian and West European Women*, 22-29

117. A. N. Ostrovsky, "Artistes and Admirers," Trans. Elisabeth Hanson, Intro. L. Hanson. (New York: Barnes and Noble, 1970), 64-5.

118. Tatiana Mamonova, *Russian Women's Studies Essays on Sexism in Soviet Culture* (New York: Pergaman Press, 1989), 98.

119. Galina V. Shtange in *Intimacy and Terror Soviet Diaries of the 1930s*, Ed. By Veronique Garros, Natalia Korenevskaya, & Thomas Lahusen, Trans. Carol Flath (New York: The New Press, 1995), 167, 181.

120. Helena Skrjabina, *Coming of Age in the Russian Revolution*, 8, 17-18.

121. See, Y. M. Sokolov, *Russian Folklore*, Translated by Catherine R. Smith (New York: Macmillan Co. 1950), 203, 209-10.

122. Hutton, 14-16 and A. E. Alexander, *Russian Folklore*, 122.

123. Sokolov, *Ibid.*, 208.

124. *The Village of Viriatino An Ethnographic Study of a Russian Village from before the Revolution to the Present*, Trans. & Ed. Sula Benet, (New York: Anchor, 1970), 140-43.

125. See Sokolov, 204 and Natalie Kononenko, "Women as Performers of Oral Literature: A Re-examination of Epic and Lament," in *Women Writers in Russian Literature*, Ed. Clyman and Greene, 22.

126. Alex E. Alexander, *Russian Folklore Anthology in English Translation*, (Belmont, Mass: Nordland Pub. Co., 1975), 50, 53.

127. "Love and Marriage," in Alexander, *Russian Folklore An Anthology*, 122.

128. Alexander, *Russian Folklore*, 71.

129. Roberta Reeder, Trans. and Ed. *Russian Folk Lyrics*, (Bloomington: Indiana University Press, 1993), 150 as quoted in Clare Keogh Olson, "Laments and Ritual Songs of Russian Peasant Women," 3.

130. Sang Hyun Kim, Prichitaniia and Rituals as Symbolic Representations of Russian Peasants' Collective Memory: A Comparative Study of Wedding and Funeral Ceremonies, *Studies in Slavic Cultures*, Issue V, (May 2006), 34-37

131. Agrippina Korevanova, *Moia zhizn'* (Moscow: Sovetskii pisatel', 1938) 10-34, as Trans. by Yuri Slezkine in *In the Shadow of Revolution Life Stories of Russian Women* Ed. Sheila Fitapatrick and Yuri Slezkine (Princeton: Princeton University Press, 2000), 174-5.

132. Korevanova, *Ibid.*, 176-7.

133. Korevanova, *Ibid.*, 177-8.

134. *Village of Viriatino*, 107-09.

135. Reeder, *Lyrics*, 136 in Olson, 11-12.

136. Reeder, *Lyrics*, 131, Olson, 12.

137. Valentina Dmitrieva, "After the Great Hunger," from "Extract from 'Round the Villages: A Doctor's Memoirs of an Epidemic," (1896) in Kelly, *An Anthology of Russian Women's Writing 1777-1992*, 160.

138. *Village of Viriatino*, 99-100, 107-8, 140-41.

139. See, N. I. Kuznetsov's reports written for ethnographer Count Tenishev,

cited by Rose L. Glickman in 'Unusual Circumstances," *Russian History*, Vol. 23, 222.

140. Herrlinger, *Working Souls*, 95-98.

141. Maria Botchkareva, *Yashka My Life as Peasant, Officer, and Exile*, 18-19.

142. Botchkareva, *Yashka*, 27-68.

143. As quoted by Ernest Poole in *The Dark People*, 203-04.

144. Poole, *Ibid.*, 206.

145. For an excellent account of women journalists in late 19th century Russia, see Barbara Norton and Jehanne Gheith, Editors, *An Improper Profession: Women, Gender, and Journalism in Late Imperial Russia* ((Durham: Duke University Press, 2001).

Notes to Chapter Three

1. For information about the impact of women's productive work affecting infant mortality, see David Ransel, "Infant Care Cultures in the Russian Empire, " *Russia's Women, Accommodation, Resistance, Transformation* Ed. By Clements, et al, 114-125.

2. Lenin, *Razvitie Kapitalizma v Rossii (Development of Capitalism in Russia)*, 88-89; Webb, *New Dictionary of Statistics*, 10; Christine Worobec, *Peasant Russian Family and Community in the Post-Emancipation Period*, Princeton, Princeton Univ. Press, 1991; Hutton, 14-18; 1897 Perepis', Vol. II, 264; and Rose Glickman, "Peasant Women and Their Work," in, *Russian Peasant Women*, 54-72.

3. Nina Berberova, *The Italics are Mine*, 12-13.

4. As quoted from P. V. Shein, *Materialy dlia izucheniia byta I iazyka russkogo naseleniia sev.-zap. Kraia* (Materials for the Study of the Mode of Life and language of the Russian Populace of the Northwestern Region, Vol. I. Pts. 1 and 2) (St. Petersburg, 1887) No. 1276 in Y. M. Sokolov, *Russian Folklore*, Translated by Catherine R. Smith (New York: The Macmillan Com., 1950) 198.

5. As quoted by A. B. Zernova in "Materialy po sel'skokhoziaistvennoi magin v Smitrovskom Krae" (Materials on Agricultural Magic in the Dmitrovsky Region, *Sov. Etnografia (Soviet Ethnography)*, No. 3, 1932 in Sokolov, *Ibid.*, 200.

6. As quoted by Sokolov in *Russian Folklore*, 268-9.

7. *Ibid.*, 288.

8. For information about women in domestic production, see Lenin *The Development of Capitalism in Russia* and Judith Pallot, "Women's Domestic In-

dustries in Moscow Province, 1880-1900," in *Russia's Women, Accommodation, Resistance, Transformation*, Ed. By Clements et. al., 163-180.

9. *1897 Perepis'*, Vol. II, 272-82 and Aleksandr N. Engelgardt, *Letters from the Country, 1872-1887*, Trans. And Ed. Cathy A. Frierson (New York: Oxford University Press, 1993), 113, 167.

10. Engelgardt, *Letters from the Country*, 167-68.

11. For information regarding the role of midwives in late 19th century Russia, see Listova, "Russian Rituals, Customs, and Beliefs," 122-145; *Perepis' 1897*, 260-61; and Samuel C. Ramer, "Childbirth and Culture: Midwifery in the 19th Century Russian countryside," in *Russian Peasant Women*, Ed. B. Farnsworth, (New York: Oxford U. Press, 1992), 107-120

12. Ramer, *Ibid*.

13. Rose Glickman, "Peasant Woman as Healer," in *Russia's Women, Accommodation, Resistance, Transformation*, Edited by Clements, 148-156.

14. See, *1897 Perepis'* Vol. II.: 268, 272-80; *Chislennost i sostav' rabochikh' Svod Perepisi 1897g* Vol. I: x, xi, 2-3; Hutton, 19-21; and Rose Glickman, "Peasant Women and their Work," 69.

15. For detailed photographs of servants and workers in the late 19th and early 20th century, see the following works: Leah Bendavid-Val, *Song without Words The Photographs and Diaries of Countess Sophia Tolstoy* (Washington D. C.: National Geographic, 2007), Chloe Obolensky, *The Russian Empire 1955-1914, A Portrait in Photographs* (New York: Random House, 1979), and *Photographs for the Tsar, The pioneering color photography of Sergei Mikhailovich Prokudin-Gorskii commissioned by Tsar Nicholas II*, Edited with an introduction by Robert H. Allshouse, (New York: Dial Press, 1980).

16. Hutton, *Ibid.*, 19-20.

17. Vera Ivanovna Malakhova, "Four Years as a Frontline Physician," in *A Revolution of Their Own, Voices of Women in Soviet History*, Trans. Sonia Hoisington, Ed. Barbara Alpern Engel and Anastasia Posadskaya Vanderbeck, (Boulder: Westview Press, 1998), 184. In her interview, Malakhova cites her mother's words about her childhood in pre-revolutionary Russia.

18. Maria Botchkareva, *Yashka*, 8-14.

19. Botchkareva, *Yashka*, 16-18.

20. Botchkareva,19.

21. Botchkareva, 20-29.

22. Botchkareva, 28-31 and 35-68.

23. Botchkareva, 71-207

24. See, "Mariia Bochkareva," in *Encyclopedia of Russian Women's Movements*, Ed. Norma Noonan and Carol Nechemias (Westport, Connecticut: Greenwood Press, 2001), 7-8.

25. See, E. A. Oliunina, ""The Tailoring Trade in Moscow and the Villages of Moscow and Riazan Provinces: Material on the History of the Domestic Industry in Russia, edited and translated by Victoria Bonnell in *The Russian Worker Life and Labor under the Tsarist Regime* (Berkeley: University of California Press, 1983) 33-4, and 153-83
26. Oliunina, 172.
27. Oliunina, 171.
28. Oliunina, 170.
29. See, Michael Melancon, *The Lena Goldfields Massacre and the Crisis of the Late Tsarist State* (College Station: Texas A & M University Press, 2006), 34, 50-60, 84, 188.
30. See, E. Blinova, *Pesni ural'skogo revoliutsionnogo podpol'ia (Songs of the Revolutionary Underground in the Urals)* (Sverdlovsk, 1935) and V. P. Biryukov, *Prerevoutionary Folklore of the Urals*, (Sverdlovsk, 1937), as quoted by Sokolov, *Russian Folklore*, 583.
31. A. V. Gurevich, *Folklore of Eastern Siberia* (Irkutsk, 1938) in Sokolov, 608.
32. A. M. Gudvan, "Essays on the History of the Movement of Sales-Clerical Workers in Russia," Edited and Translated by V. Bonnell in *The Russian Worker*, 185-208, especially 194 and 198.
33. Gudvan, *Ibid.*, 195-6.
34. Gudvan, *Ibid.*, 195.
35. Gudvan, *Ibid.*, 195.
36. *Perepis naselenia 1897*, Vol. II, 254-5.
37. See, "Educational statistics for 1913," in *Annuaire Statistique de la Russie 1914*. Publication du Comite Central de Statistique. Ministere de l'interieur. (Petrograd, 1915), 121-123 and *1897 Census* Vol. II, 250-251.
38. Cecilia Bobrovskaya, *Twenty Years in Underground Russia Memoirs of a Rank and File Bolshevik* (New York: International Publishers, 1934) 82.
39. Frank A. Golder, *Documents of Russian History 1914-1917*, Trans. Emanuel Aronsberg (New York: The Century Co., 1927), 422.
40. See, Olga Forsh, "Ham's Wife," as Trans. By Helena Goscilo in *Russian and Polish Women's Fiction*, 97-99.
41. Elena Skrjabina, *Coming of Age in the Russian Revolution*, 7.
42. Skrjabina, *Coming of Age*, 16-17.
43. Skrjabina, *Coming of Age*, 19.
44. Skrjabina, *Coming of Age*, 19-20.
45. Sofya Kovalevskaya, *Nihilist Girl*, Translated N. Kolchevsky and M. Zirin, (New York: Modern Language Association of America, 2000), 34-38, 48-50.

46. See, Tatiana Toporkova, *Memories of Revolution* Ed. Anna Horsbrugh-Porter (London: Routledge, 1993) 14-24 and Anna Bek, *The Life of a Russian Woman Doctor* in which she describes her education at the gentry-class institute at Irkutsk in the 1880s, pages 29-31
47. Anna Bek, *The Life of a Russian Woman Doctor*, 29-30.
48. Anna Bek, *The Life of a Russian Woman Doctor*, 30-38.
49. Mariana Muravyeva, "Russian Women in European Universities, 1864-1900," in *Women, Education, and Agency, 1600-2000*, Ed. Jean Spence, Sarah Jane Aiston, and Maureen M. Meikle, (New York: Routledge, 2010.), 83-93.
50. For information about girls' gimnazia and women's higher education in the late 19th centuries, see, Sophie Satina, *Education of Women in Pre-Revolutionary Russia*, Trans. A. F. Poustchine, (New York: 1966) especially, 50-51, 62, 74; *Memories of Revolution, Russian Women Remember*, Ed. Anna Horsborough-Porter; Helena Scrjabina, *Coming of Age in the Russian Revolution*; Nina Berberova, *The Italics are Mine*; Mariya Shkapskaya, *The Mother and The Stern Master Selected Poems*, 5; and Reginald Zelnik, *Perils of Pankratova*, (H. J. Ellison Center for Russian, East European, and Central Asian Studies, University of Washington, 2005), 13; and Ramer, 112-13
51. Khvoshchinskaya, *The Boarding School Girl*, 127-8.
52. See, "Album Graphique de la Statistique Generale de la France," *Resultats Statistique de recensement de 1901* (Paris, 1907) and Hutton, *Op. Cit.*, 61-2.
53. Bobrovskaya, *Twenty Years in Underground Russia*, 215.
54. Bobrovskaya, *Twenty Years*, 216.
55. Bobrovskaya, *Twenty Years*, 216-18, 221.
56. Sofie Satina, *Education of Women in Pre-Revolutionary Russia.*, 60 and 76.
57. Satina, *Ibid.*, 124-31.
58. Nina Berberova, *The Italics Are Mine*, 66-67.
59. Berberova, *The Italics are Mine*, 13-15.
60. See *1897 census*, Vol. I, 190-193, Table IXa "Distribution of the Population according to Educational Level and Social Estate."
61. Anna Akhmatova, "A Brief Word About Myself," *Soviet Literature*, #6, 1989: 4-5 and Reginald E. Zelnik, "Perils of Pankratova," 13-14.
62. Figner, *Memoirs of a Revolutionist*, 43-4.
63. Bek, *The Life of a Russian Woman Doctor*, 47-48.
64. Bek, *The Life of a Russian Woman Doctor*, 50-56, 58-59.
65. See *Annuaire Statistique de la Russie 1915*, de Comite Central de Statistique Ministere de l'Interieur, (Petrograd, 1916), 110-111, 127, 133; *1897 Perepis'* Vol. II, 260; and Satina, *Ibid.*, 31.
66. See, Clyman, *Russia Through Women's Eyes*, Introduction, 36-38, 158-59,

186-7, 311-12; Varvara Kashevarova-Rudneva, "My Autobiography," Trans. by Toby Clyman, especially 159, 168, 175-84, and Ekaterina Slanskaia, "House Calls: A Day in the Practice of a Duma Woman doctor in St. Petersburg," Translated by Toby Clyman, and Emiliia Pimenova, "Bygone Days," Trans. By Natasha Roklina, all in *Russia Through Women's Eyes*, 160-185, 187-216, and 312-34; Jane McDermid and Anna Hillyar, *Women and Work in Russia 1880-1930, A Study in Continuity through Change* (New York: Longman, 1998), pp. 72-80.

67. Figner, *Memoirs*, 58-9.

68. Figner, *Ibid.*, 60.

69. Valentina Dmitrieva, "After the Great Hunger," an extract from "Round the Villages: A Doctor's Memoirs of an Epidemic' 1896, in Catriona Kelly, *An Anthology of Russian Women's Writing*, 158.

70. For quote, see, Mary Zirin, , "A particle of our soul"; prerevolutionary autobiography by Russian women writers," in *A History of Women's Writing in Russia*, 112.

71. Slanskaia, "House Calls," Trans. by Clyman in *Russia through Women's Eyes*, 188.

72. Slanskaia, *Ibid.*, 190-213.

73. Slanskaia, *Ibid.*, 197.

74. Marie Grand Duchess of Russia, *Education of a Princess A memoirs*, 165-66.

75. Marie, *Education of a Princess*, 167.

76. Marie, *Education of a Princess*, 167-215.

77. Pimenova, "Bygone Days," 334, Barbara Engel, *Mothers and Daughters*, (New York: Cambridge University Press, 1983) 169, and Hutton, 96.

78. Rudneva, "An Autobiography," *Op. Cit.*, 175, and Clyman, *Russia*, 159.

79. Diana Greene, *Reinventing Romantic Poetry*, 21-37. See, page 37 for quote.

80. Rostopchina, "The Last Flower," as translated by Laura McCullough, "Evdokiia Rostopchina," in *Russian Women Writers, Vol. I*, 102.

81. See Diana Greene's discussion of Rostopchina in *Reinventing Romantic Poetry*, 90-94 and Rostopchina, "Chatskii's Return to Moscow," as translated by McCullough in Ibid., 106.

82. Ibid., 116.

83. E. Rostopchina, "How Women Must Write," Trans. in Perkins, *The Burden of Sufferance*, 48-49.

84. Karolina Pavlova, "Three Souls," as translated by Christine D. Tomei, in *Russian Women Writers, Vol. I*, 322.

85. Karolina Pavlova, "Untitled" (for Rostopchina) in *The Burden of Sufferance Women*, 39.

86. See, Jane A. Taubman, "Women Poets of the Silver Age," 171-18; Diana Greene, "Nineteenth-Century Women Poets: Critical Reception vs. Self-Definition," 95-110; and Rosenthal, "Achievement and Obscurity," 149-170 all in Clyman and Green, *Women Writers in Russian Literature*. See also, the 1897 Russian Imperial Census which indicates that there were 284 female scholars and literateurs, and 1,132 writers, translators, editors, and others in the free professions, *1897 Perepis', Tom. II:* 260, 292.

87. Gippius, "I (in someone else's name), 1901, translated by Christine Borowec, in *Russian Women Writers, Vol. II*, Christine D. Tomei, Ed. (Garland Publishing, 1999), 694-5.

88. Pachmuss, Zinaida Hippius, 19, 20, 22-25, 139, 179, 188.

89. Gippius, "Impotence," in *The Burden of Suffrance*, 83.

90. For information about the influence of Gippius on Shaginian, see "Marietta Shaginian," by Laura Goering, in *Russian Women Writers, Vol. II*, 1192-3ff.

91. M. Lokhvitskaya, *Stikhotvoreniya* (5 vols.; St. Petersburg, 1903-14), i, 98, as quoted by Catriona Kelly, *A History of Russian Women's Writing 1820-1992*, 161.

92. Mirra Lokhvitskaia, as translated by Christine D. Tomei in "Mirra Lokhvitskaia," *Russian Women Writers, Vol. II*, 429.

93. Lokhvitskaia, "First Kiss," *Ibid.*, 434-5.

94. Lokhvitskaia, "To My Rival," *Ibid.*, 435-6.

95. Lokhvitskaia, "On a White Night," *Ibid.*, 437.

96. Marina Tsvetaeva, "To Anna Akhmatova," Feb. 11, 1915, Translated by Jane Taubman and Sibelan Forrester in *Russian Women Writers, Vol. II* (Garland Publishing, Inc. 1999), 848.

97. Tsvetaeva, "To Kiss a forehead," Trans. John Glad in *Twentieth Century Russian Poetry*, Ed. John Glad and Daniel Weissbort (Iowa City, University of Iowa Press, 1992), 141.

98. Anna Akhmatova, as translated by Sibelan Forrester in *Russian Women Writers*, Vol. II, (1999), 926.

99. A. Akhmatova, "A Drive," Trans. in *The Burden of Sufferance*, 167.

100. Anna Akhmatova, in *The Portable Twentieth-Century Russian Reader*, Edited Clarence Brown, (New York, Penguin, 1985), 113.

101. Berberova, *The Italics Are Mine*, 20-41

102. Berberova, *Ibid.*

103. Olga Freidenberg, "Diary, 1912," in *The Correspondence of Boris Pasternak and Olga Freidenberg 1910-1954*, Compiled by Elliott Mossman, Trans. Mossman and Margaret Wettlin (New York, Harcourt Brace Jovanovich, Pub., 1982) 18, 28, and quotation: 37-39.

104. Regarding women's equality as writers, see Marie Zebrikoff, "Russia," 418. For Lokhvitskaya's dismay in discovering that Ivan Bunin earned more from publishers for his poetry than she did, see, "Mirra Lokhvitskaia," in *Russian Women Writers, Vol. II*, 421.

105. For good discussions of 19th century Russian women writers and their writings on "The Woman Question" and "The New Woman," see Jane Costlow, "Love, Work, and the Woman Question in Mid Nineteenth Century Women's Writing," Mary F. Zirin, "Women's Prose Fiction in the Age of Realism," and Charlotte Rosenthal, "Achievement and Obscurity: Women's Prose in the Silver Age," all in *Women Writers in Russian Literature*; also Clyman, 63; 78-91; and 149-171.

106. See, Kobiakova, "An Autobiography," 71-2 and Toby Clyman, Introducton, 1-46, 336 in *Russia Through Women's Eyes*.

107. Clyman, *Russia Through Women's Eyes*, 23-4.

108. Clyman, *Ibid.*, 21-23.

109. See, Anastasya Verbitskaya, *Keys to Happiness a Novel*, Trans. and Ed. by Beth Holmgren & Helena Goscilo (Bloomington: Indiana Univ. Press, 1999), 171-2. See also, Clyman, 41. For an excellent account of different forms of Russian Women's autobiography in the 19th century, see Toby Clyman's *Russian through the Eyes of Women*, especially the Introduction and Annotated Bibliography

110. *Verbitskaya, Ibid.*, 188.

111. Verbitskaya, *Ibid.*, 231.

112. Verbitskaya, *Ibid.*, 232.

113. Verbitskaya, *Ibid.*, 275-290.

114. Tatiana Tolstoy, *The Tolstoy Home Diaries of Tatiana Sukhotin-Tolstoy*, Trans. Alec Brown, (AMS PRESS, INC. New York, 1966) 86, Aug. 1886.

115. T. Tolstoy, *Diaries*, 106-08.

116. T. Tolstoy, *Diaries*, 132, Mar., 1888.

117. T. Tolstoy, *Diaries*, 16, May, 1882.

118. T. Tolstoy, *Diaries*, 88-89, Oct. 1886.

119. T. Tolstoy, *Diaries*, 180, May, 1891.

120. T. Tolstoy, *Diaries*, 183, July 1893.

121. S. Tolstoy, *Autobiography*, 12-13.

122. S. Tolstoy, *Autobiography*, 19.

123. S. Tolstoy, *Autobiography*, 53.

124. S. Tolstoy, *Autobiography*, 63.

125. S. Tolstoy, *Autobiography*, 64.

126. S. Tolstoy, *Autobiography*, 85ff.

127. Quote found in Mary Zirin, "A particle of our soul"; prerevolutionary autobiography by Russian women writers," in *A History of Women's Writing in Russia*, Edited by Adele Marie Barker and Jehanne M. Gheith, (Cambridge: Cambridge University Press, 2002), 100.

128. See Education Statistics for special middle schools, 1913 in *Annuaire Statistique de la Russie 1914*, 121-123.

129. As quoted by Tatiana, Mamonova, in *Russian Women's Studies, Essays on Sexism in Soviet Culture* (New York, Pergaman Press, 1989), 95.

130. Mamonova, 96.

131. *Ibid.*, 96.

132. *Ibid.*, 98.

133. For quotes by Benois and other information about Serebriakova, see *Women Artists of Russia's New Age 1900-1935*, Ed. Anthony Parton, (New York: Rizzoli, 1990), 45-50.

134. Marina Tsvetaeva, March, 1929, as quoted in M. N. Yablonskaia, *Women Artists in Russia's New Age, 1910-1935*, Ed. and Trans. Anthony Parton, 52.

135. Jane A. Sharp, "Redrawing the margins of Russian Vanguard Art," *Sexuality and the Body in Russian Culture*, Edited by Jane T. Costlow et al, (Stanford, California: Sanford University Press, 1993), 106-123.

136. As quoted by John Bowlt in *Russia Art of the Avant-Garde Theory and Criticism, 1902-1934* (New York: Thames and Hudson, 1988), 55-57.

137. Bowlt, *Ibid.*, Goncharova, "Manifesto," 60.

138. N. Goncharova, "Cubism" 1912, Trans. by J. Bowlt in *Russian Art of the Avant-Garde*, 78.

139. As quoted by Donald Goddard in "Amazons of the Avant-Garde" an essay on Russian women artists show at the Guggenheim in New York in 2000.

140. Rozanova in Bowlt, 105.

141. Rozanova in Bowlt, 105.

142. Rozanova in Bowlt, 106.

143. Rozanova in Bowlt, 107.

144. Rozanova, From Supremus mag. #1in Bowlt in *Russian Art of the Avant-Garde*, 148.

145. Rozanova in Bowlt, 109-110.

146. Stepanova in Bowlt, 139.

147. Aksenov as quoted and Trans. by J. Bowlt, *Russian Art of the Avant-Garde*, 68-9.

Notes to Chapter Four

1. In addition to Vera Broido's *Apostles into Terrorists* and Anna Hillyar and Jane McDermid's *Revolutionary Women in Russia, 1870-1917 A study in Collective Biography* (Manchester: Manchester University Press,, 2000), there are many additional works which also analyze Russian women's political activity including the following: Barbara Clements et al *Russia's Women: Accommodation, Resistance, Transformation,* Clements, et al *Russian Masculinities in History and Culture,* (New York: Palgrave, 2002), and Barbara Engel, *Mothers and Daughters: Women of the Intelligentsia in Nineteenth Century Russia* (New York: Cambridge University Press, 1983).

2. Alfred G. Meyer, "The Impact of World War I," in *Russia's Women: Accommodation, Resistance, Transformation,* Ed. Clements, 212.

3. Meyer, "The Impact of WWI," 212-13

4. Catherine Breshkovsky, *The Little Grandmother of the Russian Revolution Reminiscences and Letters of Catherine Breshkovsky,* Ed. Alice Stone Blackwell, (Boston: Little, Brown, and Company, 1919), 9.

5. Breshkovsky, *The Little Grandmother,* 17.

6. Breshkovsky, *The Little Grandmother,* 39-40.

7. Hutton, 126-7 and Catherine Breshkovsky, *Hidden Springs of the Russian Revolution* (Stanford: Stanford University Press, 1931), 8-30 and Breshkovsky, *Little Grandmother of the Russian Revolution,* ed. Alice Stone Blackwell. (New York: Little & Brown, 1917), 1-31.

8. Vera Broido, *Apostles into Terrorists Women and the Revolutionary Movement in the Russia of Alexander II* (New York: Viking Press, 1977) 146.

9. Sofya Kovalevskaya, *Nihilist Girl,* 7, 57, 99.

10. Kovalevskaya, *Nihilist Girl,* 118-120.

11. Kovalevskaya, *Nihilist Girl,* 121-137.

12. Kovalevskaya, *Nihilist Girl,* 137-139.

13. Figner, *Memoirs,* 39-45, Hutton, 132, and "Vera Figner," in *Encyclopedia of Russian Women's Movements,* Ed. Noonan and Nechemias, 20-22.

14. See, Marguerite Harrison, *Unfinished Tales from a Russian Prison* (New York, George H. Doran Company, 1923), 93-98.

15. L. Katasheva, *Natasha A Bolshevik Woman Organizer A Short Biography* (New York: Workers Library Publishers, 1934), 5-7.

16. Katasheva, 8.

17. Katasheva, 16-18.

18. Katasheva, 21ff and "Konkordia Samoilova" in *Encyclopedia of Russian Women's Movements,* Ed. Noonan and Nechmias, 66-67.

19. Vera Morozova, *The Red Carnation*, (Moscow: Progress Publishers, 1981), 86-7.
20. Anna Bek, *The Life of a Russian Woman Doctor*, 57-59.
21. Anna Bek, *The Life of a Russian Woman Doctor*, 60-61.
22. As quoted by Morozova, in *The Red Carnation*), 13.
23. Morozova, 15.
24. Klavdia Kirsanova, as quoted in *The Red Carnation*, 50.
25. *Ibid.*, 77-79.
26. See, "Table of those incriminated, acquitted, and condemned by the district courts and all the courts of justice in 1904," *Ezhegodnik, 1907, Vol. 1908*, 386-389.
27. Ludmilla Sthal, in *The Red Carnation*, 118, 148, 154-57.
28. Tatyana Ludvinsikaya, in *The Red Carnation*, 161-62.
29. *Ibid.*, 163-64.
30. *Ibid.*, 164.
31. *Ibid.*, 184-92.
32. Bobrovskaya, *Twenty Years*, 31.
33. Bobrovskaya, *Twenty Years*, 33-35.
34. Bobrovskaya, *Twenty Years*, 50.
35. Bobrovskaya, *Twenty Years*, 50-86.
36. Bobrovskaya, *Twenty Years*, 152-53.
37. Bobrovskaya, *Twenty Years*, 159-60.
38. Bobrovskaya, *Twenty Years*, 182.
39. Bobrovskaya, *Twenty Years*, 208.
40. Vera Broido, *Daughter of Revolution, A Russian Girlhood Remembered* (London: Constable, 1998) 44-45.
41. Broido, *Daughter of Revolution*, 48-49.
42. Broido, *Daughter of Revolution*, 52.
43. Broido, *Daughter of Revolution*, 59-60.
44. See, Rosalind Marsh, "Realist Prose Writers, 1881-1929" in *A History of Women's Writing in Russia*, Ed. Barker and Gheith, 177, 189, 193.
45. Filosofova, as quoted by Rachelle Ruthchild, *Equality and Revolution*, 117
46. Filosofova as quoted by Rachelle Ruthchild, *Equality and Revolution*, 247
47. Vera Levandovskaia-Belokonskaia, as quoted by Rachelle Ruthchild, *Equality and Revolution*, 41.
48. Tyrkova as quoted by Rachelle Ruthchild, *Equality and Revolution*, 11.

NOTES TO CHAPTER FOUR

49. Chekhova as quoted by Rachelle Ruthchild, *Equality and Revolution*, 48.
50. Ulianova as quoted by Rachelle Ruthchild, *Equality and Revolution*, 225.
51. Kollontai as quoted by Rachelle Ruthchild, *Equality and Revolution*, 225.
52. Laurie S. Stoff, *They Fought for the Motherland: Russia's Women Soldiers in World War I and the Revolution* (University Press of Kansas,: Lawrence, Kansas, 2006), 25.
53. Stoff, *They Fought for the Motherland*, 27-28.
54. Stoff, *They Fought for the Motherland*, 31.
55. Stoff, *They Fought for the Motherland*, 81. Stoff is quoting Krylova's views from Boris Solonevich, *Zhenshchina s vintovkoi: Istoricheskii roman (Woman with a Rifle: A Historical Novel)* (Buenos Aires: 1955), 62.
56. Stoff, *They Fought for the Motherland*), 65.
57. Stoff, *They Fought for the Motherland*), 61-66, 75.
58. Stoff, *They Fought for the Motherland*), 90. Stoff is here quoting "Vopl' zhenshchin iz derevni," (Cry of Women from the Country,") in the Russian journal *Birzhevyia vedomosti*, May 18, 1917: 5.
59. For information about liberal, bourgeois feminists, see Rochelle Ruthchild, *Equality and Revolution Women's Rights in the Russian Empire, 1903-1917* (Pittsburgh: University of Pittsburgh Press, 2010, and Linda Edmondson, *Feminism in Russia, 1900-1917* (London: Heinemann, 1984).
60. Catherine Breshkovsky, *The Little Grandmother of the Russian Revolution Reminiscences and Letters of Catherine Breshkovsky* Ed. By Alice Stone Blackwell (Boston: Little Brown and Company, 1919), 17-19.
61. See Chulos, *Converging Worlds*, 63, 91-2, 101.
62. Alexandra Kollontai, "Women and Revolution," in *Storming the Heavens, Voices of October*, Ed. Mark Jones (London: Swan Atlantic Highlands, 1987), 166.
63. Kollontai," Women and Revolution," 166-167.
64. Letter from peasant girl, quoted by Rochelle Ruthchild, *Equality and Revolution*, 59.
65. Elena Skrjabina, *Coming of Age in the Revolution*, 27.
66. Skrjabina, *Coming of Age*, 28.
67. Skrjabina, *Coming of Age*, 28.
68. Skrjabina, *Coming of Age*, 33-34.
69. Skrjabina, *Coming of Age*, 33-4.
70. Skrjabina, *Coming of Age*, 34-5.
71. Frank A. Golder, *Documents of Russian History 1914-1917, Izvestiia*, No. 120, July 31, 1917, 381-382.

72. Alexandra Kollontai, "Women and Revolution," 162-3.
73. Herrlinger, *Working Souls*, 206-07.
74. Kollontai, "Women and Revolution," 163-4.
75. Kollontai, "Women and Revolution," 164.
76. Kollontai, "Women and Revolution," 164-67.
77. Kollontai, "Women and Revolution," 166.
78. As quoted by Mark D. Steinberg, in "Workers on the Cross: Religious Imagination in the Writings of Russian Workers, 1910-1924," The *Russian Review*, Vol. 53, Ap. 1994, 227.
79. "Young Girls Fighting on the Russian Front," *Current History*, May 1916, 365-66.
80. See, "Young Girls Fighting on the Russian Front," *Current History*, May 1916, 365-67. This article was first printed in the Russian Journal *Novoe Vremya*, then in the *London Times*, and finally in *Current History*.
81. Pauline S Crosley, *Intimate Letters from Petrograd*, (New York: E. P. Dutton, 1920), 72, 132.
82. Pauline S Crosley, *Intimate Letters from Petrograd*, 132.
83. Pauline S Crosley, *Intimate Letters from Petrograd*, 156.
84. Pauline S Crosley, *Intimate Letters from Petrograd*, 210.
85. Rochelle Ruthchild, *Equality and Revolution Women's Rights in the Russian Empire, 1903-1917*, 235.

The University of Nebraska–Lincoln does not discriminate
based on gender, age, disability, race, color,
religion, marital status, veteran's status,
national or ethnic origin,
or sexual orientation.

www.ingramcontent.com/pod-product-compliance
Lightning Source LLC
Chambersburg PA
CBHW022050160426
43198CB00008B/179